D1191500

THE INVENTION OF JOURNALISM

The Invention of Journalism

Jean K. Chalaby
Research Associate
European Institute
London School of Economics

First published in Great Britain 1998 by
MACMILLAN PRESS LTD
Houndmills, Basingstoke, Hampshire RG21 6XS and London
Companies and representatives throughout the world

A catalogue record for this book is available from the British Library.

ISBN 0–333–68282–3

First published in the United States of America 1998 by
ST. MARTIN'S PRESS, INC.,
Scholarly and Reference Division,
175 Fifth Avenue, New York, N.Y. 10010

ISBN 0–312–21286–0

Library of Congress Cataloging-in-Publication Data
Chalaby, Jean K.
The invention of journalism / by Jean K. Chalaby.
p.   cm.
Includes bibliographical references and index.
ISBN 0–312–21286–0
1. Journalism.   I. Title.
PN4801.C42 1998
070.4—dc21   97–42322
                                                            CIP

This book is printed on paper suitable for recycling and made from fully managed and sustained forest sources.

10   9   8   7   6   5   4   3   2   1
07   06   05   04   03   02   01   00   99   98

Printed and bound in Great Britain by
Antony Rowe Ltd, Chippenham, Wiltshire

To the memory of my grandfather
Alfred Giordani

Contents

Acknowledgements

I would like to express my gratitude to the members of my family, friends and colleagues who have helped me in various ways to complete this project. I am grateful to Nicholas Garnham and Nicos Mouzelis whose valuable insights have provided me with guidance to turn my PhD thesis into a book. I also owe many thanks to Howard Machin, Director of the European Institute at the London School of Economics, for his support.

List of Tables

Introduction

This book pursues three concomitant objectives. First, it argues that journalism emerged as a discourse during the second half of the 19th century, and thus that journalism is a more recent invention than most authors have acknowledged so far.

Scholars traditionally assume that journalism was invented when the first gazettes and handwritten newsletters began to be published in Europe in the course of the 16th century (see, for example, Golding and Elliott, 1979, pp. 21–8; Stephens, 1988, pp. 156–67). Journalists themselves are prone to set the date of the origins of their profession as early as possible, and journalists-turned-historians often refer to the Roman *Acta Diurna*, the daily accounts of political life exposed on the walls of the Forum, as the first pieces of journalism.

However, my argument is that the profession of the journalist and the journalistic discourse are the products of the emergence, during the second half of the 19th century, of a specialized and increasingly autonomous *field of discursive production*, the journalistic field. The formation of the journalistic field had a tremendous impact on the discourse produced by the press. The relations of production which began to prevail within this emerging field originated new discursive practices and strategies, new discursive norms and new discursive phenomena. Only when these new discursive practices emerged did the press begin to produce a discourse that is distinct from other discursive forms and peculiar to the journalistic field.

Second, this book aims to contribute to the debate on the public sphere. In this debate, which was opened by Jürgen Habermas 30 years ago, many communication researchers contest the idea of a decline of the public sphere and dispute the thesis of a refeudalization of the public space by the modern media. The nature of public communication, the argument goes, may have changed over the past two hundred years, but these changes are not akin to a fall in public communication standards. Coupled with these criticisms of the Habermasian reading of the development of the public space during the last two centuries, media scholars have also identified a series of flaws with Habermas' conceptualization of

1

the public sphere (Dahlgren, 1991, pp. 3–7; Keane, 1991, pp. 35–7; Thompson, J.B. 1995, pp. 69–75; Verstraeten, 1996, pp. 349–53).

This book will not engage in a defence of Habermas' notion of the public sphere. With an alternative set of concepts, however, I will endeavour to demonstrate that the structural transformations which affected the press during the course of the 19th century not only modified considerably the nature of the discourse of the press, but did so in a way that impaired the principle of publicity that prevailed in the press of the pre-journalistic age. It is argued that during the 19th century one may observe in the British press a transition from a discourse that was political at heart and public in character, to a new discursive genre – journalism – which displayed entirely new philological characteristics.

Finally, some of the intentions of this book are theoretical in scope. This study attempts to put into practice a sociological definition of discourse. So far, discourse is essentially a linguistic category, and is either used as a synonym for text or language, or is closely associated with one of these notions. It is argued in Chapter 3 that a sociological definition of discourse should be dissociated from the linguistic sphere and refer to a *class of texts*. This definition confers upon the notion of discourse an intertextual dimension which makes it less easily reducible to linguistic or para-linguistic entities such as text or language. No longer confined to the linguistic realm, the concept can now designate a particular dimension in texts which is neither linguistic nor ideological but properly discursive.

This definition of discourse has important hermeneutic implications, as it constitutes a first step towards establishing a set of philological procedures that are fundamentally sociological and distinct from those of linguistic disciplines. The confinement of discourse within the linguistic sphere has enabled linguistic disciplines to locate the question of meaning within the linguistic structure of texts. This approach to texts may be legitimate from a linguistic perspective but is not all that valid from a sociological standpoint. Indeed, in their relationship to texts, semiologists reproduce the relationship of structural linguistics with language, and in the same way that for linguists language is a system without agents, semiologists attempt to interpret texts independently of the performing agents who produce these texts. This is the legacy of the 'abstract objectivism' of structural linguistics that Michael Bakhtin, Paul Ricoeur and Pierre Bourdieu have already criticized (Volosinov,[1] 1986, pp. 96–119; Ricoeur, 1969, pp. 233– 62; Bourdieu, 1992, pp. 272–88).

The intertextual definition of discourse addresses this problem by inducing a reading of texts which moves in two directions. The first step of the reading is intertextual as the analyst relates and compares texts within a discursive class whose outline is progressively defined by these readings. The second step is said to be 'external' as it attempts to explain some of the philological characteristics of these texts by relating these discursive units to the social and economic relations in which agents find themselves engaged at the time they produce these texts. Briefly stated, this is the hermeneutic procedure which is applied at various levels throughout the book.

This book is divided into three parts and eight chapters. The two chapters in Part I establish the rupture in the history of the British press between its public and its journalistic phases and attempt to outline the nature of the structural transformations that the press in Britain went through from the second part of the 19th century onwards. Chapter 1 attempts to change the framework of analysis relating to the pre-journalistic press and posits the use of the concepts 'public discourse', instead of 'journalism', and 'publicist', instead of 'journalist', to analyse the press of that period. The chapter illustrates these notions with the 'unstampeds' – the illegal newspapers published in London during the 1830s by working-class publicists.

Chapter 2 moves on to the structural transformation of the British press during the 19th century and examines the formation of the journalistic field in England. Section 2.1 introduces the concept of the journalistic field and specifies the advantages which flow from using this concept for our understanding of the history of the British press. Section 2.2 examines the mechanisms that created competitive struggles among newspapers from the 1850s onwards and brought into existence the journalistic field in Britain. Section 2.3 focuses on the way economic competition has structured the journalistic field and identifies the processes of industrialization, concentration and capitalization. The last section, 2.4, draws the ideal-typical portrait of an important historical figure which appeared with the formation of the journalistic field, that of the press baron.

Chapter 3, in Part II, plays a pivotal role in the book. It outlines the theoretical backbone of this research and discusses the sociological definition of the concept of discourse. The chapter also examines the philological issues raised by this definition and outlines the hermeneutic procedures employed throughout.

Part III contains the remaining five chapters of the book. As a whole, Part III constitutes an attempt to apprehend discourse as a socio-historical object and to write the history of the transformations which affected a particular discourse, journalism, during a specific period of time. The formation of the journalistic field and other related factors modified the discourse of the press in three distinct ways: they defined the ideological limits of the journalistic discourse, induced the development of new discursive phenomena and contributed to the emergence of new discursive norms, practices and strategies. Altogether, these transformations turned journalism into a discursive genre of its own.

Each chapter of Part III focuses on a particular aspect of these discursive changes. Chapter 4 examines the long and complex process of depoliticization of the British press. The emergence of proper news values and journalistic considerations on what is fit to print brought new topics to the press, such as sport and human interest stories, and reduced politics to one of the topics competing for journalists' attention. As a result, the amount of space newspapers devoted to politics diminished considerably. Particular attention is given to the decline of the parliamentary column in the British popular press during the closing decades of the 19th century. The concept of depoliticization also refers to the changing nature of political coverage during this period. Following the growing independence of newspapers *vis-à-vis* political parties, the degree of partisanship within the press declined while new discursive trends appeared in political reporting, such as the increasing focus on political actors themselves and the growing interest of the press in the spectacle that political life and politicians offered to reporters' cameras. One of the main findings is that many of the characteristics of modern political coverage whose emergence scholars often attribute to television had already appeared by the 1920s. Following the case-study of the 1922 General Election, the chapter concludes with an analysis of the consequences of the depoliticization of the press for the political process at large.

Chapter 5 examines two discursive practices, interviewing and reporting, and a series of discursive norms collectively referred to under the denomination of 'objectivity', which greatly contributed to the constitution of journalism as a distinctive class of texts. This chapter recalls the beginnings of the interview in the British press and then outlines the benefits for journalists in using this practice with politicians. Reporting is essentially a fact-centred discursive practice that journalists employ to write the news report, the discursive format most central to the profession. Objectivity designates here a bundle of discursive norms, such as impartiality, neutrality, or factuality, which began to influence the discourse of journalists in the latter part of the 19th century. Chapter 5 defines a total of nine norms related to objectivity, and argues that the implications of these norms are discursive rather than ideological. This means that journalists who abide with these norms refrain from explicit value judgements and partisanship, not that their discourse is void of ideological values. This chapter also examines the arguments that journalists brought forward to sustain their claim to objectivity, including their definition of public opinion, and finally spells out the political and economic factors which led to the development of objectivity in journalism.

Chapter 6 analyses three discursive strategies – crusadism, jingoism and sensationalism – that journalists employ to gain a competitive advantage over rivals. These strategies illustrate the influence of relations of production, and of economic competition in particular, on the discursive production of journalists. Chapter 7 documents the emergence of the division between the popular press and quality newspapers in Britain. The chapter examines the factors which provoked the polarization of the British press into two camps and discusses this phenomenon in light of the knowledge gap hypothesis.

The final chapter concentrates on the way editors and press proprietors adapt their newspapers to the tastes and preferences of their audience, and notably the methods they use to respond to readers' demand for escapist material. The chapter analyses the nature of this market-driven strategy and its philological implications for journalism. The second section of Chapter 8 concludes the book, reflecting on the overall impact of market forces on the press and the ensuing changing nature of the press's role in society. Following Warren Breed, it is argued that the press, under the influences of market forces, has essentially become a magic mirror journalists hold to society, with the effect of keeping the popular classes, in particular, in a state of ecstasy and to deny them knowledge about the world and knowledge about their position in the world.

Part I
A Tale of Two Discourses

1

'Knowledge is Power': The Working-Class Unstampeds as an Example of Public Discourse

Historians traditionally overlook the fact that journalism is an invention of the second half of the 19th century. Consequently, they comment upon the discursive production of publicists during the 18th century and the first half of the 19th century from the point of view of the discursive practices journalists began to employ at a later period in history. This tendency towards anachronism is illustrated in the assumption of historians that the norm of objectivity existed prior to the emergence of the journalistic field. Although this norm did not develop before the latter part of the 19th century (see Chapter 5), the texts publicists wrote before the emergence of journalism are often examined in light of this purely journalistic norm. Among others, Vivian Gruder criticizes the French revolutionary pamphlets of 1789 as 'propaganda' (Gruder, 1992, p. 168). But the notion of propaganda assumes a discursive norm, objectivity, which did not exist in 18th-century France. As historians generally do not acknowledge that this norm is a relatively recent invention, they treat the partisanship of public newspapers as an abnormality and a deficiency.

This chapter proposes a new framework of analysis for the pre-journalistic press, and suggests that the concepts of journalism and of journalist be supplanted by 'public discourse' and 'publicist' for the analysis of these newspapers. The concept of public discourse constitutes an attempt to analyse the pre-journalistic press in its own terms. Publicists' discursive production was largely determined by their political convictions, and the nature and intensity of these convictions matter more for the understanding of these texts than discursive norms which did not exist when publicists were writing.

This chapter introduces the concepts of public discourse and the publicist through illustration. At least one group of newspapers other than the one selected here may have been used to illustrate these concepts; they were the middle-class newspapers published during the first half of the 19th century in the north of England. Northern middle-class publicists were instrumental in publicizing the utilitarianism of James Mill and Jeremy Bentham, as well the economic doctrines of Smith, Malthus and Ricardo (notably the notions of international free trade and economic *laissez-faire*). These publicists, such as Edward Baines, of the *Leeds Mercury*, or Archibald Prentice, of the *Manchester Times*, ceaselessly advocated the political and economic interests of traders and manufacturers and defended their positions on every issue, from the Corn Laws to the ten-hour factory reform (see Read, 1961). In this book however, for reasons of space and narrative coherence, I have selected the example of the British working-class illegal newspapers, the 'unstampeds'. These journals were called the 'unstampeds' because, evading the newspaper stamp duty, they were not marked, like the legal papers, by a red stamp at the top right hand corner of each sheet. They were published in London, most notably during the early 1830s.

The first section outlines some of the economic, social and legal aspects of the conditions of production of this illegal working-class press. This press was one of the consequences of the taxes on knowledge, originally levied by Queen Anne's Tory ministers in 1712. Stamped newspapers priced 6 or 7 pence being well beyond the means of the working classes, this press could only survive by evading these imposts.

The second section of this chapter presents the discourse of the unstampeds. As public texts, unstampeds were governed by the *principle of publicity*. Public texts had the purpose of propagating political ideologies intentionally and explicitly (this is the ideological aspect of their function of publicity), and to make public facts and information relevant to public life (the practical aspect of the same function).

The last section discusses four essential philological characteristics of the public press. These philological features are related to the partisanship, the publicness, the didactic character and the ideology of public newspapers.

1.1 THE LEGAL AND POLITICAL CONTEXT OF THE WORKING-CLASS UNSTAMPEDS

The Taxes on Knowledge

In England, the pre-market period of the press is characterized by direct governmental restraints. It is in this context that libel laws and heavy duties have to be understood; that is, as two major forms of control. Indeed, the 'taxes on knowledge', first raised in 1712 but maintained for 150 years, were intended to make pamphlets and newspapers too expensive for the large majority of people.

The Origins of the Taxes on Knowledge
The 19th-century notion of 'taxes on knowledge' refers to four different taxes, all created in 1712 by the government of Queen Anne. The first of these taxes which was levied by the 10 Anne cap. 19 was the *Newspaper Stamp Duty*. This duty, 1 penny (1d.) per sheet, was fixed at 1$\frac{1}{2}d$. in 1776. Pitt's government raised it by $\frac{1}{2}d$. to make it 2d. in the year of the French Revolution, 1789 (29 Geo. III cap. 50). In 1797 the duty was increased by 75 per cent, and set at 3$\frac{1}{2}d$. In 1815, (55 Geo. III cap. 185), the newspaper duty was increased for the last time. Fixed at 4d, it yielded £383 695 that same year and £476 501 in 1825 (Collet, 1933, p. 15). The price of a stamped paper at 7d. put it definitively out of reach of the vast majority. The 1819 Act did not modify the price of the duty, which remained the same up to 1836. However, the 60 Geo. III cap. 9 reinforced the act of 1815 by extending previous constraints and making subterfuges more difficult. After an epic battle in which working- and middle-class publicists joined forces, the stamp was reduced in 1836 to 1d., before it was repealed altogether in June 1855 (Wiener, 1969).

The second tax was the *Pamphlet Duty*. Fixed at 2 shillings (2s.) per sheet for pamphlets of less than six sheets in 1712, it did not increase until 1815, when it rose to 3s. per sheet. Collecting an insignificant amount of money after the 1819 extension of the newspaper duty to all periodicals, it was the first tax to be repealed in 1833.

The third tax was the *Advertisement Duty*. It was imposed on each advertisement published in a newspaper. The tax was 1s. per advertisement in 1712, 2s. in 1757, 3s. in 1789, to reach 3s. 6d. in 1815 (Aspinall, 1949, p. 16). The tax was repealed in August 1853.

The fourth tax, of a different nature, was the *Excise Duty on Paper*. Thirty-four varieties of paper were taxed by the 10 Anne cap. 19, and the duties varied from 2 to 15s. per ream according to quality. In spite of the 50 per cent reduction allowed by the Melbourne government in 1836, it brought in more than £1 million a year in revenue by the 1850s (Collet, 1933, pp. 179–81). It may be for this reason that it was the last of these duties to be repealed, in June 1861.

The Effects of the Taxes on the Press

These taxes had two consequences. The first was to retard the development of the press in England. Priced at 7d., stamped papers were out of reach of the vast majority of people and therefore both the market of readers and the potential market were very small. These taxes were so restrictive that the number of dailies in London decreased during the four decades preceding the reduction of the newspaper stamp from 4d. to 1d. in 1836. In 1795, 14 dailies were published in London (Andrews, 1859, p. 236). In the year of the tax reduction, 1836, only 11 dailies were published – five morning and six evening newspapers (Crawfurd, 1836, p. 27). Therefore, while the population was passing from 8.9 million in 1801 to 15.9 million in 1841, the number of newspapers produced was declining (Mitchell, 1992, p. 8). By way of contrast, there were 65 dailies in the United States in 1830 (population: 12.9 million) and 138 in 1840 (population: 17.1 million) (Bogue, 1985, p. 110). The city of New York, with just about 250 000 inhabitants, had 15 dailies in 1835 (Seitz, 1928, p. 42). This represented four more than in London, a city of 1.47 million inhabitants, and one less than the whole United Kingdom, Dublin included, where the taxes were half the English rate (Weber, 1963, p. 46).

The second consequence of the newspaper duties, indirect and unintended, was the creation of an illegal press evading the imposts: the unstampeds. The appearance of a working-class press was linked to the rise of a proletarian public sphere. The industrial mode of production began to create a class of men and women whose relationship to this mode of production was so similar that they started to realize in the early decades of the 19th century that they had common interests in spite of the differences between the trades in which they worked (Thompson, E.P., 1991, pp. 781–915). Since the stamp deprived a social class of a public pulpit, its leaders began to feel the need to express this rising class-consciousness, and an illegal working-class press developed between the 1800s and the 1830s. The pauper press had two peaks. The first was in the early 1820s, the second between 1830 and 1836.

After 1836, when the reduction of the newspaper duty from 4*d* to 1*d*. created the popular Sunday market, the unstampeds disappeared. The last penny stamp on newspapers kept dailies too expensive for most people, but fostered the 3*d*. Sunday market. Therefore, in 1836, working-class political weeklies had lost the competitive advantage that the evasion of the 4*d*. stamp had given them. Unstampeds were unable to compete with better-edited newspapers which did not have a specific political calling. Sundays such as the *Illustrated London News*, founded in 1842, the *Lloyd's Illustrated London Newspaper*, 1842, and the *News of the World*, 1843, intended, above all, to distract and amuse their readerships. Against such rivals, working-class unstampeds could not compete, and many unstampeds, such as the *Twopenny Dispatch*, and the *Weekly Herald*, collapsed in 1836 (Bourne, 1887, pp. 119–26; Maccoby, 1935, pp. 419–20).

The unstampeds were not a marginal and alternative movement. Both for the variety of the titles and for their individual and aggregate circulation, the unstampeds constitute an impressive social and discursive phenomenon.

During the 1830s, more than 200 unstampeds were published. One of the most comprehensive lists has been compiled by Patricia Hollis (1970, pp. 318-28). Out of 212 unstampeds, 104 had politics as their main if not exclusive topic, and treated the subject from a working-class ('ultra-radical') point of view. Among the 15 most prominent, were Carlile's *Cosmopolite* (Mar. 1832–Nov. 1834), O'Brien's and Hetherington's *Poor Man's Guardian* (July 1831–Dec. 1835) and *Destructive* (Feb. 1833–Sept. 1836), Carpenter's *Political Letters* (Oct. 1830–May 1831) and Cleave's and Watson's *Working Man's Friend* (Dec. 1832–Aug. 1833). Twelve unstampeds focused on religion, with 'blasphemous' titles such as *Slap at the Church* (Carpenter, Jan. 1832–Nov. 1832), *Antichrist* (Smith, 1832–33), or *Devil's Pulpit* (Revd. Taylor and Carlile, Mar. 1831–Jan. 1832). Twelve were trade unionists, or organs of a working-class organization, such as the *Advocate of Artizans and Labourers Friend* (Feb. 1833–Apr. 1833), or Morrison's *Pioneer* (Sept. 1834–July 1835). Six unstampeds were Owenite, the leading one being Owen's *Crisis* (Apr. 1832–Aug. 1834). Although most unstampeds opened their columns to co-operatives, they had three papers on their own, such as the *Magazine of Useful Knowledge and Co-operative Miscellany* (Oct. 1830–Nov. 1832). Thirty-two unstampeds were published by middle-class educationists in the hope of diverting the working classes from 'seditious' and 'blasphemous' literature. The most prominent were Knight's *Penny Magazine* (Mar. 1832–Dec. 1836) and the *Chambers' Edinburgh Journal* (Feb. 1832–1854). Finally, 26 papers were labelled 'humorous', 17 of them being also classified as 'radical'. Examples include *Punch in London* (Jan. 1832–Apr. 1832), or *Figaro in London* (Dec. 1831–1839).

During the 1830s, working-class publishers printed and diffused unstamped papers which in circulation overtook the legal press (Hollis, 1970, pp. 116–24). The sales of the 15 to 20 most prominent unstampeds fluctuated between 3000 to 8000, with peaks at 10 000 or beyond for a few of them and for short periods of time. Carlile's *Gauntlet* and *Cosmopolite* and Cleave's *Working Man's Friend* sold around 3500, sometimes 5000. Between 12 000 and 15 000 copies of the *Poor Man's Guardian* were sold each Saturday for two years (1832–1833), but the sales subsequently dropped to 7000. Lee's *Man* sold between 5000 and 7000 copies.

These figures place the most important unstampeds among the leading newspapers of their time. A contemporary survey of the number of legal papers sold found that between June 1833 and June 1835 an average of 25 798 Tory and 18 915 Whig newspapers were purchased per day[1] (Maccoby, 1935, p. 141). These figures must be compared to a conservative estimate of the leading unstampeds at 100 000 per week, and of the total unstamped circulation at 200 000 (ibid.). In 1836, the six main unstampeds alone would have reached a weekly circulation of 200 000, and it was claimed that when some of these unstampeds turned broadsheet, each of these papers sold more in a day than *The Times* in a week, or than the *Morning Chronicle* in a month (Hollis, 1969, p. xxiii).

However, the sales of the unstampeds were erratic. Publishers, editors and printers faced severe prosecutions, they had their presses and stocks seized, and they could be imprisoned for months, and sometimes years. In addition, the unstampeds that were confiscated on their way to the provinces were destroyed and those caught transporting them were arrested.

The distribution of unstampeds was therefore a difficult enterprise. Since newsvendors and booksellers refused to distribute unstampeds, working-class publicists had to organize their own network of distribution from top to bottom, at first confined to London, then extended to the provinces (one-half to two-thirds of the production of most prominent London unstampeds was sent to the provinces). Entirely undercover, the distribution system relied upon tricks and stratagems to avoid seizure and arrest. John Cleave used coffins to distribute his publications (the ruse was discovered by the police the day a neighbour called them for fear of an epidemic) and Hetherington had to disguise himself as a Quaker to freely circulate in London (Grant, 1871, pp. 306–9; Holyoake, 1849, p. 3).

The actual readership of these unstampeds is estimated at twenty to thirty times superior to their sales. Unstampeds were read, discussed and debated in working-class public sphere institutions such as taverns, coffee shops, public houses, reading rooms and mechanics' institutes (Webb, 1955, pp. 33–5; Lee, 1976, pp. 35–41). The most well-known of these working-class institutions was the Rotunda, a debating club and meeting centre founded by Richard Carlile in 1830 (Harrison, 1974, p. 66). Unstampeds were also read aloud in offices and workshops. William Cobbett's reference to his 'readers or hearers' in his *Political Register* shows how the reading of unstampeds was an activity that working-class persons performed as members of a public sphere (Wickwar, 1928, p. 54).

1.2 THE PRINCIPLE OF PUBLICITY AND THE UNSTAMPEDS

The Publicist

Before presenting the discourse of the unstampeds, this section starts with an ideal-typical portrait of the publicist. Although this portrait is primarily intended to characterize the English working-class publicist of the 1830s, many of its features are characteristic of publicists in general. Having said this, it needs to be recalled that an ideal type is an '*analytical* construct' which 'cannot be found empirically anywhere in reality' (Weber, 1949, p. 90). Thus, although the following traits were thought to characterize most the figure of the publicist, no publicist is expected to conform absolutely to this ideal type.

First, publicists represent a specific political group, in general a political organization and its members. Through their writings, publicists promulgate the interests of this group and articulate its political ideology and economic doctrine. Indirectly, they also represent a social class, or one of its factions. As representative of a social class, publicists fulfil a double mission. They advocate the political interests of the social class on whose behalf they speak and in addition, they analyse the political process from the particular viewpoint of the social class they represent. With their political commentaries, publicists construct a perspective proper to a social class and thereby develop the aptitude of the members of this social class to see things in their own terms.

Publicists experience their political convictions with great strength and intensity, and the newspapers they publish not only reflect their political beliefs but also their commitment to them. They feel passionately about the cause they promote and write emotionally about it. Unlike journalists and their pretence to be objective, publicists are very combative. They also have few doubts on the rightfulness of their creed, and of its superiority over other doctrines.

Publicists are directly involved in politics. In many cases, they are prominent members of the political organizations their paper represents. Henry Hetherington offers a case in point. In the course of his political career, the *Poor Man's Guardian's* editor helped to set up the Co-operative and Economical Society (1821), the London Mechanics' Institution, the British Association for Promoting Co-operative Knowledge (1829), the Metropolitan Political Union (1830), and, in 1831, he participated to the launch of the National Union of the Working Classes (Wiener, 1969, p. 143).

Publicists feel an immense sense of duty and write to get things changed. Marx's eleventh thesis *Ad Feuerbach*, where he claimed his ambition to transform the world, and not merely to comment upon it, could be engraved not only on Marx's headstone but on the one of the 'unknown publicist'. Publicists' ultimate objective is to change not merely the lot of the social group they represent, but the whole of society according to the principles they believe in. Publicists also write to convince, to persuade, to change people's consciousness. By way of contrast, most journalists today do not entertain the hope of having any influence on the course of events or even on their readers' minds. In fact, as many journalists no longer have the possibility to express the political convictions they may have, journalists today are forced to dissociate their professional activities from their political beliefs.[2] In this respect, the publicist and the journalist illustrate the caricatural opposition, once stated by Marx, between those who live to write and those who write to live (Marx and Engels, 1975, p. 175).

Publicists, who are generally optimistic characters, have a great faith in their influence on readers and in their ability to change the course of events. Today, this faith and this belief in one's power to change things would be taken as particularly naive and adolescent. Nonetheless, publicists' optimism, force of convictions and urge to persuade confer freshness and immediacy on their texts.

The final point concerns a minority of publicists, most notably those who defended the interests of dominated classes. If some of them became prophet, many become martyr; that is, many suffered for adhering to and promoting their political doctrine. Among the British working-class publicists of the first half of the 19th century, many of them became the victim of the sustained repression of successive governments, Whig or Tory. The working-class unstamped movement is littered with accounts of trials and convictions of publishers, printers and hawkers. In an interval of three years, 1819–1821, publishers faced 120 charges for seditious and blasphemous libel (Wickwar, 1928, p. 17). In the 1820s, Richard Carlile spent almost ten years in prison on charges of seditious libel (Wiener, 1969, p. 158). In the same decade, Carlile's 150 volunteer vendors and correspondents endured a total of over 200 years of imprisonment (Harrison, 1974, p. 63). Between 1830 and 1836, there were 750 convictions related to the production and distribution of unstamped papers, most ending in jailing (Wickwar, 1928, p. 30; Wiener, 1969, p. 198). Thus, the reasons that drove them to write, fight and publish were made plain by the risks they knowingly agreed to take. Carlile launched his *Journal*, in January 1830, to 'test the real state of liberty of the press' (in Hollis, 1970, p. 308). Similarly, the *Poor Man's Guardian's* motto reveals Hetherington's drive: 'Published in defiance of "law", to try the power of "might" against "right"'. On the right hand-side of the masthead was a woodcut representing a press, which read 'Liberty of the press', and around the woodcut was the slogan of working-class activists: 'Knowledge is Power'.

Given the fact that publicists' political aims strongly determine the philological nature of the texts they write, it makes sense to examine these texts from the angle of the political function they fulfil. First, publicists formulate the ideologies and propagate the doctrines which promote the economic and political interests of a specific social group. This corresponds to the ideological aspect of the principle of publicity. Second, they publicize information relevant to readers' political activities. This information is related either to a specific political organization or to the political process at large. This is the practical aspect of the same principle. Each of these features of the public press is illustrated below with the working-class unstamped papers of the 1830s.

Ideology and Publicity: 'Knowledge is Power'

By the end of the first half of the 19th century, the working classes did not possess a body of theories either as extensive or as systematic as the one formed by the works of middle-class philosophers and economists. Furthermore, the conceptual categories of burgeoning working-class theories still owed much to middle-class doctrines. Owenism, for instance, bore the mark of Benthamism. The projects of the New Lanark cotton mills, and later, of the co-operative villages, shared with the panopticon the Benthamian assumption that progress or happiness can be produced in a mechanical way (Cole, 1953, pp. 43–90). Similarly, working-class economists, in the 1820s and 1830s, were unable to create an epistemological rupture with their main middle-class opponent, Ricardo. Yet, in spite of these theoretical weaknesses, a distinctive working-class consciousness was emerging in the early decades of the 19th century. Along with other publications, unstampeds contributed to building this class consciousness and to forming a working-class identity (Curran, 1977, pp. 195–230; Thompson, E.P., 1991, pp. 781–94). Unstampeds raised the political awareness of the dominated classes by drawing upon the consequences of the political experience of these years, by articulating ideological themes, by putting feelings into words, by expressing grievances, by proposing political modes of actions and economic solutions, by giving hope and by organizing the political activities and the political life as a whole of the working classes.

The working-class unstampeds of the 1830s may be divided into three main ideological trends: *pragmatic, utopian,* and *confrontational.* The first is composed of the trade-unionist papers, whose principal characteristic was a creed of pragmatism. The main representative of this trend was the *Pioneer,* which became, in 1834, the official paper of the short-lived Grand National Consolidated Trades Union (GNCTU). Mostly preoccupied by questions of trade, such as wages or benefit societies, this trend dissociated politics from matters of trade. Not that pragmatists completely excluded politics from their realm of action, but they acted as though social justice and equality would be obtained through collective trade actions, such as strikes. Pragmatists saw direct political struggles to be useless.

The second trend is constituted by the Owenite papers, in particular *Crisis,* and is characterized by utopianism. To a certain extent, Robert Owen was a character who had the tendency to flee from political reality rather than to confront it. Thus, he endeavoured to create a working-class world within a bourgeois society and refused to engage in conflict against the middle classes. As Owen's authority became increasingly grounded on charisma, Owenism became, even more, an inner-oriented ideology with fewer connections with the real world of political struggles and the position of the working classes within this world (Dupuis, 1991, pp. 265–8).

The last school whose themes are explored was mostly conveyed by unstampeds published by Hetherington, O'Brien, Carlile, Cleave, or Watson. By no means exhaustive, the list includes the *Poor Man's Guardian,* the *Destructive,* the *Twopenny Dispatch,* the *Republican,* or the *Working Man's Friend.* These London artisans formed the vanguard of the working classes, and their unstampeds proposed the most advanced arguments and theories of their time. They were confrontational in the sense that both their acts and their theories directly opposed the interests of labour to the combined political powers of the church, the monarchy, the aristocracy and the middle classes.

The opposition between pragmatists and confrontationalists may be illustrated by means of a few examples from the unstampeds. The position of trade unionists was that unions should be the central body of working-class struggles. Trade unions, thought the *Pioneer*, 'are of all the other means the only mode by which universal suffrage can be safely obtained, because it is obtained by practice . . .' (31 May 1834). With union members having a vote in the union, trade unions would give them universal suffrage because unions would eventually 'swallow up the whole political power', to finally become the House of Trades supplanting the House of Commons (*Pioneer*, 31 May 1834). On the other hand, James O'Brien, a confrontationalist, thought that 'the present objects of the trades' unions can never be attained under the existing government', because the government could maintain by means of law and violence the present form of society (*Poor Man's Guardian*, 7 December 1833). When masters, he further argued, combined to dismiss men and women from work, and thereby endangered the peace of the town, the social order was protected by the mayor, the magistrates, and the Dragoon Guards. Such things, O'Brien wrote, would be impossible with universal suffrage, which would 'place the magistracy and Parliament, and consequently the disposal of the military and police forces in the hands of the entire body of the people' (*Poor Man's Guardian*, 7 December 1833).

A central argument of confrontationalists was that the working classes needed a representative parliament to proclaim legislation that protected their rights and labour. While trade unionists favoured union activism to secure suffrage, confrontationalists wanted the suffrage to protect trade unions. Such were the divisions within the working-class movement. They were not, of course, absolute. Owenite unstampeds supported trade unionism, and Hetherington, publisher of the *Poor Man's Guardian*, greatly admired Robert Owen right up to his death (Holyoake, 1849, p. 6). These ideological conflicts enable us to contextualize the unstampeds within the working-class public discourse. Furthermore, they show that the making of this social class was a historical process during which initially disparate social groups who most often resisted an identification of common interests with other groups united to form a relatively cohesive social entity. During the 19th century, 'class' was a word mostly used in its plural form. This form, as in 'productive classes', 'industrious classes', denotes the awareness of the heterogeneity of the original components of a class in formation. The most far-reaching ideological effect of these unstampeds has been, precisely, the ideological homogenization of diverse social groups and diverse trades. Unstampeds played the crucial role in uniting these groups within a common political struggle. Through this process, out of separate social groups, there emerged a single and relatively united social class.

The political ideology of the confrontational unstampeds in the early 1830s represents a transitional phase in the history of working-class political thought. While the ideology of these unstampeds owed much to Jacobinism (e.g. Paine and Robespierre), they also laid the basis for Chartism. The 1832 Reform Bill, negotiated with landowners of both Houses by the Whig government and which extended the franchise to the middle classes, provides a good illustration of the concrete demands of the working classes in their journey to Chartism. The efforts of publicists to arouse a stronger working-class feeling was greatly facilitated by the £10 qualification franchise which legally delimited the working classes, in general not rich enough to qualify. However, as clear as the situation was, unstampeds had to dismiss the middle-class argument about the community of interests between both classes. The first way to do so was to explain the real structure of political alliances, namely, that Whigs and Tories were in league to deny the working class their political rights. The second was to repeat, every week, the political demands of the working classes, which included the extension of the franchise to all men over 18, the vote by secret ballot, an annual parliament and the withdrawal of pecuniary qualifications for members of Parliament.

Both tasks were undertaken by the *Poor Man's Guardian*, whose leaders between September 1831 and January 1832 mostly concerned the bill.[3] Against middle-class ideologists, who promised that once in the Commons they would be more inclined to give the vote to the working classes, Hetherington argued that the economic interests of both classes were antagonistic, as they sought to 'get the benefit of their [the working classes'] work at the least possible price' and that, therefore, the middle classes would pass laws to protect their own interests (*Poor Man's Guardian*, 8 December 1832). Claims for universal suffrage were reiterated weekly in many forms. The *Poor Man's Guardian* calculated that the new bill would not give more than 700 000 votes, and that there were 900 000 families who lived by means of the various imposts on the 'fruit of the working-class', itself of about 4.6 million families (26 November 1831). In the opinion of the *Poor Man's*

Guardian, this demonstrated that the political exclusion of the working classes was linked to its economic exploitation, and that the two realms, the political and the economic, were connected.

The lack of social justice in Britain was underlined by depicting the government as an arbitrary class power that was both corrupt and repressive. The corruption theme, which runs from Jacobinism to Chartism, via the unstampeds of the 1820s, such as Cobbett's *Political Register*, denounced state and church abuses. They include the sinecures, pensions and privileges that the government distributed among aristocrats and which made of this class an 'expensive encumbrance; an impediment to the public good' (*Poor Man's Guardian*, 23 November 1833). The attacks on corruption related to inequalities of access to public wealth, and those on repression pointed to the means that maintained these inequalities. The working classes and government were described, every week, as two directly antagonistic forces. The main function of government was to oppress people and to ensure the political conditions to maintain the present state of society with its hereditary privileges and exploitative factory system. The ideal government for the *Poor Man's Guardian* was: democratic (both Houses elected by universal suffrage); secular (the church separated from state and payments to the church not compulsory); and republican.

The demand to repeal the taxes on knowledge was associated with these claims for more political equality. The agitation for repeal was at its peak in the 1830s, and the issue was constantly addressed by the unstamped press. 'Taxation without representation', said the motto, 'is tyranny, and ought to be resisted.' All classes had an equal right to knowledge, but this right was transformed into a privilege by the 1819 Six Acts,[4] 'enacted to keep the labouring class in ignorance and delusion' (*Poor Man's Guardian*, 19 November 1831). Since the very existence of these papers was produced in defiance of these laws, in August 1831 the *Poor Man's Guardian* set up a subscription fund for the victims of the 'odious' Six Acts. The fund was used to pay a small imprisonment premium per week to street-vendors. By 13 October 1832, it had collected £233. All events related to the struggle for a free press were fully publicized. Arrests and prosecutions were reported and verbatim passages of trials published. The ideal of a free press was associated with a fairer society, in which the widespread diffusion of knowledge among the working classes would give them the power to overthrow tyranny and the moral power to make their rights prevail. With a free press, said John Cleave, 'who will dare to oppress us?' (*Poor Man's Guardian*, 30 July 1831).

As a whole, the *Poor Man's Guardian* and its readership had a clear and precise idea about the relative position of the working classes in the British social structure. A reader of this London unstamped even developed an idea which bears some resemblance to Louis Althusser's theory of state apparatuses. The reader's thesis of the 'four estates' is an attempt to offer a comprehensive view of the means used by the dominant classes to subjugate the working classes. The four estates were said to 'contribute equally towards holding things together in their present form' by maintaining the poor in their 'present state of poverty', and the rest in 'their present state of lazy enjoyment' (*Poor Man's Guardian*, 14 April 1832). The first of these estates was composed of the landed gentry, the 'land-stealers', together with the merchants and manufacturers. The second was the priesthood, or the 'tithe-stealers'. The third estate was the government, and the last, the stamped newspapers, was called the 'legitimate press' (ibid.). The anonymous author of these lines who signed the article as 'one of the oppressed' placed the emphasis on the collusion among the four estates. The priesthood was connected to the 'land-stealers', and their purpose was to frighten people with the threat of hell in order to maintain them in their submission to the landed gentry. If the priesthood was rewarded by the landed gentry with tithes, the government was rewarded with taxes. The author also developed the first critique of dominant ideology. The stamped newspapers, 'established' by the first three estates, 'mob, abuse, villify, and belie' to the extent that people neglect to demand their rights. The role of the stamped press is to disguise the reality of the system of oppression, that is, to present diverse fallacious arguments which purport to explain and justify the distress of the working classes. The press masked the dominant classes' robbery of a large proportion of working-class production: when the dominant classes could not consume enough of working-class produce, the press reasoned that there was no trade, that the working classes were too numerous, and that they had to emigrate. With several concrete examples, readers were warned against the '*seductive* language and the barefaced villainy' of the fourth estate (ibid.).

During the 1830s, the *Poor Man's Guardian* and other unstampeds began to realize that economic 'exploitation' by the middle classes was worse than the traditional aristocratic 'despotism'. The 1832 Reform Act, the 1834 Malthusian–Benthamite parliamentary reform of the Speenhamland system, and the absence of any serious piece of factory legislation that would have protected an increasing number of the working classes from inhuman working conditions led many working-class publicists to shift the focus of analysis. The middle classes in general, and more precisely the 'capitalists' and 'traders', were increasingly depicted as the main oppressors. This new class-antagonism is manifest in the following series of statements on the 'true character of the middle-class':

> It is this class which has made the condition of the British labourer worse than the brute beast. [. . .] It is this class which chorusses 'God save the King', at our theatres, and bawls 'Britains [*sic*] never will be Slaves', while slaves the most abject that ever crawled the earth, they have made our once happy labourers. [. . .] It is this class which two weeks ago, asked permission of Lord Melbourne to form a permanent armed association under the name of Special Constables [. . .] in a view to aid the police and magistracy in crushing the Trades' Unions. It is this class which made the Revolution of 1789 in France, in order to seize the estates of the French Noblesse and Clergy, and afterwards destroyed that revolution to prevent the working classes from sharing its benefits (*Poor Man's Guardian*, 30 March 1833).

By 1834, the main rhetorical and theoretical efforts of the editors of the *Poor Man's Guardian* were directed against the middle classes. They were aware that the antagonism between the two classes was based on opposite economic interests. The interests of 'capital and labour', of 'capitalists and their workmen', were perceived as being 'diametrically opposed' (*Poor Man's Guardian*, 8 October 1834). Because they grounded this class antagonism in economy, they felt the need of a proper working-class economic doctrine. The nucleus of this working-class economics was a labour theory of value. Its core hypothesis is that labour is the source of value of commodities. From this perspective, trade and capital become useless, the capitalist nefarious, and the labourer the source of wealth. Since labour is the source of wealth, the sole producer of society's wealth are the 'productive' classes, not the capitalists (e.g. *Poor Man's Guardian*, 12 November 1831). From this perspective, the inequality in the distribution of wealth is therefore double: not only do capitalists not create any wealth, but they appropriate the profit created by the labour of the working classes. As William Carpenter stated in his 'social economy': 'Mere capitalists, or persons who accumulate money by purchasing the labour of others, while they perform no labour themselves, do not add anything to the wealth of the society' (*Poor Man's Guardian*, 17 September 1831).

Competition between workers was also blamed for causing distress among them. Competition between labourers resulted from mechanization and from the legislation adapted to the economic needs of the master class. The *Poor Man's Guardian* argued that the fact that every fifth man was a pauper, and that only a proportion of labourers was fully employed showed that, contrary to the assertions of the middle class, machinery did not increase employment. Organized competition was used to reduce wages, and because there were too many labourers competing for too few jobs, many were pauperized (*Poor Man's Guardian*, 24 December 1831).

Working-class publicists did not take private property for granted. They referred to it as a 'system' and it was perceived as a source of many of their evils. Henry Hetherington criticized the attempts by the *Penny Magazine* to present the 'inviolability of property' as the 'grand stimulant of production' (*Poor Man's Guardian*, 26 January 1833). In this magazine 'wherever the institution of *property* is glanced at, it is with a view to inculcate its anti-social "rights", or rather its cannibal pretensions' (ibid.). Co-operators and Owenites attempted to set alternative models. Owen, for instance, proposed a community of property based on the equitable distribution of the fruits of labour among those who produce them (*Poor Man's Guardian*, 24 November 1832).

Such were some of the statements and opinions of the *Poor Man's Guardian*. This paper illustrates the potential of a working-class public press to voice a political and economic doctrine corresponding to what they thought were the interests of the working classes, to propagate and construct, progressively, a world vision of their own, and finally to publicly articulate and develop an ideology as close as possible to the needs of the political struggle in which they were engaged.

Publicity and Politics: 'Hear, Hear'

Public texts also fulfilled a series of roles which may be identified as having a practical character. Most notably, public newspapers performed several tasks in relation to the political organizations they represented. The first of these tasks was to keep the public informed about the activities of these societies. This role of publicity is highlighted when these papers reported at length the public meetings of such organizations. Speeches and debates were reported in indirect speech with long verbatim extracts. Audience's reactions were dutifully reported: 'shame', 'hear', 'laughter', 'cheers', 'tremendous cheering', 'roars of applause'. In the following abstract, the *Poor Man's Guardian* reports a speech on the British intervention in Belgium given at a meeting of the National Union of the Working Classes:

> The Belgians were brave men, they were not afraid to fight, but they would not fight for despotism, and so they had an English fleet and a French army about their ears to support their dear king (laughter.) He was dear to us also for he cost us £50 000 a year (hear.) The Whigs said they had honourably settled the affairs of Belgium six months ago, but was it honourable to force a king upon that country who was a pensioner of England and the nominee of the holy alliance? (hear.) The Whigs had just acted as Wellington did in respect to Turkey, and all was done to keep friends with designing Russia, cold-blooded Austria, and faithless Prussia (cheers.) (*Poor Man's Guardian*, 1 December 1832).

London unstampeds also reported the speeches of politicians, political leaders, and public activists not necessarily connected with the organization, but whose political goals were close to those of the paper. Moreover, these newspapers, whose editorial line was generally based on a very specific political doctrine, kept their columns open to sympathetic opponents. Unstampeds, and public papers in general, also gave much room to readers' letters, who exchanged their views and opinions through these columns. In other words, public newspapers organized a political debate which they structured according to their political objectives.

Another role of public newspapers was the coordination and

the promotion of the activities of their respective political organizations. Papers' columns were opened to members of different
societies reporting on their societies' activities or debating on their
goals and strategies. Future events, meetings and publications
were announced in the last pages of papers. In addition, during
the pre-telegraphic era, newspapers were the only communication medium. Therefore, they were the only means for groups
spread throughout the national territory to know about each other's
activities and to be kept informed about the headquarters. Local
clubs would have been isolated from each other if unstampeds
did not keep them informed of both national events and activities of other local branches. Without the unstampeds, the working-class movement could never have developed at national level.

To publicize, promote and coordinate are the three tasks that
were performed by public newspapers in their organic relation
to political organizations. As illustrated with the unstampeds, public
newspapers did not have an autonomous existence from the field
of politics. Combative and purposive, they were directly and
actively involved in the field of political struggle.

A second aspect of the practical character of the principle of
publicity was that public newspapers played the key role in
informing their readers about general political matters. Central
to this task was the publicizing of parliamentary proceedings.
Jürgen Habermas has already underlined the political significance
of this publicity, which he considered essential to the formation
of the public sphere (Habermas, 1991, pp. 57–73). British political
activists were the first in Europe to be granted the right to publicize
parliamentary debates, during the 1770s (Siebert, 1965, pp. 346–92).
Since this date, the reputation of a British newspaper was built
on the quality of its reports from the Houses. The first paper to
gain a reputation for excellence was the *Morning Chronicle*. After
James Perry's death, in 1821, *The Times* became, in its turn, famous
for its parliamentary columns.

It is significant that 19th-century working-class papers, whose
readers did not possess the franchise, also publicized the parliamentary debates. Among the unstampeds, the *Destructive* and the
Working Man's Friend were those which gave the most importance to parliamentary proceedings, where they appeared each
week on the first two pages. Henry Hetherington, of the *Poor
Man's Guardian*, who named the MPs the 'few elected', and the
Lords the 'self-elected', nonetheless devoted the necessary amount

of space to report the debates of the Houses, albeit in an indirect style but with accurate and complete lengthy quotations.

1.3   READING PUBLIC TEXTS

It may seem unreasonable to attribute any representativeness to this 'radical' discourse, let alone to pretend that journalism supplanted that discourse. Indeed, not all 18th- and 19th-century newspapers shared all the attributes of the public newspaper. First, it can be argued that, however exceptional, the unstampeds were not a fringe phenomenon. As seen in the first section, the circulation of the illegal press compared very well with the sales of the stamped press. In addition, other, less-known, newspapers displayed philological characteristics similar to the working-class press of the period. This was the case of the numerous Northern middle-class papers which promoted the economic doctrine and the political ideals favourable to the middle classes[5] (see Read, 1961). Finally, some of the newspapers published under government patronage, in England as elsewhere in Europe, were no less partisan, opinionated and politics-centred than the 'radical' press (see Aspinall, 1949).

To give an account of the discursive characteristics of the press before the emergence of journalism, the concept of public discourse is more appropriate than the notions of 'party journalism' and 'propaganda', which anticipate history. In addition, as will be seen at a later stage, the contrast and opposition between the public and journalistic discourse gives a dynamic and yet realistic account of the discursive changes which have occurred in the press since the 19th century. These changes are obscured by the traditional concepts used by political historians which give a false sense of historical continuity. If generalizations can be made from the empirical material presented in this chapter, public texts would be characterized by four specific features.

Firstly, public discourse is *partisan*. In their texts, publicists articulate the political vision and voice the interests of a specific social group. This partisanship is communicated through two channels. The first channel entails partisanship being conveyed by means of political discussion and commentaries. This corresponds to the ideological role of public newspapers, publicists acting as propagandists and as advocates of political doctrines and ideologies. The second channel connotes partisanship being expressed through political reporting. Publicists select facts and events which are most relevant to their political interests and then report these facts from the point of view of a specific and explicit political viewpoint. Publicists both construct and represent reality from a specific political angle. In other words, publicists do not attempt to be objective and do not separate their beliefs from their discourse. Publicists' own perception of reality is strongly influenced by their political convictions, which then inform their discursive production.

Secondly, public texts are 'public' in the specific sense that the opinions they express and the ideology they convey coincide, or are intended to coincide, with the *collective* political needs of the members of a political group. These texts are public because they do not address readers individually, they do not appeal to their subjective side. They address readers in their social and political dimension, as members of a social and political collectivity (see also Garnham, 1986, p. 48).

Thirdly, public texts are *relationally coherent*. As for popular culture, there is an 'equilibrium' between the 'ideology' of these texts and 'the actual social conditions' under which their readers live (Adorno, 1991, p. 140). Publicists' political partisanship is congruous with the political position of the class or fraction of class they speak to (and speak for) and thus there exists a *homology* between the political situation of the social collectivity to which these texts are addressed and the ideology of these texts.

Finally, publicists produce *dialogical* texts. This dialogism originates from the didactic intention of publicists, who often have as their main objective to increase their readers' political knowledge and competence. Because of this specific intention, publicists expect and demand an 'active understanding' from their audience, and, ultimately, it is this orientation towards active understanding which creates a particularly strong dialogical interaction between publicists and their readers (Bakhtin, 1981, pp. 279–81). Publicists do indeed reflect in their texts some of their readers' prejudices. However, quite often publicists take the risk of confronting readers' opinions. As publicists refuse to leave readers in their own subjective world and attempt to widen their political horizons, they have to argue and struggle against some of their readers' preconceived ideas. Publicists constantly strive to expand the limits of the field of consciousness of their readers and continuously attempt to transcend their actual political consciousness to address their 'possible consciousness' (as translated from the German *Zugerechte Bewusstein* by Lucien Goldmann, 1971, pp. 7–24). To address this consciousness, publicists have to transcend readers' immediate experience of life and explain things in their complexity and beyond their appearance.

To conclude, is it possible to assess the political impact of the public press? The general opinion among historians on the working-class press of this period is that its influence upon its public was considerable (see Curran, 1977; Thompson, E.P., 1991, p. 781). Nonetheless, the nature of this effect is difficult to appraise. Ultimately, this question refers back to the relation between culture, discourse and class formation, which is notoriously hard to conceptualize (see Katznelson, 1986; Thompson, E.P., 1991, 1995; Steinmetz, 1992; Somers, 1992, 1996).

Tentatively, several layers of effects can be distinguished. First, it seems to be beyond doubt that the unstampeds contributed to the formation of a proper working-class identity in Britain.[6] The working-class press contributed to uniting workers living an unrelated existence in different industries into a politically coherent social class by making them realize the shared and common aspects of their lives. A working-class identity was discursively constructed by a press which created 'unified fields of exchange and communication' where men and women progressively recognized each other as belonging to the same collective group by becoming aware of the identical elements in their lives (Anderson, 1991, p. 44). In other words, the working-class public discourse created a sense of sameness among people who previously perceived themselves as different and unrelated.

Working-class papers also created a sense of purpose among the working classes and played a key role in building the class consciousness of this social class. Here, the notion of class consciousness is understood as the most conscious and voluntary element of class identity, as the political dimension of this concept. Publicists fostered this class consciousness and attempted to transform the English working class into a 'class-for-itself' by articulating political doctrines and ideologies relationally coherent to the objective situation of the working classes within the class structure and by interpreting reality in a way to make workers in different trades realize that they shared the same interests and the same political objectives. This class consciousness also stemmed from the fact that publicists urged their readers to act, and to do so collectively. Publicists encouraged people to struggle for political ideals, and enabled them to unite to achieve these ideals. Publicists created a sense of common purpose and common aspiration among the people by arousing their will for collective struggle.

Finally, at the institutional level, one may follow James Curran in asserting that the unstamped press promoted working-class political organizations (Curran, 1977, p. 204). As discussed above, the link between the unstampeds and the political organizations was organic. Working-class publicists coordinated and promoted the activities of the organizations to which they belonged, published large extracts of the debates which took place at the meetings and publicized the speeches of their leaders.

2

The Formation of the Journalistic Field

This chapter aims at understanding the structural and economic causes of the transition in the British press from a public to a journalistic discourse in the course of the 19th century. It focuses on the formation of the journalistic field in Britain, as part of the argument that the journalistic discourse is the product of the emergence, during the second half of the 19th century, of a specialized and increasingly autonomous field of discursive production.

2.1 JOURNALISM AS A FIELD OF DISCURSIVE PRODUCTION

The formation of the journalistic field began when the taxes on knowledge were repealed between 1855 and 1861. As long as the taxes on knowledge were imposed on the press, stamped papers were priced at 7 pence. This price was well out of reach of the vast majority and thus the market of readers was small and too restricted to trigger market mechanisms. The repeal of the taxes between 1855 and 1861 changed all this and opened up the possibility of selling newspapers for one penny, and a few decades later, for half-a-penny. This price, affordable for more people, greatly enlarged the market of newspapers' readers. From that time on, newspaper owners and journalists have competed for shares in this market. Through diverse mechanisms, these competitive struggles have created the journalistic field.

Section 2.1 introduces the concept of the journalistic field. Section 2.2 examines the mechanisms which exacerbated competitive struggles among newspapers from the 1850s onwards and which brought into existence the journalistic field in Britain. Section 2.3 focuses on the way economic competition has structured the journalistic field and identifies the processes of industrialization, concentration and capitalization. The last section draws the ideal-typical portrait of an important historical figure which appeared with the formation of the journalistic field, that of the press baron.

The Journalistic Field and Competitive Struggles

Prior to the emergence of the journalistic field, the press was not a distinctive field of discursive production. Publicists were constituents of either a bourgeois or proletarian public sphere, and their texts were the expression of their relative positions in these spheres. This chapter attempts to demonstrate how the dynamic of economic competition created an autonomous field of discursive production which increasingly followed its own immanent economic laws.

Although the argument attributes a prominent role to economic competition in the formation of the journalistic field, it is not my intention to reduce the notion of field to its economic basis. According to Bourdieu, within a field of cultural production, agents, groups of agents and institutions compete with different types of capital and for different types of profit. They compete for recognition, legitimacy, prestige, privilege and power. Agents in struggles employ different strategies as a function of the amount of cultural, social, or economic capital they possess, as a function of the position they occupy or want to reach, and as a function of the rules of the field (Bourdieu, 1993).

Within the journalistic field, struggles occur at three different levels. First, agents struggle for positions within the same institution (for instance, several journalists within a newspaper hope to become news editor). Second, collective producers compete against each other within the same market (competition among quality papers, among tabloids). Third, there are also competitive struggles among different types of producer (between tabloids and television). Struggles among agents are relatively autonomous of economic stakes. At the market level, however (second and third types of struggles), struggles are mainly economic, the main force is economic capital, and the main stake is economic profit. Dominant and dominated positions within the same market may be rated in economic terms, such as in terms of the percentage of market shares.

From a historical perspective, the second and third types of struggle are the chief determinants of the discourse of the press. What differentiates journalism from the earlier forms of discourse produced by the press is that the texts which form journalism are the products of conflictual *relations of production*. Economic competition among collective agents within the journalistic field, a specific form of struggle, is a chief determinant of journalists' discursive practices and thus of the philological characteristics of the texts they write.

What is being argued is that economic competition among collective agents is not the only form of struggle within the field, but the most important. In the first place, economic struggles defined the limits of the journalistic field. This process can be explained the following way. The intensity of these struggles forces producers (most notably newspaper proprietors) into an increasing rationalization of their process of production. This rationalization of the process of production means that to gain shares in a market, agents must invest a great amount of energy and capital. The level of investment necessary to gain shares continuously increases, because competitors, to gain a competitive advantage over their rivals, incessantly improve their tools of production. The search for this advantage may induce producers to improve the product they offer to the consumer or to manufacture this product at a minimal cost. For this reason, the productive tasks become increasingly difficult to perform and the products delivered to the market increasingly sophisticated. After a certain period of time, the limits of a field are defined by (a) those who can sustain the necessary amount of investment to pursue the struggle and (b) those who are able to perform complex tasks and deliver sophisticated products. During the course of the second half of the 19th century, the process of production of a daily newspaper became considerably more complex. Between the 1830s and the 1890s, the amount of information to be processed, the number of copies to be printed and the number of pages per issue had considerably increased. What a handful of workers could produce in the 1830s required, by the 1890s, several hundred employees, thereby seriously restricting the number of potential players in the field.

The second reason for the importance of economic struggles within the journalistic field is that these struggles gave to this field its shape and its structure. As will be examined in Section 2.3, the processes of industrialization and concentration were themselves originated by economic competition among agents. The journalistic field is above all an industrial field, a field where the most powerful agents are corporations and where economic capital, material stakes, economic profit, and economic struggles prevail over other species of capital, profit or struggles. The latter do not disappear from industrial fields, but, in those fields, the rules of the game are predominantly defined by the economy.

Finally, the prominence accorded to struggles of an economic nature has a historical justification. In Britain, the phase of initial development of the journalistic field, which lasted until approximately the 1920s, is characterized by a strong increase in the amount of economic capital flowing within the field. The growing importance of capital, which began to circulate like blood in a living organism within the journalistic field, was a process occurring generally in the British economy. During the period appropriately named the 'age of capital' by Eric Hobsbawm, the British economy was in a phase of horizontal expansion, and economic capital was becoming a determining force in numerous new sectors which were being industrialized during this period precisely (Hobsbawm, 1975). In the press as elsewhere, entrepreneurs were discovering new sectors in which to invest their capital with an expectation of profit.

In addition, there was almost no state intervention in the journalistic field throughout this initial phase of development. From the 1920s, the entry of the BBC in the journalistic field modified, and somewhat restricted, the flow and influence of capital in the media field. However, until the 1920s, the rules of the game were plainly and directly defined by the forces of economic capital.

2.2 ECONOMIC COMPETITION WITHIN THE JOURNALISTIC FIELD

The *annus mirabilis* of the British press was 1855, in which the repeal of the last penny of the stamp duty opened up the possibility of selling newspapers for one penny. The immediate effect of this was to create a market of readers, as opposed to a public, and in consequence, to provoke competitive struggles to conquer shares in this market. This section examines the three competitive mechanisms introduced by the repeal and the subsequent creation of the penny market. These three mechanisms are the sudden growth of the number of newspapers, the increase in the average circulation of newspapers and the limitations on newspapers' ability to generate financial resources.

Growth of the Total Number of Newspapers

The first effect of the 1855 abolition was to significantly increase the number of newspapers in the United Kingdom. The characterization of what accounted to an explosion depends on: (1) the period of time considered; (2) the area of sale; (3) the character of the newspapers taken into account.

(1) Within one year of the repeal, Mitchell's Newspaper Directory registered an increase of 115 newspapers, class and trades included (Collet, 1933, p. 134). The upward trend continued well after this initial boom. In 1856, there were 530 newspapers; by 1895, they were 1798 (ibid.).

(2) In 1855, Karl Marx thought that the 'revolution . . . caused by the abolition of stamp duty' mostly concerned the provincial press (Marx and Engels, 1980, p. 281). According to Marx, four penny dailies appeared in Glasgow, and Liverpool and Manchester, hitherto without dailies, turned their weeklies into daily papers (ibid.). Between 1837 and 1887, the number of English provincial newspapers increased more than five times, growing from 264 to 1366 (Lee, 1976, p. 291). However, London also had its revolution. In the year following the abolition several dailies were launched, such as the *Daily Telegraph*, the *Morning News*, or the *Morning Star*, and numerous others were started in the following decades (Bourne, 1887, pp. 234–8). In the capital, between 1837 and 1887, total newspapers increased more than twelve times, passing from 56 to 680 (Lee, 1976, p. 291).

(3) The increase from 264 to 1366 in the provinces and from 56 to 680 in London concerns all types of newspapers as well as periodicals. The increase of dailies, Mornings and Evenings, was no less significant. From 43 in 1868 the number rose to 139 in 1886. During the 1890s, the number came to 126, and in 1900 a record of 172 dailies was reached (ibid., p. 131).

This fast and steady growth in the number of papers in the decades following the repeal helps to illuminate its effect on the press. By the 1880s, with three times more dailies than a few decades earlier, the press became an economic sector where the commercial interests of its members were bound to come into conflict. During the immediate decades following the repeal, lower prices increased demand, thus resulting in revenue gains as well as rises in profit rates. Consequently the press attracted new investors seduced by these rates of profits. However, the one-penny market was limited and, progressively, the supply started to exceed the demand. This situation originated conflictual relations of production among producers whose effect was to structure the British press into a field of competitive struggles.

With this logic, newspapers soon had to struggle not only for market shares but for survival. This new environment made agents' economic and discursive behaviour more violent, more aggressive: *Homo homini lupus*. For a newspaper to survive, its production had to be cost-efficient, its management business-minded, and its circulation important enough to reach the break-even point imposed by production costs. The first effects of this increasing competitive pressure were already felt by the end of the 19th century, when newspapers began to close down. By 1910, the number of dailies declined to 121, a drop of 30 per cent compared to the 172 dailies of 1900 (Lee, 1976, p. 131).

Increase in Average Circulation

There is no discursive production without an expectation of profit, whether it be symbolic, political, or economic. Whereas the production of public texts was, in the main, driven by an expectation of political gain, the repeal of the taxes on knowledge made economic profit an even more rational objective for press owners to pursue. Not that publicists never made financial gains out of their activities, but economic profit became, after the repeal, a legitimate and autonomous motive for owning a newspaper. Increasingly, the field attracted entrepreneurs who were primarily interested in the business aspect of journalism, and for many of them politics was well beyond their horizon. The capitalist ethos which prevailed among journalists and Fleet Street managers at the turn of the 20th century began to resonate in many of their statements. J.D. Symon, editor of an illustrated weekly, thought that the journalist is a 'man of business', 'trad[ing] in words, just as other men trade in dry or soft goods' (Symon, 1914, pp. 99–100).

The rapidly expanding circulations following the abolition of the duty reflected the pursuit of readership for purely economic reward. The press was no longer animated by symbolic and political struggles, but more prosaically by economic competition for readers and profits. Sixteen years after the abolition of the duty, in January 1871, the *Daily Telegraph* published its certified average daily circulation each day, something no newspaper in the past felt compelled to do. By the Edwardian decade, circulation figures were commented on in leaders and were topics for competitions. Once, the *Daily Mail* published on the front page, as though it were a scoop, its circulation figures for each day of the four preceding years (8 February 1908).

The 1855 abolition created a new dynamic in the press, economic competition making of newspaper production a frantic and feverish activity. In 1801, the eight main newspapers had an average circulation of 1800 copies. There was little variation between their circulations: the highest sale was that of *The Times*, at 2500, the lowest that of the *Morning Post*, at about 1000 daily copies (Wadsworth, 1955, p. 7). In 1821, with the exception of *The Times* (which by then was taking advantage of the peculiar situation created by the advertisement duty) other papers sold between 2000 and 3000 daily copies. In 1837, there was still little variation between the circulations of these eight papers, and all stood close to the average daily circulation of 3862, of 3700 in 1846 and of 2775 in 1850 (Howe, 1943, p. 13). In addition, each newspaper knew little variation in its own circulation: the *Morning Chronicle* sold 2000 in 1801 and 2900 in 1850, the *Morning Herald*, 2500 in 1801 and 3600 in 1850.

The post-repeal situation is completely different. If between 1800 and 1850 there was little increase in the average circulation, during the next half of the century the average daily circulation was multiplied by 40. From less than 5000 in the 1850s, by 1900 the average circulation had reached more than 200 000 for the leading dailies. Between these two dates, the average circulation steadily increased, decade after decade. In the 1870s and 1880s, the sales of the morning papers published in London ranged from 90 000 to 300 000 (Wadsworth, 1955, p. 21). In the 1900s, newspapers such as the *Daily Chronicle*, *Daily Express* and *Daily News* reached the 400 000 figure (Blumenfeld, 1933, p. 107).

Correlatively, the leading circulation was multiplied by 20 between the 1850s and 1900s. If *The Times'* monopoly was criticized when it reached 38 000 copies in 1850, the *Daily Mail* was selling more than 800 000 by the 1900s. During the four decades following the repeal, the *Daily Telegraph* was the leading paper in terms of circulation. The *Daily Telegraph* quickly passed *The Times'* sales to reach 141 700 by 1861 and 242 000 copies by 1877 (Wadsworth, 1955, p. 20). The next circulation leader was the *Daily Mail*, which outdid its rivals from 1896 to 1933. Within a couple of months after its launch in May 1896 the *Daily Mail* sold 200 000 daily copies. In constant growth, it reached the million mark within five years, during the South African war (Jones, 1919, p. 143). Thereafter, the *Daily Mail* stabilized at around 800 000 copies until the outbreak of the First World War (Wareham Smith to Viscount Northcliffe, 10 July 1914, Northcliffe Papers, Add. MSS 62 212).

The conflictual logic of this economic dynamic was epitomized by the notorious circulation war which broke out early in the 1930s between four popular dailies: *Daily Herald*, belonging to the Odhams group, *Daily Mail*, Rothermere, *Daily Express*, Beaverbrook, and *News-Chronicle*, Inveresk group. The strategies to attract new readers and boost circulation involved competitions, promotional games and heavy advertising. The *Daily Herald* multiplied competitions and its canvassers offered cameras, fountain pens, silk stockings, tea-kettles, or cutlery to new subscribers (Williams, 1957, p. 200). At the peak of the war, it offered the complete work of Dickens (16 volumes) to those who subscribed to the paper for ten weeks. This economic war cost millions to those who were involved in it. Employing altogether 50 000 canvassers, the total cost of promotion was £60 000 a week, or £3 million a year (ibid., p. 199). The high intensity of the competitive struggle is reflected in the sharp rise of the circulation of these papers. They doubled their readership in a couple of years to reach an average circulation of 1 800 000 in 1939, the *Daily Express* and the *Daily Herald* crossing the 2 million mark in the early 1930s (Wadsworth, 1955, p. 35).

Limitations in Generating Financial Resources

Another effect of the repeal of the taxes on knowledge and the opening of a market of readers was that prices were now directly determined by market forces. The price dynamics of the pre- and post-repeal period may be contrasted with episodes in the life of the *Daily News*, before the repeal, and *Daily Telegraph*, after 1855. At its launch, on 21 January 1846, the stamp duty was fixed at 1*d.* and the *Daily News* was priced 4*d*. After a catastrophic beginning with Charles Dickens as editor, Foster came to edit the paper, and Dilke, the manager, cut the price to $2\frac{1}{2}d$. In five months, the circulation rose from 4000 to 22 000, but at $2\frac{1}{2}d$. the enterprise proved ruinous. Foster tried 3*d.*, then 5*d.*, but the paper's circulation dropped again, and then attempted to re-establish it by going back to 4*d.* Meanwhile, the paper lost four times its original capital of £50 000 (Wadsworth, 1955, p. 10). Alternatively, one day before the stamp tax demise, on 29 June 1855, the *Daily Telegraph and Courier* appeared at 2*d.* It lost such sums in a month that, by September, the *Daily Telegraph* had to halve its price, and this move allowed it to dominate the market up to the launch of the *Daily Mail*. By 1862, its sales equalled those of all the other London morning papers combined (Bourne, 1887, pp. 234–7). The two situations reflect different economic logics. With the penny stamp, four pennies was the minimum equilibrium price for the *Daily News* as for other newspapers. Without the stamp, for most newspapers, with the exception of *The Times*, one penny was the maximum that could be charged for a copy.

Daily newspapers were among the first commodities to be mass-produced and -distributed. Indeed, the expansion of the market after 1855 generated a volume of sales sizeable enough to allow for economies of scale which reduced the production cost per copy. Economies of scale made the one penny copy possible. Competition however made it *necessary*. Both circulation leaders of their respective period, the *Daily Telegraph* and the *Daily Mail*, owed part of their success to their ability to set lower cover prices than their rivals. If the *Daily Telegraph* was the first daily to be sold for a penny in 1855, the *Daily Mail* was the first prominent daily to be sold for half a penny in 1896. By the end of the century, the rivals of the *Daily Mail* were forced to halve their price, and popular papers became the 'halfpenny press'. In 1889, 46 dailies were sold for a penny, 87 for half-a-penny; in 1913, 27 were sold for a penny, 106 for half-a-penny (Wadsworth, 1955, p. 26).

Therefore, the cover price became a determining factor in the competitiveness of a journal on the marketplace. Northcliffe, for example, after having tried other expedients, was forced to bring down the price of *The Times* (which he owned between 1908 and 1922) from $3\frac{1}{2}d$. to 1*d.* in order to compete with the *Daily Telegraph*. If the price-change, in 1913, made *The Times* gain more than 160 000 readers, to reach a circulation of above 210 000, when it went back to 3*d.* in 1919 it fell back to a circulation of 110 000 (ibid., pp. 34–5). Because of economic competition, a newspaper cannot set its price independently of rivals competing for the same market. Indeed, a press-owner deciding to halve the price of his paper may force other proprietors out of the market if they cannot follow suit: sink or swim. The cover price becomes an economic weapon which can be used against rivals. In lowering the price of one of his papers, a newspaper owner can diminish his rivals' ability to generate revenue from sales and therefore harm their capacity to re-invest the necessary amount of economic capital to sustain the competitive struggle. Such pricing strategies can kill off rivals if their production costs are higher than the level of their revenues as imposed by dominant competitors. When dominant competitors sell commodities below production costs for a period of time with the intention of annihilating rivals, this strategy is called *predatory pricing.*

In sum, the revenue itself of a newspaper is dependent upon the evolution of struggles within the field, that is, competitors using price as a means to limit others' ability to generate financial resources. Concentration of ownership in the press is the most obvious consequence of the use of such a strategy.

2.3 ECONOMIC COMPETITION AND THE PROCESS OF STRUCTURATION IN THE JOURNALISTIC FIELD

Three economic phenomena determined the boundaries of the journalistic field and defined its shape and structure: industrialization, concentration and capitalization. They can all be traced back to economic competition.

Industrialization

The way newspapers were produced in the 1900s was infinitely more complex than 100 years before. To edit, print, distribute, and promote an Edwardian newspaper demanded a wide and expensive range of sophisticated techniques. Printing, a key area in newspaper production, offers a case in point. In less than a century, progress in printing technology metamorphosed a manual craft into a mechanized industry. As in other trades, the trigger to rapid evolution was steam, introduced in the realm of the press by John Walter II, proprietor of *The Times*, in 1814. During the following years, *The Times*' Koenig machine was perfected and by 1827 the machine was capable of 4200–5000 impressions per hour. Towards the end of the 1840s, the American Hoe sold a sheet-fed rotary system to the Philadelphia *Public Ledger* and to the Parisian *la Patrie* which was capable of printing 8000 sheets per hour, and thereafter, by adding nine impression cylinders, up to 20 000 sheets.

The 1860s witnessed two technological breakthroughs. The first was stereotyping, which allowed for multiplication of the cylinders for the same page, and thus to increase the production proportionally to the number of cylinders multiplied. The second was the development of the web-fed rotary press. By the 1870s, a web-fed Hoe machine was capable of printing, on both sides of the sheet, 14 000 eight-page papers an hour, the equivalent of 224 000 impressions an hour (Howe, 1943; Compaine, 1980). Thus in less than a century printing technology moved from the hand press producing 200 sheets an hour to web-fed multiple cylinder rotary presses with an output a thousand times superior to their ancestors.

Printing illustrates the increasing complexity of newspaper production during the 19th century. What was the impact of technology on the formation of the journalistic field and, more generally, on the discourse of the press? An error many authors commit in trying to answer this question is to establish a direct relationship between discourse and technology. Neil Postman's argument is that the telegraph had an unmediated effect on newspaper contents by fragmenting the news pages and contributing to the commodification of information. When newspapers were able to receive news from anywhere in the world via the telegraph, editors began to publish news which had only an entertainment value, being unrelated to the social and political environment of readers (Postman, 1986, pp. 64–70). This technicist approach to the media, inspired by McLuhan, is blind to the fact that the impact of technology on media discourse is mediated by the internal rules of the journalistic field. The invention of a new technique does not guarantee its widespread use in the newspaper trade. The main incentive for a newspaper owner to up-date the means of production is competition: a new printing plant is expected to produce cheaper, faster, and better than the older machinery. In lowering operative costs (generally labour costs), press-owners may reduce cover price, or spend more on the editorial service. In printing, composing, or editing faster, they can increase the number of pages, or extend the existing dead-line schedules to be capable of covering late stories. The first leader of the *Daily Mail*, on 4 May 1896, helps to bring home this argument: 'Our type is set by machinery, we can produce 200 000 papers per hour, cut, folded, and, if necessary, with the pages pasted together. [...] It is the use of these new inventions on a scale unprecedented in any English newspaper office that enables the *Daily Mail* to effect of saving from 30 to 50 per cent, and be sold for half the price of its contemporaries' (*Daily Mail*, 4 May 1896).

As illustrated by this leader, the use of technology in the news-paper industry has a strategic connotation because newspaper proprietors and managers are always in search of a competitive advantage over rivals. New models of printing machines were often developed at the specific demand of a newspaper. In 1855, when the circulation of *Lloyd's Newspaper* approached 100 000, the directors of the paper contacted the Hoe company to install a rotary press whose system was especially improved to meet their requirements (Bourne, 1887, pp. 254–5). This being said, many press-owners had to upgrade their printing plant because rivals had preceded them. Once a newspaper company has upgraded its machinery, others have to emulate the initial investor if they want to keep their papers afloat. As Karl Marx stated: 'competition subordinates every individual capitalist to the immanent laws of capitalist production, as external and coercive laws' (Marx, 1976, p. 739). The industrialization of the field would never have progressed at this pace if stiff economic competition did not force newspaper proprietors to keep up with technological progress.

Regarding the process of structuration of the media field, one of the most serious consequences of industrialization is the costs it involves. During the pre-market era of the press, the costs of production were low and an enterprising individual wishing to start a newspaper would generally find the capital. Since the tool of production was limited to a hand press, the required economic capital was small. The same person could own, manage, print, and edit a paper and at the same time write many of its articles. The labour force rarely involved more than five salaries, one or two in many cases. Even the more sophisticated governmental newspapers were relatively inexpensive to buy (see Williams, 1957, pp. 57–9).

By the beginning of the 20th century, production costs included: (1) editorial costs, or expenses for gathering and editing information.

This included the costs of an editorial staff of approximately 100 journalists and editors, of telegraph contracts and of a team of foreign correspondents. (2) 'First copy' production costs (typesetting, plate production, and other production tasks necessary before the print itself). (3) Printing costs: machinery, newsprint and ink. (4) Distribution and circulation expenses. (5) Promotional expenses (advertising, competitions, etc.). (6) Administrative costs and overhead. These production costs are generally divided into fixed or variable costs. Variable costs, in opposition to fixed costs, are those which are directly generated by the production of the newspapers. Ink, newsprint and the wages of the workers on the production line are three examples of variable costs (Owers, *et al.*, 1993, p. 10).

Rising production costs and rising circulations were interdependent: ascending circulations required an increasingly sophisticated tool of production and at the same time advanced technology made mass circulation possible. New printing plants were also required to print more pages (from approximately eight in the 1880s to about 16 by the 1920s) and with more pictures. More reporters were hired to fill up these pages, and more sub-editors were needed to edit their copy. Advertising and circulation departments were created to handle the increasing complexity of what became a 'daily miracle'.

The fact that a sophisticated and efficient tool of production requires extensive capital investments is tantamount to an economic law (Picard, 1993, p. 197). Among other effects, the rise of production costs increased the period of time newspapers need to reach the break-even point. In 1876 Edward Lloyd bought the *Daily Chronicle* for £30 000 and invested £150 000 to refurbish it (Koss, 1990, pp. 203–4). In 1893, the *Westminster Gazette* cost Newnes £100 000 and then £10 000 a year for 15 years (Spender, 1927, p. 138). Between its launch in 1881, and 1894, the *Evening News* lost £298 000 (Symon, 1914, p. 153). Before the *Daily Mirror* came out, in 1903, it cost £100 000 in promotion alone (Fyfe, 1949, p. 114). In November 1904, Pearson bought the *Evening Standard* for £300 000, while Thompson lost the same amount in two years on the *Tribune*, which closed down in 1908 (Koss, 1990, pp. 464, 498). In 1917, Lloyd George bought the *Daily Chronicle* for £1 600 000, while Kennedy Jones refused a proposal for a new daily with a capital of £200 000, estimating the need for a new paper to be at £500 000 (Fyfe, 1949, pp. 186–7; Jones, 1919, p. 157). Finally, on

Northcliffe's death, in August 1922, Astor paid £1 580 000 for *The Times*, and Rothermere bought the *Daily Mail* and a Sunday paper for £1 600 000 (Koss, 1990, p. 841).

The process of industrialization made the amount of economic capital necessary to launch and run a newspaper much higher than during the pre-market era. This had the effect of restricting access to journalistic production to those who are able to invest a sufficient amount of economic capital in the means of newspaper production. In sociological terms, the boundaries of the journalistic field were being defined by the constraints of production that economic competition had created.

Concentration

The concentration of ownership in the press occurs because some titles die out, some merge and others are taken over by press conglomerates. With the costs associated with the production of modern newspapers, the break-even point of daily newspapers came to be extremely high, and newspapers need to stay above that line to survive in the market. In the early 1920s, the *Daily Herald* was not self-supporting with a circulation of 330 000 daily copies (Williams, 1957, pp. 189–91). In 1931, the *Daily News* and *Daily Chronicle* had to merge with respective circulations of 765 000 and 828 000 (Koss, 1990, p. 932).

It is easier for newspapers which do not face immediate competition to meet production costs than for those who are directly challenged. In the first case, newspapers have more flexibility in determining the cover price and have the possibility to adjust their resources to the costs of production. Such an opportunity is not offered to newspapers in a situation of competition. As mentioned above, newspapers cannot set their cover price independently of each other, and some may use pricing strategies intended to force rivals out of the market. An episode in the life of the *Daily Herald* offers a good illustration of predatory pricing. In 1919, the attacks of the government on the *Daily Herald* brought this paper to the brink of collapse as the subsequent rise of circulation, combined with the heavy price of newsprint, cost the paper a fortune. To survive, the *Daily Herald* had to raise its price from 1*d.* to 2*d.* Knowing that the cost of newsprint made other newspapers lose money as well, the managers of the *Daily Herald* asked them to do the same. They refused to move, seizing the opportunity to capture the readership of the *Daily Herald*, even at heavy cost (Lansbury, 1925, pp. 160–1). The manoeuvre was quite successful in ruining the *Daily Herald*. Heavily indebted, it lost its independence and was sold to the Trades Union Congress in 1922. In turn they sold half of their shares to the Odhams group in 1929, who turned the paper into a popular sheet. As aggressive pricing strategies exhaust the financial resources of the weakest competitors, concentration of ownership is thus likely to happen in a competitive system.

In England, the number of daily newspapers has declined since 1900. From 172 dailies that year, the figure fell to 124 in 1921, 112 in 1926, and 106 in 1931 (Royal Commission on the Press, 1949, p. 188): a decline of 38 per cent in three decades. To be exact, this decline was due to the deficit between the number of closures and the launches of titles. During the same decade the *Daily Dispatch*, 1900, the *Daily Express*, 1900, the *Daily Mirror*, 1903, and the *Daily Sketch*, 1909, were successfully started by prominent press groups, the *Daily Courier*, 1900, the *Daily Paper*, 1904, the *Majority*, 1906, and the *Tribune*, 1906–1908, failed, and accompanied the closure of five other newspapers in London, among them the *Echo*, the *Morning* and the *St James's Gazette* (Bell, 1912, p. 575).

Conglomerates grow for the same reason newspapers disappear. When two titles combine (merge), or when a group takes control of a newspaper (an acquisition), it is because one of the papers had its resources exhausted by competitive struggles and became unable to pursue the struggle by itself. In the case of business combinations (mergers and acquisitions), the expected benefit of the operation is a diminution of costs through economies of scale, which may involve four areas. First, several titles placed under the same roof can share editorial costs, which include journalists' wages and contracts with news agencies. Second, administrative expenses can be cut. This may imply a regrouping of the billing service, the classified advertisements department, or the distribution system. Third, control over several newspapers may allow the proprietor to offer a greater array of markets, differently stratified, to advertisers. Finally, a plant can be shared by several newspapers, such as a Morning, an Evening and a Sunday paper. This allows for the optimal use of plant and printing equipment. The main reason why the director of Odhams, Julius S. Elias, bought half the shares of the *Daily Herald* in 1929 was that the plant which printed Odhams' Sunday newspaper, *People*, was left unoccupied during the rest of the week (Koss, 1990, p. 892).

In the field of the daily press, conglomerates came into existence in England during the last decades of the 19th century. By 1910, the three largest groups controlled, nation-wide, 66.9 per cent of the circulation of Mornings' and 82.6 per cent of Evenings' sales[1] (Lee, 1976, p. 293). Throughout the 20th century, the proportion of circulation controlled by the three top companies remained at a similar level. In 1947, the three largest groups controlled 61 per cent of the circulation of the national daily press, 72 per cent in 1977 and 73 per cent in 1993 (Sparks, 1995, p. 186).

The rate of concentration of the UK press has been an issue for more than half-a-century. The problem was acknowledged in the postwar years, in the scope of inquiry of the first Royal Commission on the Press, which was to monitor 'the growth of monopolistic tendencies in the control of the press' (Royal Commission on the Press, 1949, p. 3). The issue was also raised by the two subsequent Commissions as well as, more recently, by other official bodies (see Sparks, 1995). In spite of all this interest, not much has been written on the relationship between concentration and competition. However, in light of the previous comments on the nature of price mechanisms in a competitive system and the subsequent difficulties most newspapers meet in their effort to match their resources to costs, there is strong evidence that the two phenomena, competition and concentration, are correlated. It is equally significant that the British press became strongly concentrated only a couple of decades after the field became competitive. Had the relation between competition and concentration been examined, and the competitive system limited by appropriate legislation, a wider variety of daily newspapers, owned and managed by a greater number of companies, would exist in Great Britain today.

Capitalization

This notion refers to a change in the type of ownership between the public and capitalist press. The ownership and management of the pre-market newspaper fits in with the pattern of production characteristic of early capitalism, when the simplicity of the mode of production limited the division of labour and when the relatively low production costs did not require large financial assets. As the press industrialized, newspaper ownership required a greater volume of economic capital, and newspapers changed hands. Over the past 200 years, the type of ownership gradually has shifted from single newspaper press-owners to global multimedia conglomerates. An important phase in this process was the emergence in the late 19th century of a group of press-owners who eventually came to be known as 'press barons'. The following section describes some of the most salient aspects of this important figure in the history of press ownership in the Anglo-American world.

2.4 NO ORDINARY PRESS-OWNERS: THE COMING OF AGE OF PRESS BARONS

A major problem with the literature on press barons is that it essentially consists of biographies. These biographies suffer from many faults, not least that they often offer an inappropriate historical contextualization of press magnates. This problem stems from the inherent sociological paucity of the biographical genre, which organizes a narrative around the life course of one figure. This leads biographers to attribute too much importance to personal and contingent factors in their biographical accounts of press barons. This approach also predisposes biographers to give much weight to press magnates' interpretation of their own acts and motives.

According to Max Weber, the understanding of human action must involve the interpretation of the meaning actors themselves attach to their own actions (Weber, 1968, pp. 4–22). However, press barons' biographers often constitute the subjective meaning actors give to their actions as the basis for understanding these actions. The subjective understanding of action Weber had in mind did not imply that the interpretation actors have of their own behaviour should form the basis of the sociological understanding of their action. The relation between action and subjective interpretation is complex and sociologists cannot take for granted that actors' own subjective interpretation of their actions unproblematically contributes to the sociological explanation of their actions. If this relation were not problematic, it would mean that actors were fully aware of the determinants of their behaviour. Sociologists, to understand human action, must take into account both the external determinants of action and the subjective meaning actors attach to it. From a sociological perspective, one needs to deconstruct the biographical account by contextualizing press baronage both historically and sociologically. A way to achieve this aim is to construct a Weberian ideal-typical portrait of the press baron and show that press baronage is a specific mode of newspaper ownership that can be distinguished from 'classic' ownership.

To get a full picture of the ideal-typical press baron, both economic and non-economic criteria should be taken into account when differentiating press barons from the rest of press-owners. In the context of this book, however, we will limit ourselves to three economic criteria.[2] Press barons can be distinguished from other press proprietors on the basis of their willingness to invest capital in the press, their ability to make profits in journalism and their aptitude for building press empires.

On the basis of the first criterion, the historical figure of the press baron may be apprehended as a *transitional figure* in the process of the capitalization of the British press, standing between pre-capitalist newspaper production and its capitalist and fully bureaucratized production. As costs escalated and newspapers modernized, few individuals owned a sufficient amount of capital to access the field of the daily press. On the other hand, very few among the individuals who possessed this amount of capital were willing to risk it in the press. Press barons were those who had enough economic capital to enter the field of the daily press and took the risk to invest this capital in newspapers. Thus the rise of press barons corresponds to a specific moment in the relation between economic capital and the newspaper press.

The patterns of investment of four British press barons reveal two striking similarities. It appears that Sir George Newnes, Sir Arthur Pearson, Lord Northcliffe and Lord Camrose followed a two-step investment strategy on their way to the daily press. Before their first foray into daily journalism, all four had experienced success with periodicals. Newnes and Northcliffe each possessed some 20 magazines before their first venture in the daily press, and Pearson had also started a series of very successful weeklies before launching the *Daily Express* in 1900 and acquiring several provincial newspapers (Simonis, 1917, pp. 258–90; Fyfe, 1949, pp. 54–6; Pound and Harmsworth, 1959, pp. 65–190). It is less commonly known that William Berry, later Lord Camrose, had 25 years' experience in the field of periodicals before acquiring the *Daily Telegraph* in 1927 (Hart-Davis, 1990, pp. 24–5).

Another common feature is that press barons followed a strategy of diversification in the newspaper market. All four spread their investment into several market segments and controlled both popular and quality dailies. Northcliffe's span spread from the *Daily Mirror* to *The Times*, Newnes launched the short-lived *Daily Courier* and the *Westminster Gazette*, Pearson owned the *Daily Express* and the *St James's Gazette* and Camrose controlled the *Daily Sketch* and the *Financial Times*. Press barons were also active in the Sunday market.

Press barons also proved able to make journalism a very lucrative activity. This observation looks self-evident by today's standards, but making money from newspapers was at this time far from the norm. Press barons stood in contrast to the numerous newspaper proprietors who lost great sums of money through newspaper ownership. Press barons supplanted the 'millionaire amateurs' as Northcliffe called them and acted as agents whose decisions were economic-oriented and rational (Northcliffe, 1922, p. 15).

This raises the question of whether the main motive of press barons was commercial or political. With few exceptions, many students of the press favour the thesis that press barons had, in the main, political motives (Curran and Seaton, 1991, pp. 49–58). To support this theory, they underline the political bias of press barons' newspapers and recall their political ambitions, the latter often illustrated with Beaverbrook's famous answer to the 1947 Press Commission, to whom he declared that he owned newspapers for propaganda purposes exclusively (Royal Commission on the Press, 1949, p. 25). The argument developed here is that notwithstanding the undeniable political bias of newspapers controlled by press barons, it is doubtful whether political interest or political conviction typifies press barons' behaviour. Press barons had marked political preferences, developed personal political ambitions at some point in their lives and were closely acquainted with the world of politics. But until the closing decades of the 19th century, so did several press-owners. However, in contrast to the classic newspaper proprietor, press barons exercised formidable independence and treaded on an equal footing with politicians. Press magnates' wariness with politicians is illustrated in Northcliffe's advice to fellow newspaper proprietors against 'a wide circle of acquaintance among people like politicians': 'The newspaper owner should always remember that while the politicians have nothing to give him, they have much to gain from his newspaper' (in Lawrence, 1903, pp. 184–6). In addition, a press baron's support for a political party was always erratic, conditional and subject to personal and egotistic considerations. This problematic relationship was epitomized by the intense animosity between Northcliffe and Lloyd George after the First World War (see Pound and Harmsworth, 1959, pp. 710–7). Similarly, when Stanley Baldwin, then Conservative leader, experienced difficulties with Beaverbrook and Rothermere in 1931, the strain appeared again and this time surfaced in Baldwin's famous qualification of newspaper proprietorship as 'power without responsibility – the prerogative of the harlot throughout the ages' (in Koss, 1990, p. 942).

Beaverbrook himself offers a case in point. In 1914, dissatisfied with the limited readership of the *Globe*, a Tory newspaper, he sold that paper and took control of the *Daily Express* two years later (Chisholm and Davie, 1992, pp. 107, 135). He then proceeded to raise the circulation of this paper to make it a successful contender to the supremacy of the *Daily Mail* in the 1930s. What differentiates Beaverbrook from the previous owners of the *Daily Express* is not that he was himself a Conservative supporter, and a Conservative MP for that matter, but that he was capable of successfully competing in the field of the daily press. As the *Daily Express* coverage of the 1922 General Election shows, Beaverbrook understood that profits and high circulation could only be obtained provided the amount of politics in a newspaper was greatly limited and its partisanship as covert as possible (see Chapter 4). Beaverbrook's prudence during these elections, despite the fact that he and Bonar Law, the Conservative leader, were intimate friends, may simply demonstrate that he was aware that hidden propaganda works more effectively than overtly ideological discourses. However, it also indicates Beaverbrook's keen understanding of the economic rules governing the field of the press and his knowledge that too much politics would have killed the paper and made him bankrupt.

The contrast between the independent-minded press baron and the politically minded press-owner for whom press-ownership was essentially a loss-making activity is further illustrated on the other side of the Atlantic by father and son, George and William Randolph Hearst. When, in 1880, George Hearst bought a Democratic political organ, the San Francisco *Examiner*, his objective was purely political and he poured $250 000 into the loss-making newspaper until he realized his senatorial ambitions seven years later (Swanberg, 1962, pp. 22, 36, 41). The *Examiner* would have remained an obscure political sheet if his son had not stepped in and transformed the costly political organ into the leading newspaper in San Francisco. After a year working as a reporter at the Pulitzer's New York *World*, he took over the newspaper, aged 24. To raise circulation and generate profit, he applied methods previously unknown on the West Coast. Knowing that the success of a paper was not based on the 'wisdom of its political opinions or the lofty style of its editorials' (his own words), he depoliticized the *Examiner* and made sure, as he explained to his father, that 'the *Examiner* destroy[s] every possibility of being considered an organ' (in Swanberg, 1961, pp. 30, 37). He also increased the amount and variety of news, enlarged the editorial team, engaged the best journalists at great expense, introduced illustrations to 'stimulate the imagination of the masses' and endeavoured to be 'startlingly original' (ibid.).

Both father and son illustrate different styles of ownership, only the latter representing the baronial style of ownership. Unlike his father, William Randolph Hearst *invested* in his papers and was able to make a profit out of journalism. Thus, even though W.R. Hearst developed political ambitions at a national level (creating the Independence Party) and held public office (becoming Senator for the State of New York), his journalistic skills and entrepreneurial abilities distinguish him and press barons from press-owners like his father.

Finally, press barons were empire builders. This characteristic singles them out because newspaper ownership does not necessarily entail empire building. During the first two decades of the 20th century, Northcliffe's was the greatest press concern in England. By the early 1920s, Northcliffe and his brothers controlled more than 100 weeklies and monthlies, 17 provincial dailies, four national dailies (the *Evening News*, the *Daily Mail*, the *Daily Mirror* and *The Times*) and several Sunday papers (Labour Research Department, 1922; Royal Commission on the Press, 1949, pp. 197–203, 217–18). In the aftermath of Northcliffe's death in August

1922, some of his assets were sold and the leading press group of the interwar years was the Berry conglomerate. Before its partition in 1937, the Berry concern incorporated 20 dailies, including three national titles, the *Daily Telegraph*, the *Financial Times* and the *Daily Sketch*, six Sundays, six weekly newspapers and more than 80 periodicals (Political and Economic Planning, 1938, pp. 99–101).

Besides the Berry group, which split in 1937 into the separate press undertakings of Lord Camrose, Lord Kemsley and Lord Iliffe, the other leading press concerns of the interwar period in Britain were the Westminster Press Group, Provincial Newspapers Ltd, Odhams Press Ltd, Thomson-Leng Group and the Newnes-Pearson Group. Rothermere (Harmsworth Group), Beaverbrook and the Cadbury family also controlled significant press concerns.

As the names which appear in this list of press concerns suggests, the empire-building strategies of press barons played a significant role in the rise of press conglomerates. By the interwar period, most newspapers belonged to press conglomerates, which had become the most common form of newspaper ownership in Britain. As a result, *The Times*, sold to J. Astor and J. Walter after Northcliffe's death, the *Morning Post*, amalgamated to the *Daily Telegraph* in 1937, and the *Daily Worker* were the only national dailies which were run independently from press conglomerates (Political and Economic Planning, 1938, pp. 96–106). A sure sign, if needed, that the press had become a capital-intensive industry dominated by profit-oriented and bureaucratic organizations.

Part II
Discourse and Method: Options for Sociology

3

Beyond the Prison-House of Language: Discourse as a Sociological Concept

The key concept in the argument about journalism emerging in the course of the 19th century is that of discourse. This notion, as many oft-used concepts, is elusive. The objective of the following pages is to explain the way I understand this notion and to indicate the contribution this concept can make, in my opinion, to the sociology of the media.[1]

Traditionally, discourse has always been apprehended from a linguistic perspective. Early linguists and semiologists used the word as a synonym for language (see Barthes, 1993 (1957), pp. 110–11; 1978, p. 30). By the 1970s the linguistic definitions of discourse had become more elaborate, but the concept remained defined along the lines of the classic Saussurian definition of language (see Todorov, 1978, p. 23; Greimas, 1990, p. 105). The most recent tendency in linguistics consists in integrating elements of Foucault's archaeology into linguistically-oriented definitions of discourse (see Kress, 1985, p. 6; Inglis, 1990; Fairclough, 1992, p. 3).

The linguistic definition of discourse is the dominant and legitimate definition of the concept in the social sciences. Although social scientists no longer equate discourse with language, they still embed the concept in the linguistic realm by defining it using the very same concepts linguists employ to define language. Laclau and Mouffe, and Purvis and Hunt, offer two cases in point. Although Laclau and Mouffe do not use 'discourse' and 'language' interchangeably, their definition of 'discourse' does not allow the notion to escape the 'prison-house of language', as Jameson put it (1972). Following Saussure's definition of a 'linguistic system' as a 'series of differences of sound combined with a series of

differences of ideas', the influence of structural linguistics is evident
in Laclau and Mouffe's definition of discourse as a 'system of
differential entities' (Saussure, 1959, p. 120; Laclau and Mouffe,
1985, p. 111).

To distinguish 'discourse' from 'ideology', Purvis and Hunt (two
sociologists) rely precisely on the fact that discourse is primarily
a linguistic concept. To them, 'discourse' 'refers to the individual
social networks of communication through the medium of language
or non-verbal sign-systems. Its key characteristic is that of putting
in place a *system* of linked signs' (Purvis and Hunt, 1993, p. 485).
Like Laclau and Mouffe, they resist the assimilation of the
concept of discourse to that of language. However, the fact that
they define discourse with the very same words Saussure used
to define language, combined with their linking of 'discourse' to
an array of linguistic and semiological notions, not only main-
tains the concept in the linguistic sphere but prevents them from
establishing clear blue water between the concepts of discourse
and language (Saussure, 1959, p. 23).

Discourse can also take on the meaning of text. Nonetheless,
even when discourse acquires a textual dimension, the concept
remains a linguistic category, employed to designate linguistic
units or linguistic phenomena. This second use of the notion of
discourse is common in three sciences of language: stylistics,
modern rhetoric, and semantics. Semanticists who attach some
importance to the notion of text (arguing that a text constitutes
a concrete situation in which language is used) often employ
'discourse' to mean 'text' (see Ducrot, *et al.*, 1980, p. 56). Similarly, text analysts who use concepts and methods taken from
these sciences of language to interpret the discourse of the press,
often employ the notions of text and discourse as synonyms (e.g.
van Dijk, 1988, pp. 1, 4, 17, 24). This formulation of discourse is
close to the one employed by social psychologists Potter and
Wetherell. Like van Dijk, they intertwine the concept of discourse
with the notion of text within a linguistic-based and linguistic-
oriented set of philological procedures (Potter and Wetherell, 1987,
pp. 7–55).

Thus whether defined as language or as text, discourse has
primarily been understood as a linguistic category. From a sociological perspective, this means that the notion has been reduced
to its linguistic dimension and confined within the 'prison-house
of language'. As a result, the concept has so far been denied

autonomy. As a linguistic category, 'discourse' is either used to refer to text or language, or is closely associated with one of these concepts, and in neither case does it stand alone conceptually. An alternative definition of discourse should therefore aim to make the concept an autonomous object of science, designating a particular empirical sphere, neither linguistic nor textual nor social, but properly discursive.

In sociology, 'discourse' should designate a *class of texts*. From this perspective, a 'text' is a text, and a 'discourse' a discourse, as both terms refer to two different realities. The first is textual. The second, wider term, is multitextual: it is *intertextual*. From this discursive standpoint, what is a text? First, the text is the basic unit of a *textual class*: it is a *discursive unit*. Second, a text is the *material manifestation* of a discourse. Unlike its individual components, a discourse is a concrete but not a material entity. As an *entirety of texts*, a discourse is not material, like its components, the texts. It is concrete however, since it is an historical and social reality.

The intertextuality of a textual class must be distinguished from the way semiologists use and define the concept in their philological task. Unlike Russian formalists, who conceived of literature as a system, and whose approach to texts was inherently intertextual, semiology has the natural tendency to abstract texts not only from their social 'context', but also from their discursive 'context'. Some semiologists, however, have attempted to modify this and it is in this sense that one can refer to a semiological intertextuality. An example of such an attempt is offered by Riffaterre. By 'intertextuality', the semiologist means that, within one text, there is an implicit reference to another. This reference is intertextual because it directs the reader to another text. This intertextuality, however, is in fact *intratextual*, as it is located, concretely, within one text. Riffaterre's use of the term 'ghost text', for instance, clearly shows that this intertextuality only makes sense at the interpretative level (Riffaterre, 1984, p. 91). A pun may be intertextual if its principle of explanation is given by another text (ibid., p. 82). Riffaterre's intertextuality designates a textual characteristic, not a textual class, and this intertextuality is a textual, not a discursive, category. Thus, in spite of the notion of intertextuality, in Riffaterre's work, as in semiology in general, a text remains a *monad*. Riffaterre clearly states that his 'basic principle' consists in regarding the text as a 'special finite context', as a 'closed entity' (ibid., p. 2). Semiologists, therefore, tend not only to detach texts from their conditions of production, but also to separate them from the class of texts to which they belong.

Analogies can be drawn between discourse as a supra-textual entity and the notion of social class. First, both concepts attempt to regroup several entities (texts in one case, individuals in the other) which possess characteristics in common. In addition, a discourse, like a social class, represents something more than the sum of the texts it contains. A social class is something which exists in itself: it has its own origins, history, fate and interests. A social class, such as the peasantry, is something specific, concrete and historical. Such is the nature of a discourse, a textual class. Its existence as a concrete entity cannot be reduced to its components. Its independent reality, as an entity, means that it develops *sui generis* qualities which are relatively autonomous from the qualities of the elements which compose it. This makes of discourse a *social fact*, in the sense that this symbolic form exists 'in its own right independent of its individual manifestations' (Durkheim, 1938, p. 13). It does not mean that a discourse is independent of its producer, but that a discourse exists beyond and independently of the texts which compose it.

Like the notion of social class, discourse must become a sociological object. As a class of texts, discourse acquires the properties which make this epistemological transformation possible. First, by differentiating the concept of discourse from those of text and language, the intertextual dimension confers on the concept its own specific dimension and gives it autonomy as regards the linguistic sphere. Second, as a class of texts, the concept becomes a positive object. Defined in this way, 'discourse' can be used to refer to a unique, concrete, specific and limited object; to classes of texts produced by real agents in concrete and specific socio-historical conditions. The identification of the positive dimension reduces the linguistic element of textual classes to a more proportionate role; relative, not absolute. This dimension dissociates, from within, discourse from language. Indeed, the positive character of a discourse deconstructs this notion as a linguistic concept and suggests that a class of texts is also a sociological object, since it possesses a socio-historical dimension which needs to be analysed with appropriate concepts.

The point here is not to deny the linguistic dimension of discourse, but to shift the focus from one dimension to another. Sociology must bypass the linguistic dimension of discourse and concentrate on its positive dimension. As Saussure put it, the point of view creates the object (Saussure, 1959, p. 8). Sociologists therefore should not only perceive linguistics' apprehension of discourse for what it is, a peculiar point of view on this object, but also construct their own distinctively sociological approach to discourse. This perspective should be more sociologically correct than the current approaches to discourse and would not necessarily operate in symbiosis with linguistic sciences.

The linguistic dimension being the *only apparent dimension* of a discourse, semiologists and sociologists have confined discourse to the prison-house of language. Both apprehend a socio-historical entity as a primarily linguistic phenomenon and ignore the positive dimension of a textual class. *Language is the means by which discourse appears, by which discourse manifests itself.* For this reason, the linguistic facet of discourse has masked its socio-historical dimension. Provided discourse is apprehended as a two-dimensional object, its linguistic dimension appears as the visible element of discourse, and its importance is relativized by the positive dimension of a class of texts. Language gives us discourse 'as it appears': it is the *discourse-phenomenon*. The positive dimension however reveals the discourse 'as it is': the *discourse-noumenon*. It is only as *noumenon* that discourse can be apprehended in its own dimension and in all its dimensions.

3.1 SOCIOLOGY AND PHILOLOGY

The sociological definition of discourse outlined in the preceding section has several philological implications. Firstly, this definition of discourse provides the opportunity to re-examine the position of sociology within the hermeneutic disciplines. With the multidisciplinary approach being in fashion, most discourse analysts claim to integrate various disciplines (among them sociology) in their hermeneutic procedures (see for example van Dijk, 1991, pp. 44–5). From a sociological standpoint, this interdisciplinarity is a myth. In discourse analysis, linguistic disciplines occupy the dominant position and both their concepts and methods are unchallenged. A properly sociological definition of discourse constitutes the first step towards a sociological approach to texts capable of keeping its distance *vis-à-vis* the linguistic hegemony in philology.

The confinement of discourse within the linguistic sphere enables linguistic disciplines to locate the question of meaning within the linguistic realm. Semiologists do not simply hold that meaning is internal to the text, they also assume that this meaning is hidden within its linguistic structure. When semiologists read a text, they dive into it, swim between its linguistic layers, and re-emerge at its surface with its meaning in their hands. From a sociological perspective, the meaning of texts cannot be given by their linguistic structure. Sociologically, meaning is external to texts. It is given by the discursive context and the conditions of production of these texts.

This does not imply that texts are not read, but that the movement of reading, instead of plunging into texts, moves in two directions. The first movement runs from one text to another within a discursive class whose outline is progressively defined by these readings. Texts are related to each other in order to observe intertextual discursive phenomena. The second movement of reading avoids abstraction of a text from social reality by relating, in a dialectical movement, the texts which compose a discourse to their conditions of production. If the social determinants creating and determining a set of discursive practices contribute to explaining the meaning of a text, it will also be necessary to know the possible meanings of a text so as to apprehend the discursive practices which produce a text. This is the sociological version of the *hermeneutic circle*: one pole is discursive, the other social. It states that to explain the meaning of a text, its social determinants must be known, and that a text must also be read to discover these determinants. The sociological approach to texts is a dialectical reading which attempts to challenge the all-too-common internalist tradition of philological disciplines.

Nor does this sociological hermeneutic procedure imply a division of labour between semiologists analysing texts and sociologists analysing the 'context' of texts. Rather it is the division between text and context itself which must be thought out again. Just as the individual is not the limit at which society stops, there are no boundaries between a text – still less between a class of texts – and its 'context', that is, its conditions of existence. In the same way that agents' cognitive structures are embodied social structures, so also a text, and a discourse, are *symbolized contexts*, that is, social structures put into symbols. There is no relationship between text and context, but only an entirety: text/context.

Not only is the 'context' in the text, in the sense that the social conditions of existence of a text are fully reflected in the text, but the 'text is context', because it is entirely made up of contexts. In a certain sense, *il n'y a pas de texte.*

To dissociate discourse from the prison-house of language constitutes the first step to an alternative to the hermeneutics of the linguistic sciences. Many social scientists thought that in the realm of philology the science of linguistic exchanges and the science of social exchanges were compatible (see for example Hall, 1977, 1980). In the last couple of years, however, most of them realized the incongruity of the attempt to combine these disciplines for a common philological task. Those who ventured onto this path were soon confronted with a series of contradictions which derive from the fact that structural linguistics extracted its object from social and historical reality. This schism between two opposite perspectives, linguistics and sociology, has meant that linguistics apprehended language from the opposite perspective to that of sociology. For in sociology, language is neither a system of signs, nor is discourse a language. So far, sociologists who used the notion of discourse in their hermeneutic activities have been drawn into linguistic methodology and lost sight, in their textual interpretations, of the sociological paradigm. A non-linguistic definition of discourse is the first step towards an alternative to hermeneutic procedures which locate the meaning of texts within their linguistic structures. Sociologists need to apprehend and interpret texts, using classic content analysis procedures if they need to, from their own perspective. Such an approach could not prevail, however, without a definition of discourse which did not overcome the linguistic dimension of this object.

The second philological implication of the sociological definition of discourse concerns the nature of the relation between texts and discourse. Which criteria should determine to which textual class a text belongs? According to Michel Foucault, these criteria are discursive in character. A group of statements form a discourse 'insofar as they belong to the same discursive formation' and provided that these statements share the same 'modalities of existence', that is, the same 'objects', 'modalities of enunciation', 'concepts', and 'strategies' (Foucault, 1989, pp. 31–70, 117).

Although it is fairly obvious that texts, to belong to the same discourse, must share certain philological properties, in the last instance, texts share these properties because of extra-discursive reasons. In practice, texts form a distinctive textual class because the discursive practices, norms and strategies with which they are written are determined by similar relations of production. Relations of production being structured by the social field, that makes the field of discursive production central both to the formation of discourses and to the understanding of the texts which compose these classes of texts.

An analysis of the way in which the process of production of texts determines their philological properties is missing both in the early and late work of Foucault. In both *Discipline and Punish* and *History of Sexuality*, Foucault shows that he is not really aware of the way in which the internal mechanisms of the 'institutions' and 'apparatuses' which produce discourses on criminality and sexuality shape these discourses. This problem has several origins.

First, it is related to the hermeneutics of the French philosopher. Foucault explicitly stated that the meaning of a discursive statement resides in the discursive formation to which it belongs. According to the ambiguously worded 'principle of exteriority', the meaning of a discursive statement is *external* to the statement but *internal* in the discursive formation to which it belongs (Foucault, 1971, p. 55). This methodological rule implies that, instead of looking at the meaning of a text within the text itself, the philologist moves from the text to the discursive formation to which it belongs. In other words, the meaning circulates within a discursive formation and the reading is internal to the discursive sphere. This rule, which confirms the internal nature of principles which govern the configuration of a discursive formation, explains why Foucault places the emphasis, as in his *History of Sexuality*, on the relations between different discursive statements within a discourse, rather than on the relations between a discursive formation and the institutions and apparatuses which produce this discourse.

The second origin of this problem lies in the excessively structuralist and functionalist concept of apparatus (Bourdieu and Wacquant, 1992, p. 102). The concept makes the analysis of the production of discourse difficult because it reifies the field of production. In spite of Foucault's claims, the notion of apparatus does not take into account, in the discursive analysis, of the relations of production in which agents, who collectively produce a class of texts, are engaged (Foucault, 1980, pp. 194–8). The concept of apparatus evacuates from the analysis agents and their struggles.

By contrast, the inherently relational notion of field, *qua* space of struggles, reintroduces the dynamic of the agent into textual analysis. Discourse analysts should never lose sight of this dynamic. Texts are weapons that agents in a struggle employ in their discursive strategies. The use of these strategies provokes *intertextual discursive phenomena* which constitute the specificity of a class of texts such as journalism.

Finally, the question of the contribution of the intertextual definition of discourse to the sociology of the media must be addressed. At first sight, the understanding of journalism as a single discourse may appear too monolithic a conception to have any heuristic value. Obviously, there is discursive diversity in journalism. Within a newspaper co-exist editorials, background commentaries, feature articles and even several formats of news stories. The conception of journalism as a class of texts does not dispute the reality of this diversity. Quite the contrary, as Part III will show, an encompassing vision of journalism offers many opportunities to the analyst to explain the origin and nature of this diversity.

The conception of journalism as a discourse however opens up the possibility of contrasting the public and journalistic discourses and then placing the emphasis on the idea of *rupture* that occurred in the history of the press towards the middle of the 19th century in Britain and America. The discursive changes that the American and British press have witnessed since the 19th century have been well documented by historians such as Alan Lee (1976), Michael Schudson (1978), Mitchell Stephens (1988) and Stephen Koss (1990). With the possible exception of Schudson, it is the idea of evolution which prevails in these writings. This conception of the history of the press is also popular with journalists, who like to think of journalism as an ageless profession. *Contra* the evolutionist thesis, this book attempts to demonstrate that the types of discursive production which prevailed in the press before and after the mid-19th century rupture are not based on the same rules and have little in common.

Although recent comparative studies between France, England and the United States made me aware of the importance of political and cultural factors in the development of journalism, this work focuses on the economy as crucial to the emergence of journalism (see Chalaby, 1996a). It is claimed here that, from a general perspective, the emergence of journalism is related to the development of the capitalist market economy. Although the market economy cannot be considered to be the sole factor, this book attempts to demonstrate that capitalism was ultimately the main determinant in the development of journalism in England and America.

The impact of the economy on culture was first studied by the members of the Frankfurt School in their writings on mass culture, and then this framework of analysis was applied in various ways to the media by British political economists (Adorno, 1941, 1991; Adorno and Horkheimer, 1979; Murdock and Golding, 1977; Garnham, 1990; see also Boyd-Barrett, 1995). Following this tradition, I attempt to develop the economy argument in a systematic way and to understand in the most accurate way possible the relationship between economy and discourse. Obviously, it is too crude an assumption to believe that the economy *directly* influences journalists' discursive production. This research shows that the mediating instances between economy and discourse are the notions of field and of relations of production. As explained in the previous chapter, the journalistic field itself has been structured by market forces, but the internal dynamic of the field deflects the influence market forces have upon journalists' discursive production. Within the field, the competitive and antagonistic relations of production which prevail between agents constitute the second mediating instance between discourse and the economy.

In this study, it is argued that for all their diversity, journalistic discursive practices are determined, albeit in a deflected way, by market forces. Insofar as the discursive transformations which affected the press during the 19th century can be read as the transition from a public to a journalistic discourse, journalism can be considered as the commodified form of public discourse. From that angle, this book constitutes an addendum to Karl Polanyi's thesis, according to which the 19th century witnessed the commodification of land, money and labour (1957). This work simply adds a fourth element to Polanyi's list: discourse.

According to this thesis, the 19th century commercialization of the press led to the commodification of its discourse. From organs of publicity for combatants in politics newspapers became industrial undertakings. Progressively, the discourse of the press became informed by economic-oriented practices and the exchange value of this discursive production became more important than its use value. The subordination of discursive practices to economic exchange transformed the function of the discursive production of the press – at first a purely political one – into an economic one; it metamorphosed the public discourse and created a new discursive form. It is not being argued that this new discourse is completely separate from politics or even devoid of all ideology, but that at one point in history, politics and ideology ceased to be the sole determinant of journalists' discursive practices and to be supplanted by market rules.

Part III
Discursive Transformations in the British Press, 1850s–1930s

The aim of Part III is to examine and document the discursive transformations which affected the British press between the 1850s and the 1930s. The formation of the journalistic field and the development of the market economy in general changed the discourse of the press in three distinct ways: they defined the ideological limits of the journalistic discourse, induced the development of new discursive phenomena and contributed to the formation of new discursive norms, practices and strategies. As a whole, this series of transformations made journalism a discursive genre on its own. As detailed in the general introduction, each chapter focuses on a particular aspect of these transformations.

Part III also refers from time to time to the development of journalism in the United States. These excursions are used to draw parallels between the development of journalism in America and England. Furthermore, journalism being an Anglo-American invention, these parallels allow us to present a fuller picture of journalism as a new discourse emerging in the course of the 19th century.[1]

4

Press and Politics:
A New Relationship

Chapter 2 pointed to the difficulty of accessing ownership of newspapers due to the economic mechanisms regulating the journalistic field. Two of the effects of these mechanisms were to restrict access to the public sphere and to define the ideological and political boundaries of the journalistic discourse. The following section looks at both aspects of the impact of the formation of the journalistic field upon the discourse of the press.

4.1 JOURNALISM AND SOCIAL IDENTITIES

In terms of access to the public sphere, one of the major effects of the development of the journalistic field and in particular, of the process of industrialization was that the working classes progressively lost the means of control over newspaper production. Considering the strengthening of working-class institutions during the second half of the 19th century and the extension of their political rights, this progressive exclusion from the public sphere may seem paradoxical. Indeed, despite the fact that the second and third Reform Acts widened the franchise in 1867 and 1884, and that there were 1168 trade unions totalling 2 369 000 members by 1909, the working classes did not control a daily newspaper during this period and had lost all significant means of publicizing their point of view to a wide audience (Cole and Postgate, 1946, p. 484). Contrary to the situation prior to the emergence of the journalistic field, where the unstampeds helped to raise the class consciousness of the general working-class public, late Victorian and Edwardian mass working-class movements, such as Socialism and New Unionism, had enormous difficulties in establishing a press of their own.

It could be argued that working-class organizations published around 800 periodicals between 1890 and 1910 (Pugh, 1993, p. 79). However, the greatest majority of these periodicals were newsletters, not newspapers, and carried very little news other than that which was connected to the publishing organization. Trade union periodicals mostly reported news directly related to the trade union movement. For all practical purposes, these newsletters had, in the main, a housekeeping role and did not fulfil the same function as the general press. Limited to the production and diffusion of newsletters of a modest circulation, the Victorian working-class organizations did not have at their disposal a public pulpit that could project beyond their immediate sphere of influence. With few exceptions, they did not possess publications whose readership would expand beyond the core groups of militants who already adhered to working-class organizations. The second half of the 19th century witnessed the progressive disappearance of the proletarian press as a legitimate and general purveyor of news to the working classes to the advantage of the popular Sundays from the 1840s onwards, the halfpenny evening newspapers since the 1890s and the halfpenny morning newspapers during the following decade.

The few working-class periodicals which attempted to establish themselves on the marketplace faced constant, and in most cases insurmountable, financial difficulties. The intensifying economic competitive struggles among newspapers made the necessary investments too heavy a burden for the dominated classes whose journals could not survive in such a hostile milieu. The inability of the working-class press to generate revenues from advertising (because of the relative lack of means of its readership and sometimes the boycott of advertisers) and its difficulty in deploying the necessary amount of economic and human capital to sustain the economic struggle, meant that working-class papers were invariably unprofitable. In consequence, these newspapers often owed their precarious existence to the voluntary work of devoted militants.

The difficulties experienced by the working classes in having a daily press of their own during the second half of the 19th century is illustrated by the fate of two papers. First came the *People's Paper* belonging to Ernest Jones, with whom Karl Marx shared the editorship in the summer of 1852. Launched in May 1852, it became the largest working-class newspaper ever produced. In spite of its excellent circulation figures, the funds raised were not enough to compensate for its continual loss, and it ceased publication in September 1858 (Harrison, 1974, pp. 137–9).

Then came the *Beehive*. It was launched in 1861, when George Potter, leader of a small union, realized that he could not publicize his point of view in the London dailies and weeklies. It became the semi-official organ of the First International, of the London Trades Council, and of the Trades Union Congress. Influential among working-class public opinion, it expired for lack of finance in 1876, after 15 years of success (ibid., pp. 141–2).

It has often been argued that the fate of working-class newspapers follows the fate of working-class movements. By the beginning of the 20th century, however, the circulation of the working-class press was more restricted than ever whereas the working classes had never been better organized. There was an apparent contradiction between the growth of trade unions and the creation of the Labour Party in the 1900s on the one hand, and the absence of a working-class-controlled daily press on the other. During these years, even the most prominent working-class organizations met strong difficulties in their attempt to establish a daily newspaper.

After five years of discussion, the Labour movement, without the Trades Union Congress, launched in October 1912 the *Daily Citizen*. Although £150 000 was sunk in the project, it was no longer enough to launch and run a newspaper. The staff of 50 journalists and 60 employees was too tiny compared to that of its competitors. In spite of decent circulation figures (claimed to be at 120 000), the paper remained unprofitable, largely because it could not generate enough advertising revenues. The restrictions on advertising imposed by the outbreak of the First World War did not harm the paper, which was closed in 1915 by government decree (Hopkin, 1988, pp. 236–8).

The *Daily Herald* was more successful than the *Daily Citizen*, but its short survival as an independent working-class paper was described as the 'miracle of Fleet Street'. Started in April 1912, its existence was extremely precarious until it turned weekly between September 1914 and March 1919, which made things easier. But as soon as it came back to a daily routine, the paper was losing heavily and appealed for £400 000, which it did not get (Lansbury, 1925, p. 17). In 1922, it was sold to the Trades Union Congress, for which the paper proved too expensive. In

1929, the TUC sold half of its shares to the Odhams group. The fate of the *Daily Herald* shows that, even with a political organization in support, it was nearly impossible for the working classes to control a daily newspaper.[1]

The inequality of access to newspaper ownership and by way of consequence to the public sphere in general has made of journalism, as widely acknowledged, an essentially middle-class discourse and institution. Many have argued that journalists' discursive production reflects the values and ideology associated with that social class. Paul Beaud's argument, which summarizes this position, is that the power of the media mainly consists of the ability for journalists to delimit legitimate political problems and thereby define political reality. This representation of reality is biased in favour of the middle classes, which by this means achieve influence over the political decisions affecting their own needs and interests (Beaud, 1984).

The Glasgow University Media Group have developed a similar line of argument. Analysing the broadcasting coverage of industrial life, they noticed there is little connection between the reality of industrial life and its journalistic representation. Along with other evidence, they showed that there is no relationship between the severity of the stoppages and the amount of news coverage they get. In fact, the stoppages that are the most consistently covered are those perceived as threatening for the middle classes. Thus a long strike might be totally ignored, while a symbolic one might receive extensive coverage (Glasgow University Media Group, 1976, pp. 140–204). The research group concluded its series of case studies with the observation that 'the news was organized and produced substantially around the views of the dominant political group in our society' (Glasgow University Media Group, 1980, p. 111).

Numerous other media analysts have reached similar conclusions. Herbert Gans summed up the point when introducing the results of the fieldwork he conducted in American newsrooms for more than a decade: 'Indeed, as I was writing about the journalists, I felt that my book was as much about the dominant culture in America, and about its economic and political underpinnings, as about them' (Gans, 1980, p. xv).

A concept worth considering in referring to the values and ideology the media discourse conveys is Pierre Bourdieu's concept of *arbitrariness*. The French sociologist refers to two dimensions when applying this concept to pedagogical action. Primarily, the notion of arbitrariness refers to the subjectivity and peculiarity of a class's culture, and more specifically to the fact that this culture 'cannot be deduced from any universal principle [. . .] nor being linked by any sort of internal relation to the "nature of things" or any "human nature"' (Bourdieu and Passeron, 1990, p. 8). Secondly, the notion of 'arbitrary' designates the fact that the culture of a social class does not give itself as a culture specific to a particular social group. In the education system, the culture of the dominant class imposes itself upon dominated social groups as universally valid.

This concept can be applied to the media with great profit, as analogies in this respect are apparent between pedagogical communication and media discourse. In both cases, the values of the dominated classes are conspicuously absent from systems of communication which, in the main, carry the culture and ideology of the dominant classes. Furthermore, in the education system as in the media, cultural producers hold claims to cultural and political objectivity and neutrality.

This chapter will examine several aspects of the political arbitrariness of the press. Meanwhile, an interesting question to raise is the long-term impact, in Britain, of the political and cultural arbitrariness of the journalistic discourse on dominated groups' social identity and class consciousness. It may be impossible to demonstrate this influence in a direct way, but it seems a plausible hypothesis to conjecture that in the absence of a sustaining ideological discourse, the political elements of the working classes' identity and class consciousness were bound to weaken. According to this thesis, the political arbitrariness of the journalistic discourse, and correlatively the difficulty for the working classes in developing a narrative which represents their values and aspirations, must be accounted one of the factors which played a part in the decline of the English working class's political identity in the course of the 20th century.

Furthermore, it can be assumed that the political arbitrariness of journalism has also favoured the emergence of social identities which are not, in the main, hostile to the dominant social and political order, or at least to capitalism in general. Gender and ethnic identities in contemporary Britain are mostly assimilatory in character and oriented towards integration into the market economy. Contrary to the pre-Second World War working-class political identity, the newly emerged gender and ethnic identities are broadly integrative rather than oppositional to the existing economic order. What role did the media play in the formation of these new identities? It is a difficult question to answer, but it is conspicuous that in the media women and members of ethnic minorities are welcome to occupy new roles and swap existing roles and occupations with others, but are not encouraged to create altogether new roles or even to change or redefine the roles they newly occupy. In sum, it could be that the long-term effect of the political arbitrariness of the media discourse has been to deconstruct social and political identities hostile to capitalism and to contribute to the formation of identities that may be distinct from each other but rather integrative with regard to the dominant economic order.

Commencing with the next section, Part III will attempt to corroborate these remarks which may at this point seem speculative. Many a facet of the evolution of the British press since the 19th century may be pointed out to support the argument that journalism is not only an invention of the market economy, but that *journalism is the narrative form capitalism took to become a historical force.*

4.2 THE DEPOLITICIZATION OF THE BRITISH PRESS

Depoliticization is a major discursive phenomenon and refers to a compound of discursive trends which can be observed in the British press from the 1850s onwards. To begin with, it designates the progressive de-selection of politics as a journalistic topic. During the second half of the 19th century, editors began to reduce the amount of political news and to fill newspaper columns with lighter topics. Gradually, politicians' speeches and parliamentary debates were supplanted by sport and society news. Although the trend was particularly marked among popular newspapers, this tendency also affected quality papers. Another trend this concept refers to is the depoliticized treatment of politics. This is in itself a complex issue which refers to a multiplicity of phenomena. Broadly speaking, the journalistic coverage of politics became increasingly focused on personal issues and on political figures rather than on political issues and political principles. A major aspect of the personalization of public life by journalists was the disclosure of politicians' private life, a phenomenon which can be traced back to the 1880s in the British press.

Depoliticization should not be confused with de-ideologization. It is false to assume that a depoliticized newspaper conveys less ideology than a political organ. Depoliticization does not entail that texts are politically neutral. The difference is illustrated with the advice given in 1885 by a 'Conservative journalist' to Conservative supporters interested in the establishment of a newspaper: 'The anxious Conservative politician who is deploring the state of the Conservative press in the provinces will ask, what about politics? I answer, the less the better' (A Conservative journalist, 1885, p. 825). With regard to newspapers which claim to be independent and impartial, depoliticization does not even imply that they are ideologically non-arbitrary. In these cases, ideology manifests itself in different ways and may be expressed in a more oblique manner. The ideology a text conveys becomes an object of inquiry for the analyst only when discursive producers do not directly state their ideological values or when they entertain the illusion that their discourse is value-free. The rise of ideology as a hermeneutic issue is correlated to the decline of political discourse.

Evidence shows that the proportion of space devoted to politics sharply decreased in the British press from the second part of the 19th century. By the 1920s, almost half the space of newspapers was filled with advertisements; features and news evenly sharing the remaining space. In 1927, home news on politics, economic and social affairs constituted 14 per cent of the total news space of *The Times*, 10 per cent of the *Daily Mail* and 10 per cent of the *Daily Mirror* (Royal Commission on the Press, 1949, p. 250). In 1937, these figures dropped, respectively, to 12, 6 and 5 per cent (ibid.). Although these figures rose in the immediate aftermath of the Second World War, they dropped again in the ensuing decades. According to the 1974 Press Commission, in 1975 political, social and economic home news occupied 13 per cent of the total news space of *The Times*, 9 per cent in the *Daily Mail* and 4 per cent in the *Daily Mirror* (McQuail, 1977, p. 26). As noticed by Colin Sparks, the figures for 1975 showed that 'unequivocally serious news took up around 15 per cent of the news content of the two most widely read papers, while sport took up more news space than "political, social and economic in general" material in every national daily paper they looked at bar the *Financial Times'* (Sparks, 1991, p. 59).

The contrast with the public press is stark. The public discourse revolved around politics. Publicists sought above all to inform their readers on public life and many working-class publicists had as their sole aim the raising of political awareness in their readers. Working-class publicists usually gave much importance to the notion of 'knowledge', and perceived the diffusion of political information as the crux of their activities. In a characteristic way, Henry Hetherington wrote that '[w]ithout knowledge there can be no union – without union, no strength, and without strength of course no radical alteration in the system' (*Poor Man's Guardian*, 22 December 1832). Although this statement may sound outrageously radical to modern ears, it reflects the mood in which many working-class and middle-class publicists wrote during the first half of the 19th century. Of this spirit, not much remained 50 years later, when editors of popular papers deliberately avoided politics. By the outset of the 20th century, journalists and editors, competing to 'brighten' their newspapers, were actively looking for alternative subjects to politics. As the necessity to entertain readers superseded the urge to propagate knowledge, sport, society news and features progressively supplanted political information. The following pages analyse and describe the factors which contributed to the depoliticization of the discourse of the press.

News as a an Instrument of Competition

News became an instrument of competition when leading press-owners and editors began to use news coverage to gain a competitive advantage over rivals. At the same time, news became a constraint for all news organizations as none of them could afford to omit facts and events published by rivals. Nothing illustrates the competitive role of news better than press-owners' and editors' constant attempts to scoop competitors and their simultaneous fear that rivals may come up with news they passed over or that remained unknown to them. 'The *World*', wrote Pulitzer, the American editor, in a note to his journalists in 1899, 'should print not only all the news worth printing, but should have, daily, some striking development or feature in the news line that will lift it away from its competitors and make it talked about' (in Juergens, 1966, p. 48). Northcliffe used to read all morning papers and ring his editors to 'cross-examine [them] about the contents of the rival morning papers' (Clarke, 1931, p. 127). Clarke, the editor of the *Daily Mail*, therefore had to read them all as well, and could learn, on the phone, 'whether [he] had won or lost the previous day in the incessant quest for "scoops"' (ibid., p. 126). Every morning, Julius Elias, the director of the *Daily Herald*, spread on the floor of his office the three rival papers he was competing with (the *Daily Mail*, *Daily Express* and *News-Chronicle*), to spot differences in the treatment of news, and to check if rivals had published news disregarded by the *Daily Herald* (Williams, 1957, p. 184). This race for news had a serious impact on news-gathering techniques.

Newspapers as News Organizations

With the competitive pressure forcing press-owners to offer an extensive news coverage to their readers on a daily basis, New York and London leading papers became, first and foremost, news organizations. Although opinions could still be voiced in newspapers, information became the prime element of newspapers and the main commodity in the trade. Journalists may not have invented news, as Mitchell Stephens argues (1988), but never before the appearance of the modern newspaper had the concept acquired such a dominance within a class of texts. Press-owners and editors devoted increasingly important resources to collect information from local, national and international sources. To satisfy their growing needs in news supplies, leading newspapers developed complex and expansive information-gathering services. Dailies had two means of collecting information: through their own reporters and special or permanent correspondents, and via news agencies.

(1) *Correspondents*. Although many editors conferred on foreign news an exceptional importance, until the closing decades of the 19th century only the leading papers were able to meet the cost of permanent correspondents abroad. By the 1880s, the main source of foreign news for many newspapers were the cables of the news agencies, such as the Associated Press in America and Reuters in England (Palmer, 1978; Blondheim, 1994). Nonetheless the second half of the 19th century witnessed the emergence of the special correspondent, and most notably, of the war correspondent.

Among British newspapers, *The Times* had the largest foreign news department. In 1857, the list of foreign correspondents and agents employed by *The Times* included 19 names (The Office of *The Times*, 1939, pp. 275, 568). *The Times* could even afford to go to the great expense of sending special correspondents to remote areas for several months, such as China, where a correspondent travelled for nearly two years (1857–8) (Cooke, 1859). Although such a team of correspondents was beyond the means of *The Times'* rivals, by this decade, most London papers had the resources to dispatch war correspondents. The special correspondent the *Morning Advertiser* sent to the Crimean War cost this paper £1500, and the expenses for the coverage of the Franco-German war amounted to £10 000 per newspaper (Grant, 1871, pp. 247–59).

(2) *Reporters*. During the period of time which coincides with the transition from the public to the journalistic press, the right granted to journalists to sit-in on Parliament contributed to developing the profession of the reporter. Towards the end of the 18th century, the *Morning Chronicle* was the first London newspaper to have a team of parliamentary reporters. By the 1830s, around 60 reporters sat in the Gallery of the House of Commons, and that number had increased to 105 by 1870 (Grant, 1871, p. 173). During the 1870 parliamentary session, *The Times* had 19 reporters following the debates, the *Standard* had 14, and the *Morning Advertiser* and the *Daily News* nine each (ibid., pp. 172–3).

Besides parliamentary reporters, London dailies also had reporters who sat in the various courts of law, and they also accepted copy from the numerous 'penny-a-liners' (ibid., pp. 260–97).

(3) *News agencies* rapidly occupied a central position in the news supply business, and newspapers had to rely on their wire services for much of the information they decided to publish. From the 1850s onwards, Reuters swiftly developed into an imposing news organization, acting as a news supplier for newspapers throughout the British Empire. A crucial moment in the development of the news agency was when *The Times* finally accepted Reuters' services, in October 1958. At first, *The Times* had declined Reuters' offers. Significantly, only once Julius Reuter had successfully offered his services to *The Times'* rivals did he overcome the resistance of the London paper (Read, 1992, pp. 22–6). Henceforth, the London press published the agency telegrams on a daily basis and in great numbers.

Journalistic Considerations in the Process of News Selection

In the course of the 19th century the extent of press coverage grew enormously. Since the 1830s in New York and the 1850s in London, the news covered an increasingly wide range of topics, expanding from politics to 'all spheres of life', as editors then said. Again, it seems that economic competition had some influence on the extension of press coverage to new areas. New press topics were always developed in competitive markets and during periods of intense rivalry between newspapers. James Gordon Bennett, the owner of the New York *Herald*, introduced society news during the early days of the penny press, in the 1830s; and Joseph Pulitzer, proprietor of the New York *World*, developed the sports section during the 1890s, one of the most competitive periods of the demanding market in New York (Seitz, 1928, pp. 58–9, 66; Juergens, 1966, p. 120).

These changes reflect the evolution of journalists' news judgement. On which basis, therefore, did journalists and editors deem an item newsworthy? According to Herbert Gans, news selection is an elaborate process which entails numerous considerations by journalists and editors, notably on the importance of the story, its format, its suitability for the medium, its quality and its novelty (Gans, 1980, pp. 146–81). Two considerations in the process of news selection appear to have played a crucial role in the discursive transformations which affected the press throughout the 19th century: readers' interest, and timeliness.

At least one apparent reason why the criterion of readers' interest in the news selection process was instrumental in modifying newspaper content, is that publicists selected facts and events on an entirely different basis. What publicists judged relevant for their readers was usually determined by the set of moral, political or religious principles that publicists adhered to. Publicists held a principled vision of reality, and unless they could connect facts and phenomena to the principles they believed in, they did not perceive the need to report these events. The gauge on which publicists judged the importance of a fact was not readers' interest but their own political or moral principles. As new economic circumstances induced journalists to take into account audiences' taste and the performance of competing newspapers, journalists detached themselves from publicists' principled and dogmatic relation to reality.

As a result, politics lost its privileged access to publicity. Although journalists still judge facts on their intrinsic importance, this criterion became gradually less relevant in the process of news selection. As reflected by the widening gap between the news selections of popular and quality dailies, journalists increasingly took into account the presumed interest of their respective audience in their considerations on story suitability. Thus political facts came to be judged on the same criteria as other events and lost their priority over non-political matters. In the media in general, but most distinctly in the popular press, politics had to be as entertaining as cricket and football.

The fact that newspapers' columns could be devoted to nothing else but politics may sound incongruous today, but things were not that obvious to contemporary journalists. Kennedy Jones, editor of the *Evening News* and Northcliffe's associate, thought it necessary to justify Northcliffe's news policy for his popular dailies and wrote that 'we neither live for politics nor by politics' (Jones, 1919, p. 158). Northcliffe himself had to reiterate on many occasions to his staff the necessity of reducing the amount of politics in his newspapers. 'We must not let politics dominate the paper' said Northcliffe to an editor of the *Daily Mail*, '[t]reat politics as you treat all other news – on its merits. It has no "divine right" on newspaper space' (Clarke, 1931, p. 197). At the *Evening Standard*, Simonis was told that although lighter subjects were preferred, political facts could be published, provided 'they were directly interesting to the general reader' (Simonis, 1917, pp. 103–4). By all accounts, journalists did not rate politics as a very interesting topic. When the 1947 Press Commission asked press-owners and journalists which events they valued as interesting, politics was not even mentioned. First came sport, then news about people, followed by news of 'strange or amusing adventures', then tragedies, accidents, and crimes (Royal Commission on the Press, 1949, p. 104).

The second fundamental journalistic consideration in news selection is timeliness. Since time immemorial the speed of news transmission has been important. Everyone prefers fresh news to old. However, modern means of transportation, combined with the electric means of communication, have dramatically reduced the time lag between the occurrence of an event and its account in the press. During pre-telegraphic times, the circulation of information was slow and entirely dependent on physical means of transmission.

Improved means of communication accelerated the pace of news flow and newspapers could soon 'palpitate with actuality' on a 24-hour basis (Stead, 1902, p. 479). Rivalry between journals made the printing of timely news all the more crucial, editors soon realizing that '[t]he public are apt to take the paper which has the first news' (Horace Greeley to the Select Committee on Newspaper Stamps, 1851, in Blondheim, 1994, p. 23). Thus timeliness became one of the most decisive criteria taken into consideration during the process of news selection.

As competing newspapers concentrated on the latest news, their relation to the time frame changed. Only most recent events were likely to be deemed newsworthy by editors, to the detriment of events which occurred before the last edition was printed. This new criterion of selection meant that the events of the day gave pulse to the dailies. 'Old news' being 'no news', the rhythm of news accelerated and past events progressively disappeared from newspapers' columns.

With this new frame of reference, past events lost all newsworthiness. Journalists' focus on the last couple of hours could only undermine politics' old central position in the discourse of the press. Politics being a continuous process, journalists' 'fetishism of the present' became particularly unadapted to this topic (Schudson, 1986, p. 81). To report politics, the past needs to be constantly reactualized and this proved increasingly difficult for journalists whose time reference concentrates on the last 12 or 24 hours. Thus, with the advent of journalism press and politics ceased to revolve in the same time frame. As the present became perpetual in the news, political events had to be as timely as other subjects, and politics lost its privilege in publicity.

Journalists' considerations in the process of news selection are thus different from those applied by publicists. Publicists had a dogmatic approach to reality, based on political beliefs and principles. Not that journalists never apply political considerations in the news selection process, but timeliness and above all readers' interest became the prominent criteria over those previously applied by newspaper writers. In particular, journalists' attitude to the audience became very different from that of publicists. As will be seen in the following chapters, journalists are very audience-conscious and their approach to reality is mediated in a fundamental way by what they perceive as the tastes and desires of the audience.

For a complete definition of news that can be inferred from the process of news selection, numerous factors should be taken into account. Nonetheless, in the context of our discussion, a piece of news may be defined as *a discursive statement about a real event which is both recent and of presumed interest to the audience.*

A New Relation to Facts and Events

Economic rivalry among newspapers has not merely changed journalists' considerations in the process of news selection, it has profoundly modified the way journalists relate to reality. As mentioned in the last section, publicists held a principled relationship to reality and they reported facts insofar as they could relate them to a theory, a doctrine and an ideology. But as a sense of rivalry emerged among journalists, they developed a more instrumental relationship to events. Newsworthiness ceased to be defined by principles, and events began to be reported because journalists had a competitive advantage to gain by publishing them. This strategy became apparent when journalists began to pay for exclusives, probably in the 1890s. But the instrumental aspect of this new relationship to reality was made even more conspicuous when journalists' keen interest for people's misfortunes began to surface. In 1896, Nansen received £4000 from the *Daily Chronicle* for his account of his North Pole expedition. But a news agency paid £5000 for Scott's story as the 'tragic end of the expedition [. . .] added considerably to the money value of the story' (Simonis, 1917, p. 169). The case of war is archetypal. Following an excellent coverage of the Franco-Prussian war in 1870 during which the circulation of the *Daily News* trebled to 150 000 daily copies, the editor was told that 'you and Bismarck are the only persons who have gained by this war' (Bourne, 1887, p. 281). The circulation of the *Daily Mail* reaching new peaks during the First World War, the editor of the popular daily did not look too distressed by the conflict: 'For four years, the war had been the daily "big story" ready-made every night' (Clarke, 1931, p. 120).

As the motives to report certain facts became less political and more commercial, newsworthiness became almost external to events. Increasingly, the news value of an event was not defined by its intrinsic significance but more simply by the presumed interest that the readership may find in it. A distinctive effect of this news policy was the progressive disappearance of the parliamentary column.

Decline and Fall of the Parliamentary Column

Until the end of the 19th century, Parliament occupied a central place in the press. As mentioned earlier, the right to publicize the debates greatly contributed to the development of the reportorial profession. The Parliament was the foremost beat for reporters, where more than one hundred of them worked in the 1870s. Still, in 1881, 10 boxes were added to the 19 already existing in the Reporters' Gallery to accommodate representatives of the provincial press (MacDonagh, 1913, p. 416). Late into the 19th century the profession of parliamentary reporter kept its prominence. For instance, a handbook on journalism published in 1890 devoted no less than four chapters, out of seven, to parliamentary reporters (Pendleton, 1890).

Since Marx, many philosophers and political analysts have agreed in saying that the publication of parliamentary proceedings is a *sine qua non* for a regime to be identified as non-authoritarian.[2] The publication of the debates introduced the possibility for *criticism* on the one hand, and for the *participation* of the citizenry in the process of political decision-making on the other. The possibility for criticism implies the existence of a rational discourse as the expression of the ideal of reason in the public sphere. Citizens' participation to the process of political decision-making is only possible when individuals are in possession of the appropriate information. The publication of the parliamentary proceedings fulfilled this role and enabled citizens to form for themselves an opinion on public affairs and hence to express this opinion when they deemed necessary. Political information allowed individuals to enter into the political arena and to actively participate in the process of decision-taking. In the final analysis, the publication of the debates of the Houses empowered individuals by giving them the possibility of becoming rational political actors.

Media analysts today refute these notions as idealistic, but then if the publication of parliamentary proceedings is of no significance for the democratic process, why do authoritarian regimes not allow for the publication of parliamentary proceedings? For example, a century after reporters were tolerated at the British Parliament, France's Second Empire still restricted the publication of parliamentary debates. Following the 1860 reform, newspapers finally acquired the right to publicize parliamentary proceedings, but only with considerable delay since they were just allowed to copy the debates from the regime's official newspaper (Choisel, 1980, pp. 375, 382; Bellanger *et al.*, 1969, p. 413). Thus the publication of parliamentary reporting in the British press bears historical significance not simply at the discursive level but for the consequences it implies for the nature of the political public sphere.

In the newspapers read by the upper classes and political elites, the parliamentary reports remained untouched until the mid-1860s. Daily newspapers devoted nearly one page in great format to parliamentary reports when the Houses were in session. The layout was particularly unattractive, proceedings being printed in long columns of small characters uninterrupted by headlines or subheads. The debates of the House of Lords could be given half to one-and-a-half columns; those of the Commons could reach five columns. The reports were fairly extensive with long verbatim abstracts.

The first quality morning to shorten the length of the parliamentary reports was the *Daily Telegraph*. The latter paper, of more recent origin than *The Times*, was one of the most ambitious papers of the post-repeal period. Founded in 1855, the *Daily Telegraph* was selling more than a quarter-million copies on average by the late 1870s, much more than *The Times*. The *Daily Telegraph* achieved this circulation by lightening its contents and by printing significantly more sporting and sensational news than its rival. It is in this context of commercial rivalry that the *Daily Telegraph* reduced the length of its parliamentary column. Progressively, the *Daily Telegraph* began to be more selective and more concise in its printing of the parliamentary reports. Whereas *The Times* would still devote a full six-column page to the debates in the 1880s, the *Daily Telegraph* would divide the equivalent news page with, on average, two to three columns of foreign news, one to two of criminal reports and one to three of parliamentary information.

According to the limited content analysis on parliamentary reporting conducted by Lucy Brown, the parliamentary reports of the *Daily Telegraph* began to become shorter than those of *The Times* in the 1860s. Selected dates in 1865 showed that the reports in the *Daily Telegraph* were approximately two-thirds shorter than in *The Times*. By 1895, the gap had increased, and while *The Times*' reports on 4 and 26 April were 41 250 and 11 750 words long, those in the *Daily Telegraph* were respectively 2000 and 2500 words long (Brown, 1985, p. 246). Commenting on the changes that affected Victorian papers, Brown noted that '[t]he most conspicuous decline was in parliamentary reporting' (ibid.).

Among the evening papers, two classes of paper can be distinguished. The London gazettes, such as the *Globe* or the *Pall Mall Gazette*, summarized the proceedings and never devoted more than a few columns of a small format page to the debates. The evening papers aiming at upper-working-class and lower middle-class readerships, such as the *Star* or the *Evening News*, sub-edited their parliamentary reports even more heavily. However, these short summaries conformed to the essentially local and recreational vocation of the evening papers, which were of less importance than the morning dailies. In addition, the London gazettes recruited a substantial part of their readers in clubs and were most certainly read as a complement to the morning papers.

The most serious breach of the principle of publicity of parliamentary debates came with the launch of the *Daily Mail*, in 1896. 'The Busy Men's Daily Journal', as its front-page masthead stated, heavily restricted parliamentary reporting at its inception. One of the first advertisements for the *Daily Mail* enticed readers to buy the paper by promising that '[f]our leading articles, a page of Parliament, and columns of speech will *not* be found in the *Daily Mail* on 4 May [1896], a halfpenny' (in Taylor, 1996, p. 32). In its early years the *Daily Mail* kept reporting the debates in a systematic way, albeit in a very reduced format. The average size of its parliamentary column, in its first month of existence, was seven lines for the Lords, and eight for the Commons. During the following years the reports rarely exceeded two short paragraphs. Towards the 1900s the *Daily Mail* ceased to report the debates on a daily basis, and henceforth summaries appeared sporadically. Northcliffe had set a precedent, and the popular daily papers which were launched during the Edwardian decade rarely bothered with Parliament. When they did, the reports were never longer than a few lines.

These changes of discursive practice had one major impact on the process of political communication. The decline of the parliamentary column limited the amount of *unmediated political discourse* in newspapers. As long as politicians' speeches and interventions at the Parliament were recorded in the press, politicians enjoyed direct access to their constituents. Once editors began to omit or summarize these speeches and interventions, politicians became more dependent upon journalists to access the public. This dependence created a new role for journalists in the process of political communication, that of gatekeeper between politicians and the audience. This role gave them the power to regulate both the amount and the type of publicity politicians would get in the press.

The decline of the parliamentary column was not induced by structural changes in the political system. Nothing in the closing decades of the 19th century can lead us to conclude that the parliament was losing its importance in the process of political decision. Quite the contrary, since the extension of the suffrage from the 1830s onwards made the Parliament a more democratic institution and in theory a more legitimate and accountable one. The three Reform Acts of 1832, 1867 and 1884 enlarged the electorate by 50, 100 and 75 per cent respectively (Cox and Ingram, 1992, p. 541). More than six million men were enfranchised by 1885, 58 per cent of the adult male population (Butler and Butler, 1994, pp. 239–40). If anything, this increase in voters would have made the wide publicity of parliamentary debates even more crucial in the 1900s than in previous years. In addition, parliamentary activity was boosted during the second half of the century by the augmentation of competitive constituencies (Cox and Ingram, 1992, p. 542). MPs anxious to show their prowess during the session to their constituents participated more frequently in the debates. The average percentage of MPs participating in parliamentary discussions rose from 30 to 37 per cent before the first reform to 80–90 per cent after the 1884 Reform Act (ibid., pp. 539–40). MPs also introduced a greater number of bills, and from an average of 50 bills per session in the 1820s, the number rose to an average of 132 bills in the late 1870s and to 214 after the third Reform Act of 1884 (ibid., p. 543). Considering the extension of the suffrage and the fresh zeal of MPs, the amount of parliamentary publicity should have increased instead of dwindling the way it did.

The reason for the decline of parliamentary reporting has to be searched for in the press. As seen above, twice in the course of a couple of decades it was the most ambitious newspaper and actual circulation leader which initiated the movement towards the reduction of the parliamentary column. First came the *Daily Telegraph*, which dominated the market from the 1860s to the 1890s, then the *Daily Mail*, which occupied a similar position from the 1890s until the early 1930s. The role of the two successive circulation leaders in the decline of the parliamentary column shows that the relations of production which prevailed in the competitive journalistic field were detrimental to the publicity of the debates. This concurrence supports the thesis according to which economic competition within the journalistic field played a crucial role in transforming the nature of the discourse of the press, and, in this particular case, perverting the principle of publicity. These two newspapers proceeded with a different logic from that of the public sphere. What mattered for these papers and their owners was to perform well in a competitive market, and editors did not judge the contribution of the parliamentary column to circulation figures significant enough to keep it in the paper. Subjecting political information to market judgements, journalists weakened the principle of publicity and with that democracy as a whole.

The Policy of Diversity

The depoliticization of the press was also the result of a specific discursive policy whose objective was to diversify the content of newspapers. As a result, the range of topics touched on by newspapers expanded enormously, to the point that today journalism is a discourse which is characterized by the variety of subjects it deals with.

This policy had two aims. Editors of mass circulation papers felt obliged to cater for a great range of interests, and the diversity of topics was conceived to please the disparate taste of massive readerships. At the turn of the century, for instance, editors of popular newspapers were making a particular effort to attract readers among women. They were reputed to hold the household purse, and department stores were pleased to know that they were reading their advertisements. Secondly, this policy also had the objective of distracting readers. One of the greatest fears of editors was to be told by the proprietor that the journal was boring and tedious. This was considered a serious offence, and editors of popular dailies were at great pains to find news stories which would amuse and entertain readers. As tickling the public became the popular press's first priority, frivolities and trivialities progressively supplanted political information.

Memoirs and biographies of contemporary journalists often relate the pressure from the proprietor to 'brighten' the paper with lighter topics. These journalists directly experienced the process of depoliticization, and could tell the difference between a political organ and a modern daily newspaper (see, for example, Symon, 1914, pp. 290–2; Simonis, 1917, pp. 103–4; Spender, 1925, pp. 104–5; Fyfe, 1949, p. 181). An excellent illustration of this policy of diversity pursued by newspaper owners is given by Northcliffe, who once advised the editor of the *Daily Mail* to '[m]ake the paper a happy one, fresh and free from dullness' (Clarke, 1931, p. 197). Northcliffe had also precise orders concerning the main news page, which he used to call the 'surprise page' (Clarke, 1950, p. 181). For that page, editors had to 'get more news and more varieties of news', to create 'contrast' (the 'salt of journalism'), and to 'catch the reader's eye' with short articles and distinctive headings (ibid.). This is exactly how the news pages of Northcliffe popular papers looked. Two representative pages of the *Daily Mirror* on 13 October 1908 contained no less than 33 news items. On these pages, readers could learn about the divorce of the Earl of Yarmouth, the opening of a school of orators by an anti-socialist union, the charge of cruelty to a cat brought against a lieutenant-colonel by the Humanitarian League, the story of a woman killed while trying to save her dog from a motor-car, a romance between an Italian Duke and an American, the death of Ireland's alleged oldest inhabitant, a taxicab dispute, a balloon race accident, the journey of the King to Newmarket, British warships' movements near Spain, and so on.

The policy of diversity even affected *The Times* when Northcliffe owned it. To the editorial staff of the paper, the press baron asked for more topicality, more 'readability', lighter contents, and 'fewer and shorter articles on politics' (in The Office of *The Times*, 1952, pp. 140–1). A telegram read: 'Humbly beg for a light leading article daily until I return – Chief' (ibid.). Northcliffe's aim in following this policy of diversity was that his newspapers should 'touch life at as many points as possible' (in Fyfe, 1930, p. 286).

Among the topics this policy contributed to introducing to the press, four appear particularly prominent. These are sport, society news, sensational news and human interest stories. This list is not exhaustive, but has no other objective than to highlight some of the most salient changes that this discursive policy brought to the press.

Sport

The pioneers of sports coverage in Britain were the Sunday papers. In the 1820s, the *Weekly Dispatch* and, as its full title read, the *Bell's Life in London and Sporting Chronicle*, devoted one to two columns of news and results on horse-racing, wrestling, regattas, cricketing, pigeon-shooting, pedestrianism and hunting. The Sundays launched in the 1840s, notably the *News of the World* and the *Lloyd's Illustrated London Newspaper*, devoted up to one column to sporting news, mostly horse-racing. In the 1880s, sports coverage in the *Weekly Times* and *Lloyd's Weekly Newspaper* expanded to football, athletics, cycling, rugby and tennis.

In the daily press, the *Daily Telegraph* was the first paper to pay close attention to sport and to arrange the sports news into a 'sporting intelligence' section. This section began to be regularly published in the 1860s. By the late 1880s, most daily newspapers had a sporting editor gathering and selecting information for several columns every day. The growing interest for sport shown by the press was related to the development of professional forms of spectator sports in the closing decades of the 19th century. Virginia Berridge estimated that cricket became very popular during the 1870s and suggested the mid-1880s for the beginning of mass interest in football (professional football being legalized in 1885) (Berridge, 1976, pp. 145–50).

By the Edwardian decade, sport had acquired its modern prominence in the media. Sports sections grew bigger and were increasingly well displayed. Most papers had assigned specialists to leading sports and big sporting events began to be reported on the front page. Popular newspapers, such as the *Daily Express*, began to publish gossip columns on 'soccer celebrities' (*Daily Express*, 5 September 1906). Depending on the season, *The Times*, the *Evening Standard* or the *Evening News* could devote half a page to a page to sport, the *Daily Dispatch*, *Daily Mail*, or *Daily Express*, one page or more, and the illustrated dailies, the *Daily Mirror* and *Daily Graphic*, sometimes two pages.

The Times' sports coverage stood in contrast to the rest of the press, as many of the sporting events reported in this paper were non-professional. A special interest was given to university competitions. *The Times* also offered a much broader sports selection than the other dailies. Within a week's time, it could report on a wide array of sports including golf, croquet, lacrosse, polo, yachting, archery, fencing and shooting. Popular papers focused on professional sports; racing, cricket and football were the staples of sports news in the popular press.

From that time on, sport has been the leading journalistic topic. Between the 1920s and 1970s the amount of sports coverage in *The Times*, the *Daily Mail* and the *Daily Mirror* remained fairly constant and these three papers respectively devoted 17, 32 and 37 per cent on average of their total news space to sport in 1927, 1937, 1947 and 1975 (Royal Commission on the Press, 1949, p. 250; McQuail, 1977, p. 17). In 1975, with the exception of *The Times*, the *Financial Times* and the *Morning Star*, sport was by far the largest news category in the national press (McQuail, 1977, pp. 24–5). In 1975, the *Daily Mail* and *Daily Mirror* respectively devoted 32 and 50 per cent of the total news space to sport (ibid.). As an indication, the next largest news category came to be legal and police news, occupying 10 and 9 per cent of the news space of the *Daily Mail* and *Daily Mirror*, followed by political, social and economic news, respectively given 9 and 7 per cent of the total news space in these newspapers (ibid.). The 1975 figures for the *Daily Express* followed those of the *Daily Mail*, and the *Sun's* news structure was almost identical to that of the *Daily Mirror* (ibid.). Sport therefore has been the most popular topic in the press throughout this century. The advent of television and the possibility of live coverage has added to the prominence of sport in the media.

In addition to the need for diversity, there are specific reasons why sport especially became so central to the media. A first series of factors is that sport always provides good copy:

(1) The sports privileged by the media are spectacular and offer strong visuals. Since the early days of sports reporting, images have played a key role and early this century journalists took advantage of the aesthetics of sporting activities.

(2) Sporting events can be reported as narratives. These events include all the ingredients of a good drama: they have the actors, the stage, the plot (created by the suspense of the contest) and the clear-cut ending delivered by the result. The win-or-lose situation of sports contests contributes to the building-up of tension and produces unambiguous endings. The audience also appreciate that winners and losers are clearly identifiable.

(3) Sport gives much freedom to reporters to interpret sporting events in the way that they want. For this reason journalists often dramatize the contest they report, even though the competition may lack any dramatic ingredient. Playing up on drama and suspense, journalists are able to stir up intense feelings and spur emotions in the audience. To raise the interest of readers or viewers, journalists frequently recall the glorious past of a team, the past exploits of a sportsman or woman, or the prestige of a competition. In a general way, journalists use the past to raise the importance of stakes at play. Sports events also provide the opportunity for a flow of pre- and post-analyses, background commentaries and retrospectives. Finally sport is about people, and this gives journalists the opportunity to write star portraits and competitor profiles.

(4) Sport is safe to cover. A sporting event is primarily a spectacle, and controversial issues which may be associated to a sport, such as drug cheats and boardroom power struggles, rapidly fade behind the glamour of sports contests. Moreover, news organizations are rarely accused of bias against a club or a sportsman or woman. In the media, sport is a consensual issue and journalists do not risk offending anyone while covering a sporting event.

(5) Sport can offer a platform for jingoism.

A second series of factors is associated to the fact that sports events are *predictable*. Few spectacles are as safe and as convenient to cover as sports contests. News organizations know that sports competitions generate news, and that reporters and journalists sent to cover these events often collect enough information to write several articles. Predictability is also decisive in improving television coverage, as producers are able to install cameras and to test the best shots and angles. Television coverage also improved from one year to another: producers build on experience, and avoid past mistakes. This comes from the fact that sporting events are staged and journalists can be fully prepared to cover them. Finally, predictability allows media to conveniently pre-sell advertising time or space as well as pre-advertise the event to the audience. As the media know beforehand the time a competition starts and finishes, this comes in handy in establishing the programme schedules.

Staging means that situations are rehearsed and actors revolve in tightly defined roles. The predictability of roles and situations makes the encounter between journalists and participants unproblematic.

Unsurprisingly therefore, sportsmen and women are probably the most media-friendly people journalists have to deal with. But even more friendly than the contestants are the organizers themselves. In today's world, they fully realize that the media are an integral part of sports contests, that sport and spectacle are entwined. In some cases, as with the tie-break in tennis, rules have been modified to suit media needs. Organizers are particularly aware of these needs if they themselves come from the media field. In fact, many sports events have been staged by the media themselves. James Gordon Bennett created 'Bennett Cups' in various sports, and the Gordon Bennett car race was one of the most prestigious races of the early decades of the 20th century (Seitz, 1928, p. 251). The Tour de France was also created in 1903 by a sporting paper, *L'Auto* (Bellanger *et al.*, 1972, p. 384). The Tour de France is today owned by the Amaury press group, which also runs Paris–Dakar, the African rally. In sum, professional sports competitions are pre-organized and pre-sold media events where contestants perform well-defined roles and fully and willingly participate in the success of the show.

A third factor which explains the prominence of sports coverage in the media is that sport can give a decisive competitive advantage to dominant media groups over rivals. The key element here is that since *ownership claims* can be made on sports events, transmission rights can be asked for to broadcast these events. Thus successful bidders hold exclusivity rights on the sports events they buy from sporting federations, and this privilege gives them the opportunity to capture audiences and advertisers henceforth unavailable to rival organizations. Dominant media groups often actively pursue a strategy of buying sports events' exclusivity rights.

Finally, sport is a highly suitable material for advertisers. Advertisers' need for inconsequential and uncontroversial entertainment has played a significant role in promoting sport to the status of most popular newspaper topic. With sport, advertisers find the right mix of entertainment, drama and spectacle. Advertisers also prefer the cheerful atmosphere of sporting events to the general news which sometimes distresses the audience with bleak economic bulletins and reports on seemingly unsolvable political problems.[3]

Society news

Gordon Bennett, Sr can be credited with the invention of society news, as he was the first editor to report on the social events of the high society of New York (Seitz, 1928, pp. 58–9, 66; Schudson, 1978, p. 28–31). The New York elite received the first newspaper accounts of balls and dinners coolly and perceived these reports as to be quite an unacceptable intrusion into their private lives.

Society news was not widespread in the British daily press until the appearance of popular papers towards the end of the 19th century. A landmark in the history of this news category in England was the society column of the *Star*, the London evening paper launched in 1888 by T. P. O'Connor. The Irish MP, eager to divert his audience, introduced in the *Star* a society column, 'Mainly About People', which soon became so famous that a periodical was launched in the early 1890s after its name.

Equally significant was the launch of the short-lived *Daily Courier* in April 1896. Sir George Newnes, the owner, made of society news the staple commodity of the penny paper. The leader of the first issue revealed the rationale behind this decision: 'In exact proportion as the wealthiest and the most cultivated classes take the lead in the social life of their generation, their tastes, their pursuits, their movements, and their amusements become, under existing conditions, matters of reasonable interest to multitudes who are unconnected with society, and make no attempt to enter it' (*Daily Courier*, 1 April 1896). More pages in the *Daily Courier* were devoted to the social life of the nobility than to any other type of news. Each section of the paper reported the activities of high society in different settings, in town, in the country and abroad. The first couple of pages were exclusively devoted to life at the Court and to the comings and doings of the aristocracy. Important Court events were described in all their pomposity and minor ones in a wealth of detail.

In the 1900s, all popular papers followed the activities of the social elite very closely. For the *Daily Mirror* and *Daily Graphic*, society news became one of the most common news categories. From 1905 onwards, these two newspapers frequently had up to a quarter of their main news pages devoted to society and celebrity news. Popular dailies also ran columns of society titbits, entitled 'Stories About Well-known Men and Women of the Day', 'This Morning's Gossip' or 'In the Social World' in the *Daily Mirror*, 'Court Circular' in the *Daily Dispatch*, 'Social and Personal' or 'Social Echoes' in the *Daily Graphic*, 'In Society' in the *Daily Express*, 'People Who Are Talked About' in the *Sun* and 'To-night's Gossip' in the *Evening News*. Members of the aristocracy and royal families across the world were given particular attention, followed by singers and comedians. In third position came politicians and prominent public officials.

Today, society news is an industry of its own. A century after the launch of the first society magazine, *Mainly About People*, numerous magazines across Europe are entirely devoted to the activities of celebrities and other 'well-known for their well-knownness' people. These magazines are *Gala* and *Point de Vue Image du Monde* in France, *Gente* and *Oggi* in Italy, *OK!* and *Hello!* in England, the latter magazine being modelled on the Spanish *Hola!* Chequebook journalism is today the norm in society and celebrity news and magazines now sign contracts with celebrities for exclusive rights over pictures of ceremonies. Some of these contracts allow magazines to stage-manage the event and sometimes prevent guests from taking pictures of their own at the ceremony.

Society news comprises two dimensions. First, society columns focus on personalities, namely, individuals whose social background, connections, professional activities or position in society make them eligible for journalists' interest. Once the celebrity of a person has been established by the media, he or she may reappear in the news for no other reasons than his or her fame. Society news also involves a second dimension, that of the social event itself. Journalists write quantities of portraits or feature articles on celebrities without the peg of a special occasion, but society *news* generally reports on famous people at particular occasions or in particular circumstances. Journalists concentrate on three different types of events.

The first type are public and official activities such as ceremonies, state visits, appointments and high-profile charity events. At these ceremonies personalities perform official duties and carry out public roles. The press is more than welcome to report on personalities at these public functions for two main reasons. The first is that when these individuals perform these roles they represent an institution and thus they acquire a symbolic and emblematic function which is meant to be publicized. The second is that the publicity these persons get while performing these roles reinforces their investiture in the office.

The second kind of event is more informal and concerns entertainment venues and other specific social events in the society calendar. During the Edwardian decade, these events comprised balls, shooting parties and premieres at Covent Garden. The role performed by the nobility at these occasions may not be official but their presence nonetheless bears a ritualistic character, and is what makes the event so special. Photographers and journalists are welcome.

The third variety of event is the family type. Depending upon the family event, and also the family itself, the presence of reporters at these occasions may become problematic. With a few exceptions, journalists are allowed to attend weddings but certain families may choose to restrict access to funerals or christenings. Thus on these occasions reporters need to negotiate with the family. When no privacy law protects individuals from breaches of privacy, some newspapers may decide to publish accounts of the event without family approval.

What is the difference between society news and gossip? The notion of gossip may be restricted to pieces of information which reveal something about well-known people that they would rather have kept from the press. Most often this information touches intimate details or unpleasant episodes in the lives of these people. Reporters obtain this information by indirect sources and generally from persons who have an interest in revealing this information. Gossip seems to be popular with readers for two reasons. First, there is the breach of privacy itself, which gives an aura of mystery and secrecy to the information the press divulges. There is also the fact that gossip often reveals the ill-fortune of otherwise healthy and wealthy people, and commoners who sometimes envy the life-style of the nobility may get some satisfaction learning that everybody gets their share of trouble.

Sensational news
In this book a distinction is made between sensational news, a content category, and sensationalism, a discursive strategy. Sensationalism will be examined at a later stage, and this section examines the nature of sensational news. Sensational news is an ambiguous news category. Scholars and journalists alike tend to be descriptive rather than analytical when it comes to sensational news and in most cases eschew giving a definition of the category. Implicitly, most authors relate this category to the crime

reports and murder stories of the popular press (see, for example, Stevens, 1991).

Sensational news is also a category that is difficult to quantify and content analysts operate with definitions which greatly differ from each other. The '[l]aw, police and accidents' category used by the 1947 and 1974 Press Commissions does not discriminate between crime news and 'proceedings in all courts of law' (Royal Commission on the Press, 1949, p. 242; McQuail, 1977, p. 9). Thus in the 1977 report this news category includes reports on industrial relations disputes settled in courts, news of the British police engaged in Northern Ireland and sex-related court proceedings (McQuail, 1977, p. 9). Although the primary aim of the commissioners may not have been to quantify the amount of sensational material in the national press, the implications at least are that this category would include a fair amount of sensational news.[4] On the other hand, Virginia Berridge used a more classic definition of sensational material in her analysis of the *Reynolds' Newspaper*, *Lloyd's Weekly Newspaper* and the *Weekly Times*, using this category to refer to police news, accounts of violent deaths and scandals (Berridge, 1976, p. 193). This disparity indicates that the quantification of sensational news strongly depends upon the definition of the category, which varies from one researcher to another.

The following pages offer an exploratory definition of sensational material as a news category. An encompassing definition of sensational material would include the news coverage of essentially two sorts of events: those which present an extraordinary character, and crimes. Extraordinary events comprise happenings which are unusual, rare and infrequent; those which are bizarre and uncanny – this includes the coverage of unexplained phenomena (Carey, 1986, p. 168); events which are atypical and abnormal, that is, events which deviate from a norm, break a routine or end a tradition; and finally, events of a violent nature.

There was a net increase of this type of news in the late-19th-century popular press and the Edwardian halfpenny papers devoted a fair share of their news space to happenings of an extraordinary nature. Editors kept an eye for: (1) natural disasters, such as floods, earthquakes and volcanic eruptions; (2) accidents, such as steamship explosions, railway tragedies and fires; (3) violent social and political conflicts such as strikes, mutinies, riots and wars; (4) novelties such as technological innovations and weather records; (5) unusual and odd forms of behaviour with a marked preference for acts of heroism; (6) incidents of all sorts and in particular those involving celebrities; (7) alleged supernatural phenomena, miraculous healings and tales of exorcism and spiritualism.

Since time immemorial the press has published accounts of this sort but with the advent of the popular daily paper it reached the heart of the news values of editors and of the journalistic philosophy of press proprietors. It can be assumed that any extraordinary event would get immediate coverage in the Edwardian popular paper. If one day nothing of the like was published, it was certainly not much to do with any editorial decision but rather with the fact that, on this day, nothing exceptional had happened.

Thus, this emphasis on the exceptional was the result of deliberate editorial decisions. Press barons liked their papers to cover extraordinary events because they brought diversity to the news pages and added an element of surprise and excitement to the reading of the paper. Extraordinary events allowed them to publish vivacious papers. This news policy was illustrated at best with the legendary saying '[w]hen a dog bites a man, that is not news; but when a man bites a dog, that is news' (attributed to Amos Cummings, one of Charles Dana's editors, see Romano, 1986, p. 64). Most renowned press owners had their own version of this journalistic adage, and Northcliffe once defined news as 'anything out of the ordinary', adding that this is '[t]he only thing that will sell a newspaper' (in Fyfe, 1930, p. 86).

One type of happening which encompasses all qualities of extraordinary events is natural catastrophes and spectacular accidents. In the pre-journalistic age of the press, the accounts of these events were matter-of-fact. The reports of tragedies and deadly accidents were kept simple and succinct. Words were not employed to dramatize or add pathos to the news story. With the advent of the popular daily press, these accidents became *media events*. Editors learned to make the most of each accident and catastrophe, which eventually were 'splashed' on front pages and reported at length in the inside pages. Correspondents especially dispatched to the scene reported every detail of these events, drawing maps, interviewing witnesses and public officials and suggesting hypotheses on the cause of the accident.

On 16 October 1907 the *Daily Mirror* reported a railway accident at Shrewsbury in which twenty people were killed and forty injured. The account of the accident can be deconstructed into nine elements: (1) six headlines, of which three read as follows: 'Deadly Curve', 'Scenes of Horror', 'Thrilling Stories'; (2) and (3) a detailed account of the accident with accompanying pictures, of which two covered the entire front page; (4) list of names of the persons killed, seriously injured, and slightly injured; (5) a plan detailing the geography of the accident; (6) and (7) 'survivors' stories' plus a lengthy witness account entitled 'A Thrilling Moment'; (8) an article advancing hypotheses for the accident; and (9) a list of previous railway disasters, with the number of people killed in each case. The story had a follow-up, and the disaster was mentioned on several occasions during the following days.

The *Daily Mirror* style of reporting accidents and catastrophes was based on a regular pattern. The whole set included the headlines, the detailed account of the accident, the pictures, the plan or map, the accounts of people involved in the accident (witnesses, survivors, public officials), the hypotheses, the summary of previous disasters, and the follow-up to the story.

The second type of sensational material is essentially crime news, it being understood that all crime coverage is not necessarily sensationalized. In the popular press of the 1900s, this category included accounts of murders, sexual assaults, suicides and other events involving violent or sudden death. Accounts referred to the crimes themselves, to victims and criminals, to the consequences for the actors of the drama and finally to the case once it arrived in court. Most popular dailies launched in the Edwardian decade devoted a full page to crime news and police reports. In addition, sub-editors scattered crime reports across the pages of the paper, most certainly to sustain readers' attention. Great trials became major media events.

In the course of the 20th century, the range of violent acts covered by the press has much expanded, to include drug-related crimes, terrorism and child abuse (Schlesinger *et al.*, 1991, p. 407; Soothill and Walby, 1991). With the introduction of sound and the moving image, television has pushed the limits of the genre further. Today, programmes such as *Crimewatch UK*, *Crimestoppers* and *Crimebusters*, on the one hand, *Casualty*, *The X-Files*, *In Suspicious Circumstances*, and *Out of This World*, on the other, embrace the full spectrum of sensational news, insofar as the melange of fiction and reality, drama and entertainment, has anything to do with news (Dauncey, 1996). In addition, many talk shows often touch upon sensational issues. These programmes, big in resources and big in audiences, attest to the vitality and importance of this news category in contemporary media.

Myths and Narratives in Journalism: Human Interest Stories
In the course of the transformation from a public to a journalistic press, the development of the human interest story in the daily press is a significant phenomenon. As with society news, journalists explored new territories with human interest stories and reported aspects of personal and social life previously unrecorded in the daily press. The label 'human interest story' appeared in the New York *Sun*, then owned by Charles A. Dana, in the early 1870s[5] (Mott, 1962, p. 376). The development of human interest stories in the American and British press typifies the changes in journalists' considerations about story suitability. News items came to be selected for their entertaining value and their capacity to hold readers' interest and attention. Human interest stories are the primary example of this policy and epitomize the shift away from politics and the understanding by press entrepreneurs of the importance of content diversity to satisfy current readers and attract new ones.

Human interest stories are not best characterized as a topical category, although they often relate amusing, moving or unusual episodes, incidents or experiences in ordinary people's lives (Gans, 1980, p. 156). Helen Hughes noticed that stories on life's little ironies, animal stories, dramatic changes of fortune and romantic adventures are perennial (Hughes, 1940, pp. 184–216). Human interest stories do not have a definite format. They can be published as titbits or become full-page features. For instance, many human interest stories appeared in columns entitled 'Items of Interest From All Quarters' in the *Daily Express* or 'Happenings of Interest in All Parts of the World' and 'Bright News From Everywhere' in the *Daily Mirror*. Nor do human interest stories have a precise status in newspapers as they stand at the frontier between news and features.

It is difficult to define an archetypal human interest story, but many share three elements. First, the recurrent underlying themes in these stories are universal and the feelings and emotions evoked in these texts, such as love, sense of loss, or extreme surprise are experienced by most readers. Another common point of human interest stories is their narrative dimension. These stories frequently open with a tense or painful situation produced by human actions or natural forces and proceed to narrate the resolution of the problematic situation. A typical story contextualizes the situation, briefly explains why and how it occurred, and details what actors did to sort themselves out of this situation. When actors have been successful, stories lay the emphasis on the phase of resolution of conflicts and disorders and underline the happy ending of the problematic situation. Finally, many human interest stories seem to mediate between the 'micro' and the 'macro' by relating the particular to the universal. Events related by these stories often allegorize principles, feelings and archetypes which are commonly experienced and universal in character. These allegories were the staple of popular culture. Much of folk-tales and fairy-tales consisted of symbols which represented universal archetypes. Human interest stories are the journalistic equivalent to earlier forms of popular discourse, sharing the same narrative format and providing the same link to the universal through symbols and allegories.

Politics and the Trivialization of Content

In certain newspapers, the insertion of new material did not prevent politics and other 'serious' topics from being published too. In the early years of the 20th century, the editorial policy of the *Standard* and the *Daily Telegraph* was to keep politics and other 'heavy' news for the main news pages and to make concessions towards 'lightness' in the last two pages of the paper. By way of contrast, popular dailies, including the *Daily Mail* and *Daily Express*, had second thoughts before selecting a political item for publication. Politics was deliberately kept to a minimum in these papers. In the 1900s, while major sports contests and great trials were frequently 'splashed' on the front page, politics was confined to the inside pages, no matter how important a political event would be. The day Campbell-Bannerman announced the new Liberal government (following Balfour's resignation), neither the *Daily Graphic*, the *Daily Dispatch*, the *Daily Mirror*, nor the *Star* modified their usual pagination (11 December 1905). They kept politics away from the first page, and did not devote more space to politics than usual. The *Star* took the exceptional measure of devoting its leader, three paragraphs of anecdotal comments, to the new government, but did not pursue this concession any further. Except for the list of the new members of the Cabinet, and half-a-column of gossip on the subject, the *Star* was free of politics. The editors of these papers deliberately adopted the strategy not to let politics 'invade' the newspaper and to give priority to more entertaining news.

This discursive strategy is manifest in the selection of topics for leading articles. In many newspapers, politics was diligently confined to a *pre-determined* proportion of leaders. As the copies from September to December 1905 show, the *Daily News* adopted a policy that one out of three leaders should not concern politics, and the *Daily Graphic*, four out of five. In the *Star*, the *Evening News*, the *Sun*, the *Morning Advertiser*, and the *Daily Mirror*, politics was extremely rare, and leaders were routinely devoted to the most trivial topics.

In the *Daily Mirror*, five leaders, out of 119, were vaguely political between 1 October and 31 December 1908. The first 'political' leader discussed side aspects of the Women's Social and Political Union (14 October 1908), the second the physical endurance of candidates running for the American presidency (28 October 1908), and the third criticized the government for the way it had tackled the traffic problems in the capital (18 November 1908). The theme of the fourth leader was that some old Conservative politicians were once radical young men. As strong as the ideological message was, the leader presenting Conservatism as the ideology best corresponding to the course of natural life, its framing, was in fact depoliticized (26 November 1908). The only openly political leader was directed against the suffragettes. It argued that the method of struggle of 'militant suffragettes', 'battle-axes', 'whips', 'chains' and 'piercing war-cries', was disgraceful, offending, and inefficient, especially as men would retaliate 'without restraint or pity' (8 December 1908).

The remaining 96 per cent of *Daily Mirror* leaders revealed a genuine effort to avoid politics. The very day of the American presidential election, the leader's topic was marriage (4 November 1908), and when 15 suffragettes were arrested, the 'journal for men and women' denounced the 'intolerable tyranny' of women's hairdressers (29 October 1908). The most regular topics included the weather, marital affairs and sport. Ceremonies, commemorations and other public celebrations received due coverage. The single most talked-about topic was Christmas, appearing

13 times during the three-month period. Out of a 'desire to be first in the field', readers were wished a merry Christmas on 9 October. Between 16 and 29 December 1908, out of 12 leaders, 10 had Christmas as their subject.[6] In other words current political problems were deliberately avoided. Leader-writers were asked to be creative and to come up with original topics to write on. And it certainly requires more imagination to write on these subjects than to simply comment on the political issue of the day.

The policy of diversity therefore brought in an entire range of new topics to the press, from sensational news to human interest stories. In the process, politics lost its priority over other news, becoming 'only one of many competing subjects' struggling for space in modern popular papers (Spender, 1925, p. 104). How is this process of depoliticization to be interpreted?

First, there is the tempting charge of triviality. This imputation must be handled with extreme care, since this is not only judgemental but also subjective; what is trivial for someone is not necessarily perceived as such by someone else. In particular, sociologists who advance this criticism face the accusation of being unreflexive in their relationship to the products of the culture industry. Moreover, it is hardly an original observation. In 1910, a critique analysed a New York daily using four categories, 'trivial', 'demoralizing', 'unwholesome' and 'worthwhile', to find out that only 40 per cent of the news content of the paper fitted in the last category (Holsti, 1969, p. 54).

Nonetheless, the diversification of newspaper content was as a matter of fact the product of a policy which gave priority to inconsequential news over controversial and serious material. In addition, one may wonder whether being trivial was not exactly the way press magnates wanted the public to perceive their papers. In the 1900s, untapped segments of readers had still to be induced into the habit of newspaper reading, and newspaper proprietors were trying to create an attractive image of their daily paper. Press-owners and editors were precisely seeking to supplant the image of the newspaper as a political organ for that of the entertaining and amusing daily. In some way, these papers offered the guarantee to their readers that they would never seek to convince them on any particular point or advocate any serious cause. The implicit contract between journalists and readers was that the paper would never attempt to challenge their beliefs or change their opinion. To readers these papers offered the promise of frivolity and inconsequential news; as opposed to the risk of interfering with their stereotypes and the displeasure of creating cognitive dissonances. Triviality was a commercial strategy, a point press-owners and editors wanted to make to the public.

This attitude stood in sharp contrast to that of publicists and their commitment to political debate and political ideas. Such a rapid change could only be provoked by alterations in the economic base of the field of discursive production, namely, the emergence of the journalistic field and the development of competitive relations of production among journalists. By the 1900s, the struggle for survival had made it particularly dangerous for a daily to be perceived as ideologically menacing and intellectually challenging. This would have been a serious weakness in the newspaper market and rivals would have taken immediate advantage of this failure to entertain readers.

The second discursive outcome of the policy of diversity which needs interpretation is the *discursive fragmentation* this policy provoked in newspapers. Short news items, titbits, headlines and illustrations replaced seemingly endless columns written in small print. In addition to the profusion of news and features, topics freely mixed with each other and ceased to be hierarchized. In the popular daily press, police news and politics were given an equal status and placed side by side in the news pages. Bubbly and cheerful, the daily newspaper acquired a distinctively modern touch early this century.

With this phenomenon of fragmentation one can observe in these newspapers the emergence of one of the most significant discursive developments of the modern media. Indeed, the news philosophy which produced the fragmentation of the media discourse was at a later stage greatly encouraged by the development of new media, mainly television, primarily geared towards entertainment. But it must be noted that these journalistic dispositions were already distinctive in the Edwardian popular paper.

Aspects of the fragmentation of the media discourse have been commented upon by numerous authors. Postmodernists relate this discursive trend in the media and elsewhere to the end of ideology and the 'master narrative', the loss of a unique set of references and the production of simulacra by the media (Baudrillard,

1981; Quéré, 1982, pp. 153–75). The point is that postmodernists not only dissociate these discursive phenomena from the capitalist economy, but also regard these trends as the proof of a coming out of the post-capitalist era and as the symbol of the end of the society of production. Postmodern culture is even sometimes portrayed as part of an emancipation movement from the iron cage of modernity (Bell, 1976; Baudrillard, 1977, 1985).

The argument of the separation between the economy and 'postmodern' cultural phenomena, such as the fragmentation of the media discourse, is somewhat difficult to believe when one takes into account the empirical reality of the origins of these phenomena. The fact that these discursive trends first emerged in the popular press early this century throws some doubt on the claim that the phenomena related to 'postmodern' culture are in a state of rupture from the norms and values of the modern era. The phenomenon of discursive fragmentation was initiated by the transfer of the newsworthiness of an event from its intrinsic significance, political or otherwise, to the presumed interest readers would find in it. This principle is still very much applied by journalists today with even more energy and rigour than during the past decades. The assertions on the post-capitalist nature of this culture also seem to stretch the boundaries of credibility, given that the policy of diversity was initiated by the most commercially minded press-owners. The discursive developments that occurred in the media industry for the last couple of decades are best understood if related, but not necessarily reduced to the progress in the commercialization of culture and the commodification of discourse. The postmodern argument offers many exciting features, but closing the door on the economic base of contemporary media discourse is not necessarily the best step to take in order to comprehend the historical specificity of modern culture.

Making Politics Entertaining

The process of depoliticization is about the decline of politics in newspapers, as examined in the previous pages, and secondly about the way the modern press handles the topic. Political coverage changed greatly from the 19th century to become itself depoliticized. Before the rise of journalism, politics 'contained' the discourse of the press. Public texts were the unmediated symbolic expression of political intentions. Publicists followed a political agenda and verbatim publication of speeches and parliamentary debates gave politicians direct access to the public. Following the formation of the journalistic field, the relation between press and politics reversed and politics became one of the contents of journalism. Journalists began to report politics according to their own needs and interests, covering the topic from their own perspective and own professional values.

In recent years, scholars and politicians alike in Europe and America have been critical of the evolution of political coverage in the media. In certain European countries the trend has been accentuated in the last couple of years by the privatization of television networks. In France, researchers have begun to analyse 'la médiatisation du politique' and Italian scholars attempt to come to term with the re-framing of politics by commercial television and the 'trionfo della politica-spettacolo' (Neveu, 1995; Véron, 1995, p. 201; Statera, 1994, p. 7). In England, although academics and politicians are more familiar with the depoliticized media treatment of politics, the latter recently voiced (again) their discontent with the evolution of political reporting. On 12 June 1996, a parliamentary motion signed by 51 MPs deplored the 'steep decline in serious reporting and analysis of politics and current affairs in the United Kingdom; not[ing] that this decline has gathered pace in recent times, with increasing emphasis on personalities rather than policies, and on trivia rather than substance'. The following pages attempt to identify early forms of the depoliticized treatment of politics and to relate these forms to more recent manifestations of the same discursive phenomenon. Three aspects of the re-framing of politics by journalists are particularly salient.

Politics Trivialized
From the 1880s onwards, the focus of political coverage progressively shifted from issues raised by politicians to aspects of the political game itself. Gradually journalists paid less attention to the substance of the political debate and began to report events which they found newsworthy for reasons other than their political significance. This trend in political coverage first emerged in the London evening gazettes, then spread to the popular press during the 1900s and finally reached the quality morning papers later in the century.

Signs of this new relation to politics transpired in the *Pall Mall Gazette* of the 1880s. Among the 33 competitions that the evening newspaper ran between 1886 and 1887, several had politics and politicians as a topic. One of these competitions asked contestants to rate members of the Commons in 12 categories, including 'best orator', 'best debater', 'greatest bore' and 'most eccentric' (*Pall Mall Gazette*, 13 October 1886). Two aspects of this competition are revealing. The first is the entertainment twist, while the second is the interest in politicians' performance and ability to communicate effectively. This manifests a shift of attention from the content of the message to the way politicians delivered it.

Concomitant to this trend was the growing interest by the popular press for the trivia in politics, amusing occurrences and other anecdotal incidents. Typically, on 4 May 1896, the *Daily Mail* informed its readers that half-a-dozen MPs came to Parliament by bicycle, but failed to tell them what was discussed in the Houses that day. Interest in trivia was encouraged by the introduction of the photograph in the daily press in the late 1900s (on the development of news photography in Britain, see Twaites, 1996, pp. 20–4). In England, the *Daily Mirror* pioneered the use of illustrations in daily journalism and henceforth pictures of politicians delivering a speech supplanted the report of that speech. Sometimes, the theme of the address was mentioned in the caption below the picture of the speaker or the audience. Politicians were routinely photographed going to or coming from Downing Street, attending a luncheon, meeting colleagues and members of the government. As for the press the interesting part of politics became its paraphernalia, not its subject matter; the substance of politics disappeared behind the everydayness of it.

One of the modern equivalents of this frame of reference is the focus on campaign issues, as opposed to policy issues, in election news. Political communication scholars have widely researched the media interest for the campaign game (the events and strategies associated to electoral contests) and have labelled it 'horse racism' (see, for example, Patterson, 1980). With horse-racism, journalists focus on the strategies candidates employ to undermine the legitimacy of the opposition, to win voters' confidence, or to close the gap with their opponents in the polls. Journalists also assess candidates' performance, commenting on their rating in the polls and speculating on the effectiveness of their latest campaign gimmicks. Finally, journalists report on campaign teams' activities and spin doctors' manoeuvres to get their candidates favourable coverage. The problem with this type of coverage is that politicians find it increasingly difficult to get their message across to the electorate. As journalists' news values divert them from the substance of the political debate and lead them to focus on the political game, political coverage today increasingly interferes with political discourse itself.

In recent years, horse-racism has become quite pervasive in the British media. A study on the media coverage of the 1987 British General Election showed that during the five weeks preceding the election 15 per cent of election news was devoted to the campaign process (Miller *et al.*, 1990, p. 208). The authors also noticed that 25 per cent of election news items were 'unfocused', a category which included 'multi-issue' and 'campaign-trail' items (ibid., pp. 208–9). Five years later, the horse-race and campaign issues had become one of the leading topics in the television coverage of the 1992 General Election. Horse-racism clearly dominated the ITN coverage as 31.6 per cent of the election news stories during the four-week official campaign preceding the election were devoted to opinion polls and the horse race itself, followed by 15.4 per cent of news stories on how the campaign was conducted and 15.4 per cent on the economy (Nossiter *et al.*, 1995, p. 88). On the BBC the leading topic for the duration of the campaign was the economy, accounting for 19.5 per cent of news stories, followed by horse race and opinion polls, with 18.4 per cent of news stories (ibid.). During the last week of the campaign, however, the horse race had become the leading topic on BBC too, with 27.8 per cent of stories on the subject, plus 11.5 per cent on how the campaign was run (ibid.).

Public Life Personalized
The 'personalization' of public life refers to the fact that political reporting concentrates on individuals rather than on the political process itself (see, for example, Graber, 1989, pp. 212–15). Part of this 'peopling of the press' involves a process of 'personification' of politics, well-known personalities becoming 'surrogates for institutions' and historical forces being anthropomorphized (Sigal, 1986, pp. 12–15). Another aspect of the focus on personalities is the interest the media pay to politicians' private lives.

The disclosure of public officials' private life is specific to journalists, as publicists, in England at least, never ventured into this territory. For all their political virulence, unstampeds, for instance, never invaded a politician's private sphere. A contemporary observer, who had otherwise little sympathy for the unstampeds, acknowledged that '[o]ne thing may be remarked of all of them [the unstamped papers], that they refrain from personal scurrility and private scandal' (Crawfurd, 1836, p. 38). Charles Dilke, chosen by the Liberal Party as Gladstone's successor, was the first political figure to be forced out of national politics due to press agitation following publicity about his private life (Jenkins, 1958, p. 212). Alleged to be Mrs Crawford's lover, Charles Dilke was named as the co-respondent in the trial for divorce initiated by her husband (ibid., p. 214). At the conclusion of the first trial the press campaigned against him on the ground of debauchery and perjury and obliged him to retire from the political scene (ibid., pp. 235–60). Particularly vocal during the campaign was W.T. Stead, the editor of the *Pall Mall Gazette*, an independent evening paper which leaned towards the Liberal Party. The Dilke scandal marked the beginning of a trend which developed from strength to strength in the 20th-century press. Today, the time lag between press allegations and the resignation of a public official is a matter of days.

What encouraged Stead and other journalists to turn this trial into a major scandal? Was it the Victorians' liking for public displays of morality, or the keen rivalry at that time between London gazettes? Although both points are valid, there is more to it than the *Zeitgeist* thesis or the economic argument would suggest. By the end of the 19th century, all prominent daily newspapers claimed to be formally independent of political parties. As long as newspapers were openly tied to political parties, their legitimacy to hold a discourse on political matters rested on the party whose principles they advocated. But when newspapers became more autonomous, they had to find a new *basis of legitimacy* in order to comment on politics from a position external to the political field, from a viewpoint which claimed not to be directly involved in the political struggle. One of the new sources of legitimacy became morality. As such, morality was (and continues to be) particularly convenient for journalists because moral virtues, such as integrity and forthrightness were considered to be valid in both private and public spheres. Thus, journalists could justify disclosures of private affairs by claiming that they, and the public, could draw useful inferences from these revelations.

Similar to today's tabloids, Stead defended himself in the aftermath of the Dilke affair arguing that the vices of the elite should not be covered up and are relevant to the public and the political process at large (*Pall Mall Gazette*, 5 February 1887). In addition, the supposed universal validity of moral categories also allowed journalists to express opinions on politics and elected officials with categories taken as valid in the political sphere but which were not openly politically connoted. In other words, on the ground of morality, journalists could not only justify breaches of privacy, they could also comment on politics with seemingly a-political categories. These two combined advantages were the main incentives for journalists to invade public officials' privacy and to put an end to the former distinction between private life and the public arena.

Politics as Spectacle
The contrast between public discourse and journalism is at its most stark when the relationship between each of these two classes of texts and politics is compared. Publicists discussed politics as a process in which both themselves and their readers were directly implied. Not that all readers were active in politics, but public texts conveyed a sense of immediacy to politics giving their readers the feeling that they were part of the political process. This feeling gave readers a political identity and publicists a sense of purpose which was made plain from the enthusiasm with which they discussed political matters. Journalists have developed a different relationship to politics, all too manifest by the cynicism many observers have noticed in the newsroom and the detachment journalists affect when reporting on politics (see, for example, Breed, 1980, p. 149). Journalists operate on the basis of a marked distinction between themselves, politicians and the 'general public'. Although journalists depict neither themselves nor the public as direct participants to the political process, they still give themselves a role to play in the public sphere, that of observer of the political game and watchdog of democratic values. This distribution of roles reserves the most passive part for the public. The audience is invited to watch, not to participate in the political game. Journalists give the public the opportunity to voice their opinions in talk shows and to a lesser extent in opinion polls. But this is as far as journalists go to give the public the illusion that they are connected to politics. The way politics is framed by

the news, the implication is that politicians act, journalists report, and the audience watch, and sometimes react.

The aspect of the framing of politics which may be singled out as particularly related to this tendency is that of journalists' emphasis on the spectacular, eventful and dramatic ingredients of politics. As for journalists' interest in the political game, the possibility for newspapers to reproduce same-day photographs was a major step towards the coverage of politics as a spectacle. Thus, the big break towards the spectacular treatment of politics occurred at the turn of the century. In the 1900s, the popular press coverage of political events became radically different from that of the quality newspapers of the same period. The *Daily Mirror*'s coverage of the Opening of Parliament in February 1904 illustrates this point. In sharp contrast to the established tradition, the *Daily Mirror* exclusively focused on the pageantry of the ceremony and ignored the Queen's speech. Northcliffe's paper devoted half the front page to a picture of the royal coach and the entire last page to a portrait of the late Queen Victoria. The *Daily Mirror* coverage also included a map of the route from Buckingham Palace to Westminster and two articles detailing the procession and the decoration of the carriage. On this day the leading article discussed politics, but jumped on the occasion to excuse the paper's lack of interest in politics. Parliament was characterized as a 'talking-shop which has very little real influence upon the course of events' (*Daily Mirror*, 2 February 1904). The elegance of this remark can be fully appreciated knowing that in 1904 women had still not received the franchise and only 58 per cent of the adult male population had gained the right to vote (Butler and Butler, 1994, p. 240).

The *Daily Mirror* never departed from this style and based all its subsequent political reporting on images. The Russo-Japanese conflict in 1904 essentially consisted of sensational drawings of naval battles. A few years later, the *Daily Mirror* used the same technique to report on the Portuguese republican revolution. The *Daily Mirror* published scores of pictures and readers could admire panoramic views of Lisbon, palaces, yachts, the King's relatives, the King's highly ranked officers, and so on. King Manuel alone appeared in 16 pictures over three days (*Daily Mirror*, 5–6, 8 October 1910). On 12 October 1910, the popular daily gave the same picturesque treatment to the newly installed President of the Portuguese Republic.

In the 1900s the coverage style of the *Daily Mirror* was still unusual but soon other papers aiming at a lower middle-class audience followed suit. This type of coverage also pre-figured the 'tabloidization' of the leading popular papers in the early 1930s. Photographs have two qualities that made the struggle between words and images uneven. Images made their way into journalism because, quite simply, they are easy to understand and require no mental effort from readers. Readers process them as they see them and satisfy their curiosity instantly. Images are also self-explanatory, or so they seem, and a short legend is often enough to provide the context. This was a determining advantage for press-owners, like Northcliffe, who requested from their journalists that they '[m]ake [their] story read so that a man coming off an Atlantic liner to-morrow can understand what it's about' (Clarke, 1931, p. 32). The second advantage of images is that because of their proximity to events they are inherently more dramatic than words. Unlike words they directly represent the event they depict. For the same reason, images are very useful in adding a human interest touch to news stories.

The first problem with the shift from words to pictures in political reporting is that there is not much to see in politics. Images are of little help in comprehending argumentative political debates. Images are signs whose relationship to the object is non-arbitrary (Barthes, 1964). Thus images can represent objects, but cannot signify them. This makes images effective in certain applications in medicine and engineering, but remains of little use in conveying the meaning of political controversies. Consequently, political reporting which relies on images concentrates on what fits within the image format, and more often than not, passes over the substance of politics. The same reliance on the image led journalists to over-report events with strong visuals such as public ceremonies and public officials inspecting disaster areas, to the detriment of less spectacular but possibly more significant political events.

In addition to the use of images, a second mechanism turns politics into spectacle in the media. Since timeliness became an essential criterion in the process of news selection, media and politics evolve in two different time frames. The time frame of the media is at the same time more restricted and more hurried than that of politics. The frantic pace of news combined with the focus on events that are a few hours old tends to transform politics into a spectacle, politics being presented as a carousel of discontinued and decontextualized events. This disjunction between the two time frames creates a contradiction between journalism and politics. Politics cannot be reduced to a series of disconnected events. Politics involves the resolution of complex problems within a conflictual environment. It intertwines with social structures, economic phenomena, antagonistic ideologies and divergent political interests. It is also a field with its own rules, specific structures and actors. Politics is a world of complexities, conflicts and divergences and the rapid pace of news cannot do justice to this reality. In politics, more than anywhere else, the past is the key to the present, and invisible structures explain recent events. As the past fades away behind images, as news separates the present from its past and as the past ceases to explain the present, the conflict between spectacle and history becomes apparent. By making history disappear from the present, spectacle erases memories.

4.3   THE 1922 GENERAL ELECTION

The 1922 General Election illustrates two of the main points of the present chapter, the political arbitrariness of the British press and the discursive phenomenon of depoliticization. This section starts by examining the relationship between the press and the three main political parties contesting the 1922 General Election, and then points to the depoliticized aspects of the coverage of this election.

The editor of the Liberal *Westminster Gazette*, J.A. Spender, wrote that the Labour Party became a political force in England because its members were working 'behind' the newspapers (Spender, 1925, p. 122). In view of the lack of support the Labour Party got from the press in 1922, it may have been more correct to write that the Labour Party became the second political force in the country 'against' the newspaper press. The Labour Party achieved this position in 1922 by getting 29.5 per cent of the vote, against 29.1 for the two Liberal lists and 38.2 per cent for the Conservative Party (Butler and Sloman, 1980, p. 207). From our perspective the relevant fact is the discrepancy between these results and the support political parties received from the press. Only one national daily, the *Daily Herald*, supported the Labour Party, as compared to five for the Liberal Party and 12 for the Conservatives (see Table 4.1). In terms of circulation, the balance also tipped

Table 4.1   Press partisanship and newspaper circulations at the 1922 General Election

Conservative	Liberal	Labour
Large circulation (200 000 and higher)		
Daily Mail	*Star*	
(1 800 000)	(550 000)	
Daily Mirror	*Daily News*	
(1 000 000)	(500 000)	
Daily Sketch	*Daily Chronicle*	
(950 000)	(250 000, estimated)	
Evening News		
(900 000)		
Daily Express		
(750 000)		
Daily Dispatch		
(460 000)		
Evening Standard		
(350 000)		
Daily Graphic		
(250 000, estimated)		
Medium circulation (50 000–200 000)		
The Times	*Manchester Guardian*	*Daily Herald*
(160 000)	(50 000)	(150 000)
Daily Telegraph		
(160 000)		
Small circulation (50 000 and below)		
Morning Post	*Westminster Gazette*	
(20 000, estimated)	(20 000)	
Pall Mall Gazette		
(20 000, estimated)		

Sources: Wadsworth, 1955; *Newspaper Press Directory*, 1922, 1923. The circulations of the *Daily Graphic*, *Daily Chronicle*, *Morning Post* and *Pall Mall Gazette* had to be estimated on the basis of partial indications and comparisons with similar newspapers. Prewar circulation figures have to be taken cautiously as some papers appear to have inflated them. (On advertisers' complaints on this matter, see *Truth About Circulation*, a pamphlet issued in 1924 by the Incorporated Society of British Advertisers.)

in favour of the Conservative Party, with approximately 81 per cent of the press supporting the Conservatives, 17.1 per cent the Liberals and only 1.9 per cent the Labour Party (see Table 4.2).

A brief look at the ownership of popular papers in 1922 is enough to confirm the improbability of Labour getting substantial support from the press. Following Northcliffe's death in August 1922, the *Daily Mail*, *Daily Mirror* and *Evening News* became the possession

Table 4.2   Aggregate circulation of press partisanship and results of
the 1922 General Election expressed in percentages

	Conservative	Liberal	Labour
% votes	38.2	29.1	29.5
% circulation	81	17.1	1.9

Source: Butler and Sloman, 1980, p. 207.

of his brother and associate, Lord Rothermere, widely acknowledged as the most right-wing press lord; in the 1930s, he supported Oswald Mosley, the Fascist and totalitarian regimes in Italy and Germany (Koss, 1990: pp. 944–5, 970–2, 1025–8; Taylor, 1996, pp. 279–98). In 1934, Rothermere's friendship with Hitler was such that Rothermere, his son and a close collaborator 'were three of four foreigners among only two dozen guests who attended Hitler's first dinner party given in his official residence in Berlin' (Taylor, 1996, p. 294). The *Daily Express* was the property of Beaverbrook. Beaverbrook was himself a Conservative MP and he and the leader of that party, Bonar Law, were intimate friends. Bonar Law became Prime Minister in October 1922, but for a short period only, as poor health forced him to retire in May 1923. In 1922, the *Evening Standard*, to be bought in 1923 by Beaverbrook, the *Daily Sketch*, to be bought the same year by Rothermere, and the *Daily Dispatch* were still in the hands of the Hulton group, whose newspapers were traditionally Conservative. Since 1920, the *Daily Graphic* was part of the Berry conglomerate, the most important press group in Britain after Northcliffe's death. Seymour Berry (later Lord Buckland) was a close friend of Stanley Baldwin, Law's successor and three times Prime Minister, and his younger brother, William Berry (later Lord Camrose), developed a lifelong friendship with Winston Churchill (Hart-Davis, 1990, passim). Moreover, the huge industrial interests of the Berry brothers in steel and coal mining, most notably, gave them no particular incentive to support the Labour Party. In addition to the daily press, most popular Sunday papers were owned by one of these groups. Rothermere possessed the *Sunday Dispatch*, Beaverbrook the *Sunday Express*, Hulton the *Sunday Illustrated Herald* and the Berrys the *Sunday Graphic*.

Northcliffe was the only press lord who had kept an open mind towards Labour. Stephen Koss attributed Northcliffe's openness to Labour to his discord with David Lloyd George (Koss, 1990, p. 789). Other factors which need to be considered are Northcliffe's complex personality and, more prosaically, his keen commercial sense. In the late 1910s, as Northcliffe had asked the *Daily Mail* to take into account the Labour stance in the newspaper's coverage of industrial disruptions, the press baron received a note from the circulation manager approving the decision as commercially sound and stressing that the 'coming force in this country is undoubtedly Labour' (Valentine Smith to Northcliffe, 13 January 1920, Northcliffe Papers, Add. MSS 62 211). Had Northcliffe lived through 1922 and witnessed an excess of four million people voting Labour, he may have decided to re-examine the political leanings of one of his daily newspapers.

In 1922, the relationship between the Labour Party and two of the Liberal papers from whom they could have hoped for support, the *Star* and the *Daily News*, had in fact deteriorated. In 1919, the Labour Party had obtained some help from the Liberal press. Arthur Henderson, the Labour Party Secretary, having obtained a 'Labour column' from Liberal newspapers, could thank the editor of the *Daily News*, A. G. Gardiner, for the 'fair play and sympathetic consideration which the *Daily News* has shown towards the Labour cause' (Henderson to Gardiner, 3 January 1919, Gardiner papers). In 1922, however, the Liberal Party was attempting a revival, and the 'Labour column' disappeared from Liberal dailies.

As a result, the 1922 press support for Labour was limited solely to the *Daily Herald*. Succumbing to its debts and out-distanced in terms of circulation by the leading popular titles, it was taken over by the Trades Union Congress in September 1922, two months before the election. This take-over limited the usefulness of the *Daily Herald* by tainting the ownership of the paper, which, in contrast to other newspapers, was officially controlled by a political organization.

In sum, press support for political parties was unequally distributed during the 1922 General Election, the balance strongly tilting in favour of the Conservative Party. As Table 4.2 shows, the Conservative bias of the press did not reflect public opinion, and there was a strong discrepancy between the ideological stance of the press and election results. In terms of aggregate circulation, approximately less than 2 per cent of the press supported the Labour Party, while more than 29 per cent of the electorate voted Labour.

During the interwar period there was not much change in the ideological preferences of the press. The *Daily Mirror*'s shift of policy during the Second World War in favour of Labour was the most significant change in the pattern of press partisanship since the Great War. Thereafter, the balance of partisanship has remained relatively stable. Between 1945 and 1992, the Conservative circulation has averaged 59.4 per cent of total circulation, against 34.6 per cent for the Labour circulation (Butler and Butler, 1994, p. 499). The gap between the two circulations peaked in 1983, with the Conservative circulation at 78 per cent of total circulation, against 22 per cent for Labour (ibid.). Significantly, the average total Conservative circulation (59.4 per cent) has always been above the total Conservative vote (43.2 per cent), but the total Labour circulation (34.6 per cent) has always been below the Labour vote (41 per cent) (ibid.). Therefore, ever since the formation of the journalistic field the press has shown a constant bias in favour of the Conservative Party. The perenniality of this leaning towards the Conservatives suggests that the bias is structural rather than partisan and derives from the economic structure of the field. As mentioned above, constraints in the field imposed by economic competition have reserved access to the journalistic field to the very few news organizations which have the financial resources to sustain the competitive struggle. The discrepancy between the opinion of the public and the opinion of the press proves that the difficulty of access to news production prevents non-dominant viewpoints from expressing themselves and impairs the diversity of voices in the public sphere.

The press coverage of the 1922 General Election also illustrates that a politically arbitrary press can be depoliticized. The two phenomena are not contradictory, since the depoliticization of the press does not refer to political opinions *per se* but to the decrease in the amount of political reporting and to a series of trends in the political coverage of the press. In 1922, none of the popular dailies showed a great deal of enthusiasm for the elections. During the three weeks preceding the General Election, the popular papers did not increase in any notable way the amount of space they usually allocated to politics, and political information was almost as scarce as ever. As a result of this patent lack of interest, it is not that obvious to the modern reader that the nation was on its way to a General Election. This problem was clearly perceived by the authors of a study on the press published by the Labour Research Department in 1922. Unexpectedly, the report did not criticize the 'Harmsworth press' for its bias in favour of the Conservatives, but for 'anaesthetising the public mind' with an overflow of inconsequential news and trivial titbits (Labour Research Department, 1922, p. 46). It is significant for the press coverage of the election that the report singled out for criticism the lack of political information in popular newspapers rather than the partisanship of the press. The researchers for the Labour Party may have realized that the political ignorance popular newspapers were manufacturing was more prejudicial in the long term for the Labour Party than the political bias of the press.

Other aspects of the depoliticization of the press were manifest in several popular newspapers during the weeks preceding the General Election. The coverage of the *Daily Express*, for example, illustrates the extreme circumspection of the popular press when articulating political opinions. In spite of Beaverbrook's intimate friendship with the Conservative leader, Bonar Law, the support the *Daily Express* gave to the Conservative Party was oblique rather than explicit. The *Daily Express* favoured Bonar Law by way of news selection and devoted more space to his speeches and activities than to those of the other candidates. The *Daily Express* also published favourable economic reports and made claims about good economic prospects in the event of a Conservative victory which was presented as certain (*Daily Express*, 8–14 November 1922). On polling day, the leading article gave no other reasons but 'safety' to vote Conservative, and claimed that the journal had 'no personal allegiance to any politician or set of politicians' (*Daily Express*, 15 November 1922). Lack of frank political opinion, absence of openly political statements, unbalanced news selection, biased news treatment and claims of independence and neutrality characterized the *Daily Express* coverage of the General Election, illustrating a form of 'depoliticized political bias'.

The *Daily Mail* and *Daily Mirror* were more virulent than the *Daily Express* against the Labour Party but were even less argumentative. They urged readers not to vote Labour with a series of unchecked assertions and plainly false allegations against that party. The *Daily Mail* and *Daily Mirror* based their discourse on stereotypes and played on people's fears. The two dailies sought to persuade their readers, but without arguments or debates. This made their discourse politically arbitrary, but without the political substance that characterized the public press. This political coverage was pure violence, without reason, pure propaganda, without information.

Rothermere's dailies strove to associate the Labour Party with Bolshevism. In the leading articles of the *Daily Mail*, the most frequent words employed to designate Labour were 'Reds', 'Socialism', 'Communism' and 'Bolshevism', and their coming to power was commonly associated with 'ruin', 'misery', 'unemployment', 'starvation' and 'robbery'. A leader claimed that 'if the Labour Bolshevists once get control we shall all be irrevocably dragged along the Russian Road to Ruin', and added that since Labour 'assail' the 'whole principle of private property', 'they threaten every man's house and furniture, and every woman's clothes and jewellery, as was done in Russia' (*Daily Mail*, 1 November 1922). These statements were misleading and did not reflect Labour policies at that time.

The *Daily Mirror* made the message more visual for its readers with a series of six cartoons. The first showed a Cossack, 'Bolshie', and his dog, 'Wolfie', preparing themselves for the election by veiling their Russian origin in British garments. The Bolshevik in disguise became 'Labourski' and 'Wolfie' was re-named 'Snap'. The series showed our two protagonists trying to steal people's property by ruse (*Daily Mirror*, 3–9 November 1922).

Rothermere and the editorial staff of the *Daily Mail* and *Daily Mirror* may have had excellent reasons to believe that the Labour Party once in power would steal everybody's property, but unfortunately never stated them. 'Common sense' and the 'interest of the nation' were the main two arguments they gave readers to not vote for Labour. They tried to inspire a visceral hate of the Labour Party in their readers, without providing arguments or even information on party programmes and policies that could have helped readers make a reasoned choice.

Aside from the anti-Labour bashing, the *Daily Mail* and *Daily Mirror* never made it very clear whom they stood for. The only vote recommendation the two papers gave was not to vote Labour. The two papers found Bonar Law a decent Prime Minister, 'wise' and 'experienced', but that was as far as they went with their compliments. The only party Rothermere papers wholeheartedly supported was Rothermere's own list, the Anti-Waste League, which campaigned on an anti-tax programme.

The *Daily Mail* opposition to Labour and evasiveness on the other political parties is reflected in the polling-day leader article, entitled 'Don't forget to vote today against Socialism':

The common sense of our people repudiates the Socialism and the Bolshevism of the Labour leaders. The first result of their capital levy would be wholesale unemployment, the second starvation and the third chaotic revolution. [. . .] Our final counsel to the electorate of both sexes is: Vote for the Bonar Law Party (the probable victors) or the Lloyd George Party, or the Asquith-Grey Party, if you will, but don't vote Socialist! (*Daily Mail*, 15 November 1922).

Finally, the popular press placed much emphasis on personalities during the election campaign. Not much information was given on party programmes and not much was said on policy issues, political principles and ideologies. Rather, the attention was firmly on party leaders. In the *Daily Mail*, the Conservative Party and the Liberal Party were generally referred to as the Bonar Law party and the Lloyd George party. Nor was much written about the 615 seats being fought for during this General Election. Moreover, it is quite manifest that the personalities of candidates were becoming a strong point of interest for the popular press. Numerous pictures showed the candidates at different moments in their private lives. The *Daily Mirror* published a series of special issues on each candidate, and the one on Bonar Law contained three full pages of pictures. Bonar Law was photographed performing public duties, but also playing golf or tennis. His relatives, and daughters in particular, appeared in many pictures (*Daily Mirror*, 8 November 1922).

The coverage of the 1922 General Election displays many characteristics which became the usual features of modern political reporting. Certain traits have changed, but the focus on personalities, the tendency to drift away from substance, the circumspection in expressing values and opinions, and the structural bias in favour of the Conservative Party, indicate that several aspects of modern media political coverage were established well before the Second World War.

4.4   CONSEQUENCES OF THE DEPOLITICIZATION OF
THE PRESS ON POLITICS AND POLITICAL DISCOURSE

The effects of the media on public life is one of the most researched areas in media studies, and probably the most problematic. Taking into account the methodological background of this book on the one hand, and the fact that many aspects of the media's effects are still open to discussion, this section has no other aim but to suggest possible liaisons between the discursive phenomenon of depoliticization and certain features of modern political life. Since the section discusses these liaisons at a fairly general level, it incorporates recent data when deemed relevant to the argument.

Many political scientists have noted the lack of interest in politics by the population, and some have even voiced their surprise that democratic systems have survived with such low levels of participation in political affairs (Miller *et al.*, 1990, pp. 204–5; McCombs *et al.*, 1991, p. 87). In Britain, the average turn-out at the general elections between 1945 and 1992 was 76.6 per cent (Butler and Butler, 1994, pp. 216–19). Considering the low frequency of elections in Britain compared to other modern democracies where the ratio of elected officials by public appointment is much higher than in Britain, this rate implies that nearly a quarter of eligible voters in Britain have no degree of interest in politics. Electoral and political behaviour is extremely complex and to single out the media and even the process of depoliticization of the press as the main culprits for the low degree of involvement in politics would be far too simplistic. However, if the agenda-setting hypothesis is correct, that the press 'may not be successful much of the time in telling people what to think, but it is stunningly successful in telling its readers what to think *about*', the process of depoliticization therefore must not have encouraged people to think about politics (Cohen in McCombs and Shaw, 1972, p. 177). Neither the small quantity of political reporting in the media nor the way politics is framed induces citizens to increase their participation in politics.

The mere fact that journalists act as non-partisans and rarely explicitly engage in political debate themselves produces a climate which is not propitious to raising levels of engagement and participation in politics. Moreover, journalists' cynical attitude towards politicians may turn people further away from politics. The media emphasis on strategy and the shift away from the substance of politics also act as a disincentive for the citizenry to engage in public life. Among the reasons why the focus on strategy drives people away from participation, Kathleen Jamieson has mentioned that the 'strategy schema invites audiences to critique a campaign as if it were a theatrical performance in which the audience is involved only as a spectator' (Jamieson, 1992, p. 187).

Media intrusion into politicians' private lives has had a series of impacts on the political system itself. First, the fear of media inquisition into one's private life may have reduced the number of political vocations, and at the very least the number of people able to embark on a political career. Second, as illustrated by the Charles Dilke affair, the media's self-appointed right to reveal intimate details of someone's life has curtailed the power of political parties to select their own candidates. On the other hand, politicians and their spin doctors know today how to turn to their own advantage journalists' interest in politicians' private lives.

The reliance of journalists on the image in political reporting has made physical appearance a factor of relative importance in politicians' careers. It has often been said that certain old political figures would never have made it in today's image-saturated political world. Although it is not precisely known how appearance can be converted into votes, numerous politicians today watch or even modify their demeanour with the intention of looking more appealing to voters. In all cases most politicians are conscious of the image they project to the public and some of them receive professional advice from image consultants.

The process of depoliticization had an undeniable impact on political discourse. In the course of the 20th century, politicians have learnt to deal with the media and have considerably modified the way they communicate with voters. Politicians forestall the fragmentation of their discourse and no longer develop arguments but speak in soundbites. They also assert more, simplify the issues considerably, construct narratives and use strong symbols and images in order to get their point across through the media.

Finally, the process of depoliticization has changed what people know and what they understand about politics. The process of depoliticization has primarily affected the popular press and so it may well be the case that the readers of the unstampeds knew more about politics than those who read the popular press at the 1922 General Election. The main problem associated with this decline in political knowledge is that as political awareness decreases, vulnerability to political propaganda and manipulation increases. The study on the 1987 British General Election conducted by Miller and his colleagues demonstrates that tabloid readers were those most influenced by the campaign of the Conservative government during the months which preceded the election. The voting trends among voters who read a quality paper hardly changed between 1986 and March 1987. Only 9 per cent of those who read the *Daily Telegraph* and 4 per cent of those reading *The Guardian* shifted to the Conservatives during that period. Electors reading middle-brow tabloids were more influenced by the government campaign, with respectively 10, 14 and 13 per cent of the readers of the *Daily Express*, *Daily Mail* and *Daily Mirror* changing their minds in favour of the Conservatives during these months. But 30 per cent of the readers of the *Star* and 36 per cent of those of the *Sun* swung to the Conservative Party during the same period (Miller, *et al.*, 1990, pp. 89–91). Vulnerability to political propaganda and lack of political knowledge are thus positively correlated. The implications for the democratic process is that as the general level of knowledge about politics decreases, the risks of the emergence of demagogic and populist leaders increase. As Walter Lippmann wrote: 'The quack, the charlatan, the jingo, and the terrorist can flourish only where the audience is deprived of independent access to information' (Lippmann, 1920, p. 55).

Populism and demagogy, however can pervade democracies without the emergence of populist leaders. This is notably the case when politicians elected in a democratic system resort to populist methods and demagogic arguments to win electoral contests. A common feature of populist discourses is the use of people's fears and anxieties.

In England, the Conservative Party and pro-Conservative newspapers have been using this type of electioneering technique against the Labour Party ever since it became a threatening political force. As seen with the 1922 General Election, the Conservative press associated Labour with the Bolsheviks, and relentlessly played on people's fear by warning readers of disasters such as massive unemployment, starvation and chaos in the event that Labour made its way to Downing Street. At the following general election in 1924, the Conservative Party and the Conservative press pursued a similar strategy and continued to link Labour with the Bolsheviks and agitate the spectre of communism in the case of a Labour victory. The high point of this campaign was the Zinoviev letter. Released within a week of polling day on 29 October 1924, the forged document sought to scare off electors by accusing the Labour Party of being the domestic agent of the Moscow-based Communist International.

The parallels with these prewar campaign tactics and those employed recently by the Conservative Party are numerous. In February 1992, two months before the General Election, the *Sunday Times* published Kremlin files allegedly detailing Kinnock's attitude to the Soviet Union at the height of the Cold War and the relations of prominent Labour figures with the Kremlin during the Brezhnev years. Although the collusion between the Conservative Central Office and the Tory press denounced by David Hill, Labour's communications director, remains unproven, there was certainly some connivance between the Conservative Party and the right-wing press. In any case, *The Sunday Times* report included all the classic components of prewar Tory tactics against Labour: the connection between Labour and the Soviet Union, the association with Labour and Soviet-style communism and finally the implicit questioning of Labour's patriotism.

In 1996, the end of the Cold War and the collapse of the Soviet Union deprived the Conservative Party of a traditional campaign line. The Conservatives changed the substance of the attack but not the main campaign tactic and continued to play upon people's irrational fears. During the summer of 1996, one of the posters of the 'New Labour New Danger' campaign launched by the Conservatives showed two menacing red eyes drawing back red curtains, while another displayed Labour leader Tony Blair with the same evil eyes and a 'New Labour New Danger' heading. Michael Portillo, then Secretary of State for Defence, commented upon the advertisements with arguments that first surfaced during the 1922 campaign. The 'pair of red eyes', Portillo told readers of *The Times*, depicts the Labour Party 'eyeing your money, your job and your mortgage' (in *The Times*, 13 August 1996).

Manipulating people's fears can bring immense rewards for those who play with them, but the benefits are not equally spread within society. The use of the irrational in politics increases the chances of large-scale manipulation with the effect that electors influenced by these electoral tactics may not vote to the best of their objective interests. Moreover, the democratic process itself suffers in the process as the use of the irrational further debases the ideals of an enlightened citizenry and of a public sphere governed by the principle of reason. Finally, to play with people's fear is to open Pandora's box, and so far, no one who has used this strategy to conquer power has been able to predict the unattended consequences of the use of such tactics in politics.

5
Discursive Norms and Practices in Journalism

This chapter begins by examining two discursive practices, interviewing and reporting, which have been invented and developed
by journalists. The origins of these practices being neither political nor literary, they help to differentiate the journalistic discourse
from other classes of texts. The chapter then proceeds to analyse
a discursive norm, that of objectivity, which is also specific to
journalism.

5.1 INTERVIEWING AND REPORTING

Undisputedly, the interview is an American invention. The date
of birth of this journalistic practice is, however, open to debate.
To many authors, the first published interview was the conver-
sation James Gordon Bennett had with a housekeeper while
enquiring about a murder and that he reproduced in the New
York *Herald* in April 1836. Schudson, on the other hand, under-
lines that the interview did not become a common practice in
the American press before the 1860s (1994, p. 565). According to
a contemporary historian, the practice became so common by this
decade that New York dailies were specifically employing inter-
viewers (Grant, 1871, p. 427). The practice spread to England during
the early 1880s, notably thanks to William T. Stead. Stead, editor
of the *Pall Mall Gazette* between 1883 and 1890, conducted his
first interview in October 1883, and published 134 of them the
following year (Schults, 1972, p. 63; Goodbody, 1988, p. 146).

From the perspective of the comparison between the public
and journalistic discourse, it must be noted that, to a certain extent,
the interview replaced reported speech. Instead of publishing long
abstracts of politicians' speeches, newspapers would much rather

print their answers to interviews. Understandably, British politicians were quite apprehensive when the interview was introduced in this country and were at first very reluctant to grant formal interviews to journalists. William Stead had to be extremely persistent to secure his first interviews and many politicians refused him the favour (Brown, 1985, pp. 164–5). Once the interviews were published, the result was not always what politicians had expected. Gladstone, among others, twice made a complaint in 1889 about distortion of what he had said (ibid., p. 166).

The popularity of the interview with journalists finds its explanation in the benefits this practice offered to them. Firstly, the interview procured more control for journalists over politicians' discourse. Since reporters now had the opportunity to intervene directly in political discourse, politicians gave away a great deal of power to journalists. By asking specific questions, journalists could select the bits and pieces in politicians' discourse they thought most relevant to readers. With this process of selection, journalists could optimize the news value of politicians' discourse. Secondly, with interviews granted on a one-to-one basis, journalists could lay claim to exclusive news. These exclusive interviews gave editors the opportunity to differentiate the day's issue from the competition. Finally, exclusive interviews with personalities conferred prestige upon journalists to whom they were granted. Thus rivalry developed among British journalists to interview the most illustrious personalities of their time. Stead asked for interviews from Sadi Carnot, the French president, Herbert Bismarck, who both refused, and Tsar Alexander III, who accepted the offer (Schalck, 1988, p. 86; Baylen, 1988, p. 127).

Reporting is the discursive practice most associated with journalism, chiefly because it produces the news report, which is the discursive format most central to the profession. Reporting is a purely journalistic practice different in character to discursive practices employed by publicists and literary authors. In essence, reporting is a *fact-centred discursive practice*, and this explains two of its major characteristics.

First, the news report format implies the dissociation between facts and opinions. Progressively in the course of the 19th century, the difference was being established in the press between '"matters of fact men" and journalists disposed to adding "*intelligence raisonnée*", between "mere reportage" and some form of comment and interpretation' (quoted in Stephens, 1988, p. 247). As a consequence, facts and opinions began to be separated into two distinct journalistic genres. As value judgements began to be confined in leaders, facts were reported in a discursive format, the news report, designed solely for that purpose. Not that news reports were value-free, but in that format journalists abstained from explicit value-judgement.

By way of contrast, publicists did not draw such a sharp line between facts and comments. Publicists commented on and criticized the news in the same article in which they published information. In fact, publicists not only wrapped information up with their own observations but constructed articles according to their interpretation of the events that they were relating. The organizing principle of public texts was the political subjectivity of the publicist. On the other hand, news reports are constructed around facts. For example, news reports are usually written following the principle of the inverted pyramid, with the most newsworthy fact coming first in the story (Keeble, 1994, pp. 129–30).

Second, the news report format implies the dissociation between facts and emotions. In the classic format of the news report, journalists do not reveal their feelings and do not let their subjectivity come to the surface of the text. Reporters refrain from demonstrating their emotions and do not elaborate on their feelings when they report on a scene or an event they have personally witnessed. They may quote onlookers and passers-by whose statements reflect their personal views, but generally reporters step back from mediating between readers and reality and, at the discursive level at least, reporters give priority to the facts themselves. Unlike literary authors, journalists may not impose their own and subjective point of view, at least in an explicit manner, to readers.

When reporting on some particularly horrendous scenes, reporters have to dominate their emotions to be able to write their story: 'It is often remarked that the pressmen are nauseated at a hanging or an electrocution, but if a man can begin to write and fix his attention upon describing what he sees, he recovers control over the physical reactions of horror and they no longer dominate him. The reporter who writes without raising his voice has stilled all the impulses that would lead him to do something, event if it is only to take sides' (Hughes, 1940, p. 95).

Helen Hughes illustrated this impressive process of distancing from one's own feelings with Theodore Dreiser's romanticized autobiography, in which the American reporter told of his witnessing the torture of a black slave lynched by his owners. Observing the scene, the 'trained and relentless reporter' did not think much of the tortured man but of the 'colorful' story he would be able to write the following day (in Hughes, 1940, p. 98). As it appears, the news report is the outcome of a long process of the rationalization of a discursive practice whereby journalists have progressively learnt to refrain from expressing their opinions and emotions. This rationalized discursive practice produces an impersonal and distant account of reality and thus stands in sharp contrast with the opinion-oriented practices of publicists and the personal narratives of literary authors. Through these practices journalists have gained credibility but have lost the freedom to fully express their opinions or emotions.

5.2   OBJECTIVITY AS A DISCURSIVE NORM

A series of discursive norms delineates the boundaries which circumscribe the news format and defines the news report as a journalistic genre. The term 'objectivity' is a short-cut to designate two closely interrelated clusters of discursive norms and one discursive norm which greatly contributed to shape journalism as a particular discourse. The first of these clusters comprises four norms which formed during the process of separation of the press from party politics. These four norms are neutrality, impartiality, balance and fairness. The second norm is that of retreatism and is related to media organizations' and journalists' reluctance to take sides in the political process. The third cluster also includes four norms: truthfulness, factuality, accuracy and completeness.

The first cluster of discursive norms stemmed from the progressive detachment of the press from party politics. During the second part of the 19th century, when newspapers became relatively independent of political parties and had ceased to formally represent these parties, editors began to apply a policy of non-alignment towards political parties and put forward claims to neutrality and impartiality.

This process of disengagement from party politics mainly followed the 1855 repeal of the stamp duty. In the 1880s, most newly established papers claimed to be apolitical, and one-third of all papers declared themselves to be free from political ties (Lee, 1976, p. 229). At the onset of the 20th century, in the great majority, newspapers advertised themselves as news providers with no aim other than to inform their readers of the day's events.

Having said this, the norm of neutrality did not really imply that newspapers ceased to favour a party over another. Rather, it suggested that press support for political parties was more the result of an editorial and independent decision rather than an obligation due to party affiliation or financial dependence. Editors who claimed to be neutral mainly indicated that their newspapers had ceased to be the mouthpiece of a political party and that they were parting company with partisanship and militant politics. They also signalled that their newspapers' support for a party would become less vocal and more conditional than in the past. The norm of neutrality implied the end of party newspapers and the militant press, but not of press support for political parties.

The norms of balance and fairness are best understood as the modern versions of neutrality and impartiality and for this reason are mostly associated with broadcast journalism. With the advent of broadcast journalism, the norm of neutrality became more restrictive and even legally enforced. Unlike print journalists, broadcast newspeople are forbidden to show support for a political party and are legally required to provide fair and balanced coverage for all the main parties. This implies that broadcast news reports must treat political parties on an equal footing and must give a fair and balanced view of the acts and opinions of the actors in the political field. In consequence, both the amount and content of broadcast coverage each party gets is monitored. Content monitoring can include the analysis of journalists' tone and insinuations when commenting on a party platform or interviewing a candidate. Modern political systems include a formal set of procedures whereby political parties and candidates can complain if they deem themselves to have been the victims of media bias.

In sum, the norms of neutrality and impartiality emerged with the policy of non-alignment towards political parties that newspapers began to follow in the course of the 19th century. These norms were to be legally defined and enforced with the development of broadcast journalism. Only in this latter context can these norms be referred to as the obligation for broadcasters to be balanced and fair.

The second norm, retreatism, is concomitant with the first series of norms and refers to the reluctance and sometimes the impossibility for journalists of intervening as opinionated persons in the public sphere and for media organizations to be directly involved in the political process. Journalists and media organizations themselves do not engage in politics and follow what may be called a *policy of non-engagement* in the public sphere. Overtly biased statements are rare in political coverage, and in general journalists refrain from expressing value judgements and plain political opinions. The point which is being raised is that the distance journalists create between themselves and politics implies more than simply impartiality or neutrality. It entails a policy of non-engagement in politics, which ultimately signifies that journalists refuse to be directly involved in the political process.

The four norms, truthfulness, factuality, accuracy and completeness which compose the second cluster also emerged when the newspapers divorced themselves from political parties. The emergence of the first norm, truthfulness, can be illustrated with *The Times*. On 7 February 1852, following a leader published the previous day, claiming that the duties of the state and the 'fourth estate' were 'constantly separate, generally independent, sometimes diametrically opposite', *The Times* spelled out the task it assigned to itself, 'the same as that of the historian': to 'seek out truth' (*The Times*, 6, 7 February 1852). This statement must not be taken at face value, but it indicates the attempt by several newspapers in the 19th century to dissociate themselves from partisanship and portray themselves as news providers. The pretence to truth betokened a commitment to factuality, a preference to facts over opinions.

Accuracy seems to have appeared later in the 19th century when journalism professionalized further. Joseph Pulitzer, for example, owner of the New York *World*, is known to have placed particular emphasis on the demand of accuracy to his staff (Juergens, 1966, pp. 30–1). Accuracy reinforced the norm of factuality. It not only prescribed the publication of facts, but to publish them correctly.

Completeness is related to truthfulness to the extent that this norm enjoins the need to publish all the important facts of the day. At the end of the 19th century, this norm was embodied by the motto of the *New York Times*, 'All the News That's Fit to Print'. On its 10th anniversary, the *Daily Mail* in London attributed its success to the fact the journal 'prints *all the news'* (*Daily Mail*, 4 May 1906).

Each of these clusters represents a facet of the norm of objectivity. Yet, objectivity is not merely a norm. It is also an ideal because many journalists are sincere in their attempt to be as objective as they can; it is a belief because journalists, although they admit they are not totally objective, think they can improve in objectivity; and finally it is a claim, as journalists want the audience to believe they are objective. But it is as a norm that objectivity had the most potent impact on the journalistic discourse.

Felix potuit rerum causas cognoscere, and thus: why objectivity? The array of factors which prompted this norm to existence is so vast and each factor so powerful as a determinant that, similar to the Althusserian contradiction, the development of this discursive norm may be identified as 'overdetermined in its principle' (Althusser, 1965, p. 100).

Several valid reasons have already been put forward to explain the emergence of the objectivity rule. Oft-mentioned causes include the development of news agencies which began to send wires to papers with different news policies or more generally, the need for newspapers to maximize profits and audiences (Palmer, 1983, pp. 53–4; Splichal, 1994, pp. 73–8). Herbert Gans has proposed a series of organizational factors, including journalists' comfortable income (keeping them away from militancy), journalists' assumption that their values are universally valid and finally the need for journalists to protect their credibility (Gans, 1980, pp. 185–6). Michael Schudson has adopted a general view on the question and laid emphasis on macro political and social characteristics of 19th-century American market society (1978, passim). Four important factors for the development of objectivity as a discursive norm can be listed.

(1) Financial Independence

A *sine qua non* to the existence of the objectivity rule which today is often taken for granted is financial independence from government and political parties. The norm of objectivity, and more generally the autonomizing of the British and American press

from partisan politics would not have been possible if newspapers had needed political money to survive. *The Times* offers a
case in point. During the first half of the 19th century, the London
paper was notoriously corrupt, and, like the rest of the press,
received large amounts of money from the government (Aspinall,
1949, pp. 66–106; on the end of the subsidy system in England,
see Aspinall, 1949, pp. 369–84). By the 1850s *The Times* sold enough
copies (38 000 by 1850) and enough space for personal advertisements to make a profit without covert governmental aid. As a
result, *The Times* could afford in 1852 to mention objectivity as
an ideal. By the next decade, the costs of newspaper production
were such that government or party money was of little use to
keep a newspaper afloat. A daily paper would either survive from
advertising and sales revenues or perish. This was illustrated with
the *Evening News* in the early 1890s. Kennedy Jones and Alfred
Harmsworth bought the *Evening News* in 1894 for the bargain
price of £25 000 precisely because years of under-funding by the
Conservative Party had placed the paper in a difficult position.

A comparison of newspapers' advertising revenue in England,
the United States and France confirms the importance of financial independence for the objectivity rule to emerge. Advertising
has traditionally been an important source of revenue for the
British press since the 18th century (Harris and Lee, 1986, pp.
19–20). The repeal of the advertisement duty in 1853 reinforced
this trend and during the second half of the century London
morning papers, the *Daily Telegraph* and *The Times* first among
them, were crammed with advertisements and had to resort to
the expedient of publishing weekly supplements to satisfy the
demand. It was claimed that in 1870 *The Times* received twice as
much revenue from advertisements as from sales (Grant, 1871,
pp. 120–5). By the turn of the 20th century, British manufacturers began to use the press to advertise brand names and, from
then on, display advertisements invaded popular dailies. In 1910,
the expenditure on newspaper advertising reached £11.5 million
(Nevett, 1982, p. 71).

During the 19th century the advertising revenue of American
newspapers and periodicals constantly rose to reach $528 million
in 1920, 65 per cent of their total revenue (Norris, 1990, p. 49). This
growth was sustained by the near trebling of the US population
within half-a-century, which came to 106 million individuals in
1920, and by the rising standard of living, with annual income

per capita reaching $639 in 1920 (ibid., pp. 9, 12). Another important factor was the rapid development of consumer industries selling goods such as furniture, clothing, or food (ibid., p. 72). In this field, an increasing number of companies relied on advertising to promote branded goods, most notably department stores and mail-order houses.

There is limited evidence to show it but it appears that advertising revenues have been substantially higher in the United States and to a lesser extent in Britain than in France. The first indication that this may have been the case was established by Alexis de Tocqueville who observed in the early 1830s that '[i]n France the space allotted to commercial advertisements is very limited' while '[i]n America three quarters of the enormous sheet are filled with advertisements' (Tocqueville, 1990, p. 185). A check at the Bibliothèque Nationale in Paris confirmed Tocqueville's observation that for the 19th century and beyond, French newspapers contained a great deal fewer advertisements than their British and American counterparts. French industrialists, operating in a different economic and cultural context, remained reluctant to spend money on advertising for a longer period of time than their Anglo-Saxon counterparts. As late as 1962, the advertising expenditure per capita was seven times higher in America and almost three times higher in Great Britain than in France (Cadet and Cathelat, 1968, p. 40). As a result, French newspapers sold proportionally less advertising space than the British and American papers, and advertising revenue did not contribute to the finances of French newspapers to the same extent that it did in America and England. The advertising revenue of *Le Petit Parisien*, the best-established and commercially most successful newspaper of the Third Republic, averaged only 13.1 per cent of its total income between 1879 and 1914 (Amaury, 1972, pp. 472, 476).

A least one contemporary French newspaper director made an explicit link between the paucity of advertising revenues and the notorious corruption of the French press during the Third Republic (L. Marc in Bérenger, 1897, p. 775). During this period, few French newspapers were financially independent and many accepted the bribes through which government and political parties controlled them. According to an estimate, between 1871 and 1913 only, the French government would have spent one to two million FFr. a year to bribe journalists (Bellanger 1972, pp. 249–50). Since state agencies and the dominant political parties used these subsidies to exercise political control over journalists, most newspapers remained the mouthpieces of political factions. As a result, many journalists continued to produce a partisan discourse and to hold an opinionated view on political facts and events.

(2) Competition for Readers

Besides the necessity of financing themselves, the opening of a market of readers and the ensuing competition for shares in this market was probably the single most important factor for the development of the objectivity rule. In America before the 1830s and in England during the pre-repeal period, publicists wrote for a public, as opposed to a market, with clear-cut limits defined along party lines. Apart from changing allegiance and batting for a bigger and richer political party, there was not much publicists could do to expand their readerships. Competition for readers had altogether different implications for journalists. Commercially ambitious press-owners adopted a more dynamic view of their readerships. They ceased to perceive the readership of their paper as a closed universe and instead to see it as an expandable market with open and fluid boundaries. In that situation political partisanship became a liability. Why exclude individuals from a readership because of too overt a partisanship? Press-owners did not want political opinions to be a reason for readers not to buy their papers, and the principle of objectivity was well suited to a situation where newspaper proprietors needed to cross party lines to extend the potential market of their newspapers.

Objectivity became even more of a necessity once readerships did actually become bigger. When readerships began to be counted in six-figure numbers in the course of the latter part of the 19th century, they inevitably became composed of individuals with diverse, if not divergent, political beliefs. Knowing that these beliefs also differed in intensity, the norm of objectivity allowed editors to accommodate a politically eclectic audience under one roof.

(3) Basis of Legitimacy

Another factor which reinforced the norm of objectivity was the need for journalists to create a basis of legitimacy. As mentioned in Chapter 4, openly partisan newspapers did not need to advance any particular legitimacy claim to discourse on politics. Such newspapers represented a political party in the public sphere and were accepted in that capacity. Once newspapers divorced themselves from partisan politics, their political legitimacy ceased to be provided by the political party they once represented. Thus journalists had to devise a new source of legitimacy in order to report and comment on a sphere of activity from which they claimed to be detached. In addition to morality (see Chapter 4), objectivity helped journalists to maintain their legitimacy to intervene in political matters. Journalists boosted the legitimacy of political reporting and enhanced the credibility of the opinions they expressed in leaders by claiming to be neutral political observers and the impartial arbiters of political conflicts.

How was this claim sustained? As a discursive norm, objectivity taught journalists to tone down their opinions and avoid explicit value judgements. This practice gave to the journalistic discourse the appearance of impartiality and fairly large sections of newspaper readerships seem to believe newspapers are unbiased. But this is only one part of the story and journalists went to a great deal of effort to add substance to the claim of objectivity. What journalists did was to construct a representative basis *ex nihilo* which they then used to legitimate their discourse and which eventually they employed in a struggle for legitimacy against the very political parties they once represented. This representative basis became what journalists called 'public opinion', which, in due course, they claimed to represent equally, if not better, than politicians. It was common talk by the 1900s among editors and press owners to claim to 'reflect' public opinion (see, for example, Blumenfeld, 1933, p. 44; Clarke, 1950, p. 153). To confer credibility upon the contention of reflecting public opinion, journalists first redefined the notion of public opinion and then contributed to the development of the opinion poll.

As early as 1886, William Stead set out the typical journalistic argument regarding public opinion. In the first article in a series of two published in the *Contemporary Review*, Stead argued that the House of Commons, elected only once every six years, had lost touch with the people and therefore ceased to represent them (Stead, 1886a, p. 654). By way of contrast, editors were re-elected every day and had to stay in touch with their public because newspapers were bought day after day. Being close to the public, the press had become the true representative of the people, the true exponent of public opinion and so had supplanted parliament as a 'democratic debating-place' (ibid., p. 657).

In the second article, Stead had in mind to improve the credibility of his claim to exclusive representation of public opinion, and quite significantly came up with the idea of the opinion poll. Some 60 years before the *News-Chronicle* pioneered the use of the opinion poll in Britain during the 1945 General Election campaign, Stead proposed a plan whereby 1000 individuals scattered around the country would collect their neighbours' opinions and send them to the editor. Stead had not only imagined the principle of the 'exhaustive interrogation of public opinion', but he had also perceived the benefits that could be derived from this scheme. Since journalists were the 'latest to interrogate the democracy', they would know 'the opinion of the public' better than anybody else and thus they 'would speak with an authority far superior to that possessed by any other person' (Stead, 1886b, p. 675).

Implicitly, Stead gave in these texts the first journalistic interpretation of the notion of public opinion, defined as an aggregate of personal and private opinions. Characteristics of this notion are: (1) Public opinion conceived as such is an aggregate of unrelated and separate opinions which are artificially combined by the pollster. (2) The opinions collected by this method are *personal* and remain those of unrelated individuals who did not express them collectively. (3) These opinions are *private*, because individuals who hold them did not plan to publicly voice them. Altogether this is an abstract and immaterial conception of public opinion which stands in contrast to the understanding of the concept by the philosophers of the Enlightenment who unequivocally related public opinion to progress and reason (Habermas, 1991, pp. 89–140). This aggregate of private opinions also differs from public opinion as a set of themes and ideas deliberately and collectively made public by an organized and collective group, as was the case when social groups possessed newspapers advocating their views.

Opinion polls do not measure public opinion *per se* but the journalistic definition of this notion. Patrick Champagne has described with telling details the way contemporary French journalists use opinion polls to reinforce their legitimacy and undermine politicians' prestige. Journalists employ opinion polls to assert their position when they face public officials. The latter, having been elected, used to be the unique holders of political legitimacy. With opinion polls, journalists can now quote results of their own, and this not only gives them the legitimacy to confront politicians' discourse but also grants them a quasi-official status. During interviews, journalists justify their assertions by citing from polls' results. Journalists also select themes and topics for discussion with politicians because they are related to questions asked in polls to the public. Finally, journalists make use of opinion polls to assess politicians' performance in office and in the media. For instance, the French press regularly publishes polls pointing to the 'divorce' and 'misunderstandings' between politicians and the electorate, the lack of interest in politics or even the poor esteem in which the French hold their political class (Champagne, 1990, pp. 125–91). In sum, opinions polls are used by journalists not only as a representative base for their own discourse but also as a way to weaken politicians' public legitimacy.

(4) Politics

A fourth factor which has influenced the appearance of the objectivity rule is related to politics. It can be observed that in the two countries where the principle of objectivity appeared first, Britain and the United States, the political game was efficiently codified and confined within the limits of parliamentary bipartism. In both countries therefore journalists could claim to be objective simply by proclaiming to support neither of the two main political parties. In Britain, even the position of the Reporters' Gallery at the Parliament since 1835, behind the Speaker's chair and facing the two rows of benches, may have inclined journalists to neutrality.

The comparison with France provides further evidence that the efficient codification of political struggles facilitated the development of a discourse based on facts rather than political opinions. In France, journalists faced a more complex political situation as the space of political positions was much wider and the field of political possibilities was more open. Late into the 19th century political positions spanned from communism to royalism. The principles these two parties questioned, private property and universal suffrage, were both taken for granted in Washington and London. The fact that not much was taken for granted in

French politics made political questions and ideologies more crucial in France than in America or Britain.

The stability of political life may also have played an important role. In France, class struggles and political conflicts were more violent and intense than in the other two countries. This was evidenced by the Paris Commune in 1871, the Dreyfus affair and the multiple crises of the Third Republic. Within this political context, journalists could not but be directly involved in the political game. Many of them, and above all the most prominent, were engaged by newspapers and political factions to polemicize and promote political doctrines. As a result, the overwhelming majority of the 46 newspapers published in Paris before the First World War had the aim of propagating a political doctrine as their primary purpose (see Manevy, 1955; Bellanger, 1972). In Britain and America, a calmer and better codified political game meant that newspapers were not drawn into the political arena the way they were in France. It was easier for British and American journalists to detach themselves from the political process and to be less passionate about politics.

In conclusion, factors internal and external to the journalistic field induced British and American journalists to adopt 'objectivistic' discursive practices and to put forward claims to impartiality. The existence of the objectivity rule seems to contradict the findings of numerous studies that media discourse is ideologically connoted and that journalists are biased towards specific values. Here too it is acknowledged that newspapers have ideological leanings with the concept of the 'political arbitrary' (see Chapter 4). The explanation of this apparent contradiction is that the implications of the norm of objectivity are discursive rather than ideological. Thus the fact that journalists largely abide with this discursive norm does not challenge the reality of the political and ideological arbitrariness of the media discourse. The norm of objectivity essentially means that journalists refrain from explicit value judgements and partisan discourse, not that journalists' discourse is void of ideological values. Even though news policies and journalists themselves often favour certain political parties, this favouritism remains very different to the partisanship displayed by publicists in the past. The norm of objectivity had a real impact on the press, and to acknowledge this fact is to understand aspects of the specificity of journalism as a discourse.

6
Journalistic Discursive Strategies

This chapter further develops the link between economic competition and the journalistic discourse. It pursues the task set previously of establishing a causal relationship between the conflictual nature of the relations of production within the journalistic field and certain aspects of the journalistic discourse. This chapter examines three discursive strategies which are particularly connected to competitive struggles: crusadism, jingoism and sensationalism.

6.1   CRUSADISM

A crusade may be defined as *a campaign a newspaper launches to call for reform*. This broad definition of the crusade tries to encompass different types of newspaper campaigns which differ both in style and objectives. Between the 1880s and 1920s, three archetypal crusades may be identified in the British press. First came the *social crusade*, which includes campaigns with the aim of alleviating the plight of the poor and the oppressed. The typical *jingo crusade*, which appeared in British newspapers during the same period, had imperial overtones and showed concerns for problems related to national security and the overseas operations of the British army. With the popular daily press of the beginning of the 20th century came the *stunt crusade*, or crusades whose object was so silly that they had no other manifest aim but to amuse the audience for a couple of days.

In England, William Stead was among the first to make a fairly consistent use of the crusade, particularly those of the first two kinds. Soon after he became editor of the *Pall Mall Gazette* in 1883 he wrote a series of indignant articles revealing and protesting against the living conditions of the deprived in the slums of

London's poorest boroughs. The next year he launched campaigns for General Gordon to be sent to the Sudan and in support of a bigger and better Navy. In 1885 he demanded closer imperial ties. That year, he also launched his most famous campaign, the 'Maiden Tribute of Modern Babylon'. In this series of articles Stead described the evils of juvenile prostitution in the brothels of the capital and called for legislation protecting girls below the age of 16. In 1887 he ran a campaign in defence of Langworthy, a divorcee whose husband flew to Argentina without leaving her a pension, and of Lipski, a murderer. The length and intensity of these campaigns were variable. The Langworthy crusade was run without a break for 35 days, with an average of one-and-a-half pages a day. The campaign in favour of Gordon was more erratic but lasted a year, and the crusade for the Navy was a recurrent theme throughout Stead's editorship.

Northcliffe's use of the crusade was more frequent and more blatantly commercial than Stead's. The style was aggressive, abrupt, and most of his campaigns were short-lived. Northcliffe campaigned, among other causes, for wholemeal bread, a new hat shape, better roses, better sweet peas, purer milk, better houses and the conservation of Crystal Palace. However, not all of Northcliffe's crusades were mere stunts. For instance, Northcliffe thought he had a case against William Lever, a soap manufacturer, who had reduced the size of the threepenny soap bar. The campaign cost the press baron £151 000 in libel damages.

Throughout the period, Northcliffe newspapers were the most jingoistic of the British press. From the early days of the Anglo-German antagonism until the 1922 Versailles peace conference, Northcliffe ceaselessly crusaded along jingoistic lines. For many years before the outbreak of the First World War he warned against Germany, demanded a greater defence budget (already substantial) and called for rearmament and the reorganization of the armed forces. In May 1915 Northcliffe heavily criticized Lord Kitchener, Secretary for War, to whom he attributed the shortage in high-explosive shells. A couple of months before this outcry, Northcliffe had called for Kitchener's appointment, a fact that he himself recognized (Pound and Harmsworth, 1959, p. 477). Once a coalition cabinet headed by Lloyd George had replaced the Liberal government, Northcliffe campaigned for compulsory conscription, the creation of a ministry of munitions and the Allied War Council.

Was it commercial motivation or strength of conviction which urged Northcliffe to embark on these numerous campaigns? Biographers generally point out that Northcliffe was not a cynical character and felt quite strongly about the campaigns he conducted. There can be no doubt, for instance, that Northcliffe was a sincere patriot and imperialist. On the other hand, personal convictions and commercial interest are not necessarily incompatible, and evidence shows that crusadism, as a general rule, does not harm circulation.

First, three out of four of the greatest crusaders were press barons who were second to none when it came to raising circulations. With the sole exception of Stead, Northcliffe, Pulitzer and Hearst in America, were at the same time the most ardent crusaders and the most gifted and enterprising press owners.[1] What advantages did these newspaper proprietors see in the crusade to use this strategy so extensively?

First, crusades allowed press-owners to enliven the paper. On many occasions, Hearst or Northcliffe had wished to report more exciting happenings and criticized their staff for producing a boring paper. Getting vocal on selected popular topics offered them the opportunity to manufacture excitement and add thrills to the day's issue. This aspect of the crusade is related to the tradition of creating news. Press barons sponsored costly expeditions, organized spectacular races and launched crusades all with the same aim of amusing the crowd. For example, Northcliffe launched the sweet peas stunt with the explicit intention of diverting the public from a tense domestic political situation which lasted too long for his taste and which 'made today's paper look too much like yesterday's' (Pound and Harmsworth, 1959, p. 404).

Many crusades were also intended to provide sensational content. This is quite manifest with Stead's 'Maiden Tribute of Modern Babylon', where he indulged in much voyeurism when describing London's brothels. As with social crusades, these campaigns were better at describing horrendous living conditions than in analysing the causes of deprivation. Social crusaders also stopped short of proposing viable solutions to end misery in Britain. The exploitation of misery for commercial ends was equally plain as many weepy accounts of poverty in the East End were clearly written with no other aim than to arouse readers' sense of pity. Most of these crusades tackled important problems too superficially to pretend to have any motives but to stir emotions among the audience. Crusading turned poverty into a spectacle and into a gold-mine for journalists. The most sensible effect of social crusades was not so much to improve living conditions for the deprived but to make some press-owners considerably better-off.

Finally, some crusades had the virtue of making facts newsworthy where otherwise they would never have made it to the popular press. This was especially true of crusades which focused on the plight of a single person. It took a particularly unfortunate widow for the press to demand a revision of marriage laws, or the conviction of an innocent man to plead for a modification of appeal procedures. Poverty is not a newsworthy fact, neither are laws and abstract principles, and journalists need to personify general issues to include them in the news columns. Some crusades therefore served as the vehicle for the personification of issues and problems that were too abstract and too common to become news.

6.2   JINGOISM

Jingoism was another discursive strategy favoured by journalists at the turn of the century. The analysis of two different situations where the press turned particularly jingoistic shows that there exists a positive correlation between the intensity of the competitive struggle in the journalistic field and the degree of jingoism propounded by competing newspapers.

Edwardian England and the Warmongering Press

Between the Boer War and the Great War, the presence of numerous rivals aiming at the popular market (the *Star*, 1888, the *Daily Graphic*, 1889, the *Sun*, 1893, the *Evening News*, 1894, the *Daily Mail*, 1896, the *Daily Express*, 1900, the *Daily Dispatch*, 1900, the *Daily Mirror*, 1904, and the *Daily Sketch*, 1910), meant that competition between them was extreme. This particularly intense competitive struggle prompted some of these newspapers to use jingoism to reach or maintain a dominant position in the field.

Northcliffe's dailies may be singled out to be the most vocal jingoists over these years. The jingoism of one of his papers, the *Daily Mail*, surfaced in the news policy, crusades, and even serials of the journal. The *Daily Mail* called itself the 'Voice of the Empire', and its editorial policy, according to Northcliffe's associate Kennedy Jones, followed the motto 'One flag, one empire, one home' (Jones,

1919, p. 149). As a result, all foreign and colonial affairs were treated with a pervasive ideological bias in favour of the Empire. The Germans for instance, the 'Huns' in Northcliffe's papers, were copiously insulted, and the *Daily Mail* invited its readers to take as a personal offence each 'dreadnought' the German Navy built. The whole newspaper was suffused with a warlike atmosphere. Anything remotely related to the soldiery was acclaimed and the military forces were constantly praised. The paper associated values such as courage, pride, honour and loyalty to imperial and military institutions.

As mentioned above, the jingoism of Northcliffe's papers was most conspicuous in the crusades they launched both before and during the war. But even the serials published in the *Daily Mail* reflected the paper's jingoism. In 1906, the national daily serialized 'The Invasion of 1910'. Day after day the story related the inexorable progression of German corps through British territory, up to the siege of London. Nothing was spared to make it appear as realistic as possible. The episode was often placed in the foreign news page, 'official declarations' of the German Kommandatur were reproduced 'exclusive' alongside presumably authentic news. Detailed maps of the battlefields were published and, for good measure, readers were given lengthy descriptions of the atrocities the Germans committed in the occupied cities.

Contrary to the *Zeitgeist* thesis which posits a correlation between international relations and the tone of the press, many contemporaries found Northcliffe's papers much too jingoistic and bellicose, to the point that some journalists, such as J.A. Spender, editor of the Liberal *Westminster Gazette*, suggested that the press baron bore part of the responsibility for the outbreak of hostilities (Spender, 1925, p 140). This argument, presumptuous of journalistic power, reflected the contrast between the frenzy of the press and the prewar hesitations of the Asquith cabinet. In 1914, the Liberal government included several pacifists and as many isolationists as interventionists. Recently, Paul Kennedy agreed that this '[j]ingo hurricane' was out of step both with the mood of the government and of the public (Kennedy, 1980, p. 384).

The New York Yellow Press and the Cuban Crisis, 1895–98

A similar situation arose in New York between 1895 and 1898. During the 1890s, an extremely violent circulation war broke out between three newspapers, the *World*, the *Journal* and the *Herald*. The competition between these papers prompted Hearst's *Journal* (and the other papers had to follow suit) to adopt such a jingoistic stance during the Cuban crisis that the three rivals used to be one of the most oft-quoted causes for the intervention of the United States in the conflict in April 1898. When the American government still gave the appearance of remaining neutral, these papers aroused public feeling and campaigned for intervention, running headlines such as 'Our flag has been insulted' or 'The butcher [a Spanish general] sharpens his knife' for months on end (Wisan, 1934, pp. 69, 197). The discursive strategies included continuous boasts of scoops, claims of exclusives, gross exaggerations and falsifications of news. Once the war started in Cuba, while Pulitzer sent hundreds of correspondents, Hearst led a corps of fighting journalists (Swanberg, 1962, pp. 150–69). If most reports were sensationalized, scenes of tortures and of cruelty, even whole battles, were purely and simply invented (Wisan, 1934, p. 320; Brendon, 1982, p. 139). Hearst even went as far as stage-managing the escape of a girl from a Cuban prison whom he had previously constructed as the 'Cuban Joan of Arc' on the basis of 'entirely erroneous' information (Swanberg, 1962, p. 122). When a local Cuban newspaper charged the New York press with a 'systematic attempt to deceive', Pulitzer's *World* was proud to be singled out and Hearst's *Journal* took it as a 'grateful compliment' (Wisan, 1934, p. 190).

Never before had competitive struggles interfered so much with the journalists' relationship to reality. Competing for readers, press-owners became confronted with the necessity of developing consensual opinions and transcending, as far as possible, the political divisions of their vast market of readers. To this end, several discursive strategies were developed, one of them being jingoism. Those in command of mass circulation newspapers find it quite hazardous to take clear-cut and long-standing political positions on domestic issues. In a competitive environment, it becomes even more difficult for the editorial board to find not too divisive an editorial line for the paper. Both Hearst and Northcliffe knew that too partisan a position in politics would have alienated a significant section of readers and that partisan politics was a hindrance to commercial prosperity.[2] On the other hand, circulation leaders needed to attract readers' attention and to arouse their curiosity. Jingoism is one way of overcoming the difficulty of producing exciting reading material without offending any substantial group of readers. Although Hearst's and Northcliffe's jingoism proved excessive for some of their contemporaries, nationalism still gave them the opportunity to be both vehement and relatively consensual. Jingoism, in other words, brings the profits of resolute and determined political opinions without the commercial risks that such positions often imply. To a certain extent therefore, jingoism is a pseudo-opinion, or a simulacrum of opinion, which journalists employ as a substitute for commercially more dangerous political positions. Jingoism is the product of the structural difficulty for mass circulation newspapers of advocating political opinions.

These two historical situations show that there exists a strong correlation between the intensity of the competitive struggle in the journalistic field and the degree of jingoism propounded by competing newspapers. They also suggest that the ideological position of a newspaper is more dependent upon the state and intensity of the struggle within the journalistic field, and the position of a newspaper within that struggle, than on journalists' convictions or on public opinion. More generally, these cases illustrate how the relations of production within a field can provoke intertextual phenomena in a class of texts and determine important aspects of the texts which form a discourse.

6.3 SENSATIONALISM

Sensationalism is another example of the direct influence of the competitive relations of production over the nature of the discourse produced by journalists. The causal correlation between sensationalism and economic competition was made quite apparent during the same New York circulation war mentioned above. The struggle between the *World*, the *Journal* and the *Herald* for the same mass market lead to the emergence of 'yellow journalism'; a journalism which has been defined by its tendency to serialize the most torrid scandals and to depict in brutal detail the most morbid of crimes. Headlines such as 'He crucified himself', 'Condemned to worse than death', 'Murderer murdered' (*The World*, 1 March 1891), 'Is spiritualism true?' (2 March 1891), 'His wife was a man' (3 March 1891), were some of the headlines commonly employed by editors to maintain readers' attention.

Sensationalism, originating from the urgent necessity for editors to attract readers and to divert them from rivals, constitutes the most direct reflection of economic competition on journalism. The resurgence of this discursive practice during periods of intensification of competitive struggles confirms the historicity of the journalistic discourse and its dependence upon the nature of the relationships within the journalistic field. The fact that such a practice emerged against the resistance of many journalists and that press-owners such as Pulitzer and Northcliffe who employed this discursive strategy felt quite uneasy or even guilty about using it, further underscores the economic necessity of this practice (Juergens, 1966, p. 46; Fyfe, 1930, p. 64; Pound and Harmsworth, 1959, p. 416).

This argument presents sensationalism as a modern phenomenon, not exclusively journalistic but nevertheless strongly influenced by the nature of relations of production within the journalistic field. Many journalists and scholars would dispute this, saying that sensationalism is a timeless discursive phenomenon. John Stevens maintained that Ancient Rome's official court publications, the *Acta Diurna*, were the first form of sensationalism (Stevens, 1991, p. 69). In the same vein, Mitchell Stephens argued that '[a]nyone who clings to the notion that the sensationalism practised by [. . .] the most shameless present-day journalist is unprecedented could be set straight by spending a few minutes with any a number of sixteenth- or seventeenth-century newsbooks' (1988, p. 112). Journalists are naturally very defensive about the topic and similarly argue that the sensationalism of the contemporary press compares favourably to the yellow journalism of the ancient days (Jones, 1919, p. 293; Cummings, 1936, pp. 7–10; Clarke, 1950, p. 34; Williams, 1957, p. 139). The then editor of the *Daily Express* held that the 'yellowest of yellow newspapers of to-day are restrained' compared to the old popular press (Blumenfeld, 1933, p. 21). Some authors also blame the victim for the crime and mention, sometimes elliptically, the unsophisticated taste of the popular classes for the genre (see, for example, Hughes, 1940, p. 108; Stephens, 1988, pp. 127–8).

These authors are able to cite from a substantial amount of newssheets, folktales and ballads relating supernatural phenomena, sights of monsters, catastrophes, crimes of all sorts, murderers' confessions and public executions. However, these writers quite overstate their case and facts may be brought to light to suggest that sensationalism was not as widespread and as popular as they would like us to believe.

To begin with, because of the need to legitimate their own discursive practices, memoir-writing editors overestimate the importance of crime reporting in the old popular press. They quote from a large and disparate body of literature with the effect of distorting the real amount of sensational literature that was produced. With some more consideration for the homogeneity of the sample one may gauge more precisely the proportion of sensational material in the ancient popular press.

From the popular papers of the first half of the 19th century, one gathers that sensational material was not as sought after by the masses as is suggested by the authors quoted above. Among the 242 working-class periodicals published between 1819 and 1836 in England, only five were crime reporters (Hollis, 1970, pp. 318–28). Of these five papers, two died out after the first issue, the others remained in existence for periods of five, six and 13 months (ibid.). This is not quite the type of success expected from later editors who may have pandered to the tastes of the masses as much as they have moulded them.

Part of the controversy stems from what is being defined as 'sensationalism'. As proposed in Chapter 4, a distinction should be made between sensational material as a news category and sensationalism as a discursive strategy. Sensationalism refers in this case to the nature of considerations made by editors during the process of news selection and to the set of discursive practices journalists employ to write a story. These practices concern the writing style, the choice of language, the story angle, the elements emphasized in the narrative, the tone of the article and various other techniques journalists use to dramatize a story. Following this terminology the pre-market popular press was sensational to the limited extent that it included some sensational material, but there is not much evidence to suggest that the rest of the discursive practices associated with sensationalism were commonly used by newspaper writers before the development of the commercial popular press. In the vast body of literature cited by the exponents of universal sensationalism, there is a great proportion of texts composed as verses. Many of the accounts of murders and public executions taken as examples were also written in a distinctive oral style.

In the unstampeds there was not much sensationalism either.

In many instances unstampeds had a police information column, but the casual way crimes were reported was a far cry from the techniques employed by the later commercial press. These police information columns appeared infrequently and were poorly edited. Working-class publicists did not use any of the later journalistic techniques to dramatize crimes or serialize murder stories. They did not massage the facts to add mysteries and build up suspense. Crime reports were written in plain English without any linguistic artefact destined to spice the case and stir the audience's emotions. These reports were relatively short, usually no longer than one or two paragraphs. It was often the case that the emphasis was on the police handling of the case rather than the offence itself, and many of these accounts were quite simply extracts of dialogues held in police stations. This was not surprising since information came mostly from court files and police reports. The absence of sensationalism in the working-class press is illustrated in 'Murder at Northwich', a crime report published by the *Poor Man's Guardian*:

> A murder was committed on Friday week last, in the neighbourhood of Northwich, by a tradesman of that town, named Samuel Thorley, on the person of a young female named Mary Pemberton, the daughter of a widow lady residing on a farm at Leftwich, to whom he had been paying his addresses. A coroner's inquest, on view of the body, was held at the Bowling Green at Leftwich, at three o'clock on Monday afternoon. The jury, after hearing evidence, returned a verdict of 'Wilful murder' against Samuel Thorley. The funeral of this ill-fated young woman took place on Tuesday, at Davenham church. It was attended by a vast crowd of spectators, and sorrow seemed to sit on every countenance (*Poor Man's Guardian*, 21 December 1833).

This excerpt is particularly apropos since the editor of the *Poor Man's Guardian*, Henry Hetherington, is famous for once promising to his readers more 'Murders, Rapes, Suicides, Burnings, [and] Maimings' (in Hollis, 1970, p.122). Yet the passage quoted above shows that publicists lacked the skill to build upon these crimes. The extract includes material for a copious number of newspaper articles. Later Sunday commercial papers and popular dailies would have elaborated *ad nauseam* on the circumstances and motives of the crime, the profile of the persons involved, and so on. Modern reporters would also seek out extra information and comments from various sources to add column inches to the case. In addition, the trial and verdict would have been covered with a similar attention. In sum, this argument contends that working-class publicists did report a certain number of sensational facts but did not use any of the discursive methods which characterize sensationalism.

Pre-1836 Sunday papers have also been targeted as sensational sheets by modern editors, and, more surprisingly, Raymond Williams (1961, p. 176). Sundays such as *Bell's Life in London* and the *Weekly Dispatch* published indeed lengthy columns of law and police news and dutifully reported every public execution outside Newgate. But not all this material was sensational (many items in the 'law intelligence' section, for instance, concerned libel cases) and, again, these reports were written without the methods journalists use to sensationalize their stories. Moreover, these Sunday papers devoted a considerable amount of space to politics and, correlatively, criminal news was not given the prominence it acquired when competition among popular papers intensified. When Parliament sat, *Bell's Life in London* published a minimum of two full pages of engagingly written proceedings and leaders were always devoted to political discussion. *Bell's Life in London* also published verbatim extracts from important speeches and a regular column on foreign affairs. Letters to the editor generally showed a great acquaintance with political matters.

Similarly, much of the front page of the *Weekly Dispatch* was devoted to a political leader two to three columns long and entitled 'History and Politics'. The leading article, which sometimes ran onto several subsequent issues, was followed by a column on foreign affairs and by a compact page of parliamentary news. The *Weekly Dispatch* also published parliamentary sketches, reports of public meetings, large abstracts of political speeches made outside the Houses, additional political news and political commentaries. In sum, these Sunday papers were a far cry from the sensational sheets modern editors and historians have accused them of being. Although these papers undoubtedly qualify as commercial ventures and did publish a certain amount of sensational material, it would be as correct to write that they contributed to the politicization of popular culture in Britain and to the political and intellectual formation of the British working classes.

Finally, crime and police reporting was in many cases more political than sensational in character. The accounts of public executions at Newgate in the Sunday press expressed strong doubts about the law system and took sides with the convict when he or she was of a particularly young age, when his or her crime was seen as too petty to deserve capital punishment or when evidence for the offence was not clearly established. These reports also recorded the clamorous hostility of the crowd against the executioner and its sympathy for the convict when the public was unconvinced by the sentence.

In the unstampeds, working-class publicists emphasized the deprivation of those arrested for begging offences and were critical of the class-based judgements of magistrates. Publicists regularly poured scorn on magistrates accused of hypocrisy and cruelty. Court reports were also routinely dealt with as a specimen of the inequality of the judicial system. Once the *Poor Man's Guardian* compared the execution of a young man convicted of burning a stack of hay with the commutation of a death sentence to a jail term for a murderer who had deliberately shot a friend of his. A man whose crime is 'destructive of human life' escapes death concluded the unstamped, while an 'offence against property' does not: 'We cannot repress the exclamation – Is this justice?' (*Poor Man's Guardian*, 26 January 1833).

This helps to differentiate the reporting of sensational events by the early working-class press from the journalistic sensationalization of the same material. Not that no traces of sensationalism existed before the advent of journalism but sensationalism should be classified as essentially a journalistic strategy which developed in the later part of the 19th century and which reporters began to use when competition for the popular market intensified.

It leaves us with the necessity of defining this strategy and this can be done by examining the set of relations that sensationalism implies between journalists and readers on the one hand, and between journalists and reality on the other. With regard to readers, sensationalism fulfils a triple objective: it is a means to appeal to readers' emotions, to provide excitement and to arouse their sense of curiosity. The range of emotions that sensationalism appeals to is vast and extends from horror to pity. As sensationalism incites journalists to locate their discourse on the emotional plane, it also inclines them to neglect other purposes of human communication such as the transmission of information or the sharing of knowledge.

Secondly, sensationalism is a specific reading of reality which is marked by its strong intentionality. It is not, so to speak, a 'natural' form of discursive production and a writer needs to be compelled by the violence of the competitive relations of production to sensationalize reality. As a consequence of competition, a sensationalist's relation to reality is strongly mediated by the need to stir readers' emotions. This impelling force explains why the sensationalist can be driven to alter reality or even introduce some fictional elements in his or her narrative account. To a certain extent, sensationalism implies a blurring of the distinction between fiction and reality.

Finally, as a set of discursive practices, sensationalism is not necessarily related to sensational material. Although an increase in the amount of sensational news is a sign of sensationalism, any topic can be sensationalized – football, politics, and also crime reporting. This discursive strategy drives journalists at best to reorganize, at worse to modify reality in line with their need to dramatize and emotionalize facts and events.

Some of their techniques are linguistic, such as the use of certain words and grammatical structures; some are discursive, such as the selection of a particular story angle and the selection and hierarchization of facts within the narrative; finally others are journalistic and are employed during the process of news selection.

One method journalists use to sensationalize an event is to present it out of its context. Since the context of an event contributes much to its understanding, any event related out of its context will appear much more sensational than it really is to an unaware audience. It could be argued that journalists decontextualize events only because of the need for copy space. However, the following example, taken from the modern press, shows that decontextualization is not a function of space but can be achieved with a specific reporting strategy that journalists can employ if they want to sensationalize a story.

On 13 August 1994 Richard Everitt was knifed to death by a group of Asian teenagers in a street of the Borough of Camden, North London. The local paper, the weekly *New Camden Journal* devoted much space to the attack and in the process specified the circumstances and the context of the murder. The journal reported the comings and goings of the group of unemployed

Asian males the day of the attack; inserted the murder within the context of the recent racial tension in the community and recalled the recent closure of a youth day-centre in Camden due to a shortage of funds. It also interviewed social workers, police officers and community leaders. Some of the articles in the *New Camden Journal* were straight reporting, others were more explanatory in aim. All in all, the weekly paper informed readers on both the crime and its circumstances and succeeded in avoiding any trace of sensationalism in its columns.

By way of contrast, the national popular press excluded all local knowledge from their reporting. They never mentioned the context of the murder and did not spell out the social factors which contributed to the slow build-up of a tense situation in the local community. The *Sun, Daily Mirror, Daily Express* and *Daily Mail* sought to dramatize the case as much as possible. They achieved this objective by focusing on the crime itself and on the testimonies of Richard's relatives, close friends and neighbours. All four newspapers rigorously followed a similar strategy, but the *Sun* illustrated it at its best. On 15 August 1994 the headline across the front page was 'Knifed to Death for Being White', followed by a 'Fury at Lad's Racist Murder'. The main text read:

> A grieving dad told last night how his 'gentle giant' son was murdered by an Asian gang for being white. Six-footer Richard Everitt, 15, was stabbed in the back as he fled from the ten-strong Bangladeshi mob. Dad Norman, 38, said: 'I saw him lying in a pool of blood. It was too late to save him. My son didn't have an ounce of bad in him. The people who did this are the scum of the earth – they should be cut up in pieces and fed to the rats.' The murder follows an increase in revenge attacks on whites in the King's Cross area of North London. Richard's mum Mandy, also 38, said: 'All you ever hear about are racist attacks on Asians. But if this wasn't a racist attack, what is?' (*Sun*, 15 August 1994).

Pages 4 and 5 were mainly devoted to further testimonies by relatives and neighbours.[3] By focusing on the reaction of the Everitts, the *Sun* made public their grief and anger provoked by the death of their son, but it also helped the tabloid to handle the case on a purely emotional plane. The Everitts' testimony was necessarily the most emotional they could possibly get on the murder. This strategy also allowed the *Sun* to ground the story on a system of oppositions whereby a first cluster including Richard/white/family/innocence was set in contrast to a second cluster comprising Asians/mob/violence.

The *Sun*, like the other popular papers, excluded local knowledge and context so as to keep the story simple, contrasting and emotional. There was nothing in the reporting of the tabloid press which was aimed at developing readers' understanding of this crime. To put in print Richard's parents' anger and trauma did not provide readers with an explanation of why this drama happened. In the tabloid press, the case gained in being spectacular what it lost in meaning. The popular press dramatized the murder by reifying it, by setting aside the circumstances and the contextualizing evidence; everything, in fact, that may have contributed to an explanation. In light of the contrast between the local perspective and the sensational approach, one can detect an opposition between discursive producers who strive to disenchant the world and those who mainly seek to entertain their audience. Sensationalism is a strategy employed by those who attempt to re-enchant the world and substitute the sensation for the explanation.

The following section attempts to outline the history of the discursive practice of sensationalism in the British daily press since the 1855 repeal. These pages do not claim that sensationalism was invented right after the repeal of the stamp duty. On the contrary, I try to show that sensationalism took time to develop in the British press and that decades were necessary for journalists to improve on this practice. The history of this development has been divided into two periods, with the second phase opening with the establishment of the popular daily press in the course of the 1890s and 1900s.

Early Sensationalism

In the late 1850s, the reportorial policy of the *Daily Telegraph* betrayed the commercial ambition of its editor and co-owner, Edward Lawson. From this period onwards the *Daily Telegraph* increased the coverage of crimes, murders and lurid court cases. Especially when Parliament did not sit, accounts of murders, suicides, robberies and other sensational events such as fires, explosions and natural disasters were scattered across the paper, the financial page included. Page 2 of the 3 October 1859 issue included headings such as 'Frightful Death', 'Sudden Death in The London Docks', 'Double Attempt at Suicide', 'The Catastrophe in Birmingham', 'Another Tragedy in Birmingham', 'The Fatal Explosion at Lewes', 'Forty Ships and nearly 400 Lives Lost'. Every page had its share of sensational news; page 3, for example, displayed 'Sudden Death at the Bar of a Public House' and 'Suspected Suicide in the Serpentine'. The two columns of 'police intelligence' were on page 6, relating incidents such as 'Attempted Suicide and Child Murder' and 'Alleged Murder of a Child'.

There was a clear difference between the news selection of the *Daily Telegraph* and its rival, *The Times*. During October 1859, the *Daily Telegraph* regularly devoted up to four long columns to police and crime news, compared to a sporadic column in *The Times*. The latter paper was generally free of the sensational material that could be found in the *Daily Telegraph*. The police news column of *The Times* mostly reported benign offences and focused on events at the police station. The 1 October issue covered three minor offences which went unreported in the *Daily Telegraph*, and none of the crimes related by the latter paper appeared in *The Times*.

The reporting style of the two papers also differed. Much of *The Times'* crime column consisted of dialogues between police officers and offenders reported verbatim. *The Times'* reports were more concise, factual and to the point than those of the *Daily Telegraph*. The *Daily Telegraph's* reports tended to be lengthy on gory details and to use a language geared towards building up the dramatic dimension of the incident. The following abstract, which may sound innocent by today's standards but which was couched in quite blunt terms compared to similar reports in *The Times*, related the accident of a man knocked down by a train while crossing a railway track:

> When picked up the body presented a frightful spectacle, the head of the deceased being completely cut in two, and the right arm and hand being found at a considerable distance from the other remains, which were then placed in a shell and conveyed to the parish dead-house, to await an inquest. The deceased was fifty-two years of age, and has left a widow and family to deplore his untimely end (*Daily Telegraph*, 10 October 1859).

The leaning of the *Daily Telegraph* towards sensationalism was consistent with its pricing strategy. Sold three pence cheaper than *The Times*, the penny paper rapidly became the circulation leader in London and kept this position until the arrival of the *Daily Mail* in 1896. The editorial policy of the *Daily Telegraph* may have contributed to its success in the marketplace, but it was not to the taste of everyone. Contemporaries charged the paper with 'dilating on the vices of the aristocracy' and *The Times* accused its rival of imitating the sensationalism of the New York *Herald* (in Hart-Davis, 1990, p. 41).

Stephen Koss has written correctly that 'sensationalism was undeniably an integral part of the New Journalism' (Koss, 1990, p. 345). The first signs of this development appeared in the 1860s. During this decade journalists began to use this practice more liberally and in particular sensationalized the reporting of a particular social phenomenon, that of poverty. A handful of journalists had struck what would reveal itself to be a gold-mine for the press and had realized the symbolic and financial profits that could be gained by depicting the poverty and deprivation of the masses to upper-class readers. The first to try his hand at miserabilism in England was Frederick Greenwood. In January 1866, the reporter published a series of four articles in the *Pall Mall Gazette* where he related in picturesque detail the night he spent in a poorhouse. Greenwood started the 'A Night in a Workhouse' series by warning readers that 'no language with which I am acquainted is capable of conveying an adequate conception of the *spectacle* I then encountered', and then proceeded in describing the 'horrors with which [he] was surrounded' and from which there was no 'escape' (*Pall Mall Gazette*, 12 January 1866, my emphasis; ibid., 13 January 1866).

In the same month of the following year the *Daily Telegraph* established the tradition with a series on 'The Prevailing Distress' in the East End of London. The reporter of the *Daily Telegraph* was a little more adventurous than Greenwood and remained a bit longer in the East End. In the first article of the series he promised his readers that he would not only portray the workhouses 'crowded with the destitute and utterly helpless poor' and 'besieged by hundreds craving help to keep body and soul together', but he would also 'follow some of the sufferers to their squalid homes, and see how it fares with them, their wives, and their children within' (24 January 1867). During four consecutive issues, lengthy articles depicted 'these sombre scenes in all their sad monotonous gloom' that the *Daily Telegraph* reporter thought in its 'duty' to reproduce in the paper (*Daily Telegraph*, 28 January 1867).

What were the motives behind this sudden interest in East End poverty? Journalists wrote of their concern for the poor and showed commiseration for their plight. The reporter of the *Daily Telegraph* confessed that he found the task 'painful' but hopefully not 'unavailing' (*Daily Telegraph*, 28 January 1867). In the following days the newspaper had set up a distress fund and printed the names of the contributors and the amount of their donation next to the 'money market' column.

Evidence, however, suggests that it was not only philanthropy which prompted journalists to pay attention to London's most impoverished area. Greenwood was hailed as a hero by the rest of the press for his night in the outer world, and, in the process, had saved the twopenny paper from bankruptcy (Diamond, 1988, p. 31). In 1866, a year after its creation, the *Pall Mall Gazette* was on the verge of insolvency, and Greenwood, whose brother was the editor of the London evening, had hoped that his reporting on poverty would draw public attention to the newspaper. Attention he duly got, and the circulation doubled within three days (ibid.). This helped to add four pages to the eight-page evening paper, to attract better contributors and to move the paper's office near the Strand (ibid., p. 33).

The sensationalism of this reporting was conveyed by the style which aimed at adding pathos to the stories and which directly appealed to readers' emotions. The angle selected for these stories was also designed to have a maximum effect on readers' feelings. This is quite manifest when this reporting is compared to the perspective of working-class publicists on the same topic. For evident reasons, publicists did not need to describe poverty to a working-class audience. However, their analytical approach stood in contrast to the dramatized and serialized journalistic descriptions of misery. Publicists tried to understand the causes of the distress of the working classes and this attitude, which was geared towards comprehension, stands in contrast to the voyeurism of reporters. But journalists knew they had tapped a vein, and since turning poverty into a spectacle they have been reaping the material rewards of moving their middle-class audiences to tears.

During the following two decades sensationalism remained confined within the boundaries set in the early 1860s. No major new daily was launched, no breakthrough in technology was realized. Thus the press knew a relatively stable period and the positions within the field remained virtually unchanged. With regard to sensationalism, the epoch was aptly encapsulated by a contemporary who observed that '[c]ompetition between rival producers was keen enough to force them to use all their wits in seeking and winning public favour, but not yet so keen as to drive them often into unworthy ways of attracting and amusing readers' (Bourne, 1887, p. 284).

The end of this era is probably symbolized by William Stead, one of Greenwood's successors at the editorial helm of the *Pall Mall Gazette* and who kept this post until 1890. For all his sensationalism, and Stead is considered the father of British sensationalism, the *Pall Mall Gazette* editor restrained his use of the discursive strategy to moral crusades. Sensationalism for the sake of it was still not acceptable and it had to be done for a good cause. It had to be moral, purposeful and salutary. 'Sensationalism in journalism', Stead wrote, 'is justifiable up to the point that it is necessary to arrest the eye of the public and compel them to admit the necessity of the action' (Stead, 1886a, p. 671).

Stead pushed this genre to its limits and provoked quite a scandal with his notorious 'Maiden Tribute to Modern Babylon' crusade. This was an inquiry into, and a campaign against, juvenile prostitution. For this crusade, Stead interviewed brothel-keepers, young prostitutes and other people related to the trade. The style was naturalist in tone but clearly sensationalist in intention. Stead went to great pains to reproduce every single detail of the places he visited, the people he talked to and the experiences he went through. The following headings give a measure of the campaign: 'The Violation of Virgins', 'The Confessions of a Brothel-Keeper', 'The London Slave Market', 'No Room for Repentance', 'I order Five Virgins', 'The Child Prostitute', and 'Imprisoned in Brothels' (*Pall Mall Gazette*, 6–8 July 1885). The series was hugely successful and brought 80 000 new readers to the *Pall Mall Gazette* and an additional 1.5 million people read the twopenny reprint of the crusade (Mills, 1921, p. 64).

Diffused Sensationalism

However sensational Stead's crusade was, it marked the end of the first period of sensationalism. During the following years a convergence of factors prompted the development of a more achieved form of the discursive strategy. These influences were the spate of murders at Whitechapel in 1888, the development of the halfpenny evening papers aimed at a popular audience and the emergence of the press barons.

Between September and November 1888 Jack the Ripper's crimes became one of the most current topics of the national press. Papers devoted a substantial amount of column inches to the crimes and the inquest. The spate of murders was widely accounted for, discussed in leaders of all papers and debated in letters to the editors sent in by prominent personalities. The prominence of the case was such that the notoriety of the serial killer quickly spread throughout Europe and crossed the Atlantic.[4]

The nature and amount of coverage devoted to the case helped sensationalism to surface to the open air and set sensationalism as a *fait accompli* in the public mind. The attention the press gave to the case greatly increased the visibility of sensationalism, and journalists could no longer play down the significance of the phenomenon. This spate of murders has also made crime coverage somewhat more acceptable to the public who were getting accustomed to this form of reporting.

The second factor which contributed to the progress of sensationalism in the daily press was the arrival of the halfpenny evening papers. The *Evening News*, launched in 1881, the *Star*, created in 1888 and the *Sun*, 1893, were devised for a fairly popular readership and sold at a price they could afford. To impose themselves on the popular market, the popular Evenings relied on an entertaining type of journalism and a fair amount of sensational material. The *Evening News* in particular established its name in the market on the basis of its extensive crime coverage. Not surprisingly therefore the evening paper's coverage of the Whitechapel murders was one of the most comprehensive of the whole press. Between 1 September and 20 October 1888, the *Evening News* devoted 82 columns to the series of murders out of a total of 688 columns of editorial material in these 43 issues. This represented nearly 12 per cent of the paper's available editorial space during this period. The *Evening News* further pushed out the boundaries of decency in the daily press and set the standard for years to come. When Northcliffe, in association with Kennedy Jones, bought the newspaper in 1894, the new controllers pursued the same policy of sensationalism (Jones, 1919, p. 310; Fyfe, 1930, pp. 63–6).

Finally, the advent of press barons was a major influence on the development of sensationalism. The commercial ambition of press magnates greatly contributed to the sensationalization of the press. However, equally crucial to the push for circulation was the expertise that the press barons brought with them to the newspaper press. Newnes, Pearson, Northcliffe and Camrose all had solid experience in the trade of popular magazines before their foray into daily journalism.

George Newnes was the first in the popular magazine trade with *Tit-Bits*, which he launched in 1881 and which became the model of many new ventures. By the next decade he possessed some twenty periodicals including *Home Notes*, *Woman at Home* and *Girl's Realm*. He became involved in the daily press during the 1890s with the *Westminster Gazette* (which he launched in 1894) the *Daily Courier* (1896) and a string of provincial newspapers (Simonis, 1917, pp. 285–90; Fyfe, 1949, pp. 54–6).

The future owner of the *Daily Express*, the *St James Gazette*, the *Evening Standard*, the *Standard* and five prominent provincial dailies had also started his career with magazines. Arthur Pearson had successfully launched periodicals such as *Pearson's Weekly*, *Pearson's Magazine* and the *Royal Magazine* before venturing into the world of the daily press (Simonis, 1917, pp. 298–301).

Northcliffe came from a similar background. He started his career as newspaper proprietor with the fairly sensational *Answers to Correspondents on Every Subject under the Sun*, an improved version of *Tit-Bits*. Within the next decade Northcliffe and his brothers were the controllers of a prosperous magazine business with evocative titles such as *Comic Cuts*, *Illustrated Chips*, *Forget-Me-Not*, *Marvel*, *Funny Wonder*, *Home-Sweet-Home* and *Union Jack* (Clarke, 1950, pp. 56–78; Pound and Harmsworth, 1959, pp. 65–190).

As mentioned in Chapter 2, Camrose had twenty-five years' experience in the field of periodicals before acquiring the *Daily Telegraph* in 1927. Prior to this acquisition, Camrose had launched several periodicals which included *Boxing*, *Penny Illustrated Paper* and *Health and Strength* (Hart-Davis, 1990, pp. 24–5).

The years of publishing popular periodicals were very formative for these newspaper proprietors. In this business they formed for themselves an opinion on what made the public buy newspapers and experimented with methods of giving readers 'what they wanted'. Northcliffe had learnt from his experience with periodicals 'that it was necessary for me to arouse the curiosity of the public at which I aimed, to make them talk about *Answers*, some days praising it, other days abusing it, all days wondering what it would do next' (in Fyfe, 1930, p. 44); a method he applied with success and consistency to the *Daily Mail*.

Press barons also imported to the daily press selling techniques they had previously applied in their magazine business and in effect they originated the idea that the sales of a daily newspaper could be promoted by means of competitions. These press entrepreneurs showed considerable ingenuity in devising promotional schemes for their publications. Newnes once offered houses as competition prizes and Northcliffe promised £1 a week for life for the nearest guess of the amount of cash held in the Bank of England. Some competitions, such as Pearson's 'Missing Words', would run several months consecutively (Pound and Harmsworth, 1959, pp. 141–5). Newnes was also the inventor of the fateful insurance scheme, whereby each copy of *Tit-Bits* was converted into a insurance policy against railway accidents. The scheme was later adopted by press barons to promote their daily newspapers and reduced the profits of their papers until the 1920s.

When expanding their concerns towards the daily press, these newspaper proprietors transferred managerial and editorial staff from periodicals to daily journalism. This transfer of personnel allowed press barons to apply to the daily press some of the journalistic techniques and discursive rules they had used with profit in the periodical trade. The editorial staff coming from the magazine part of the business had the expertise in selecting the most sensational story-angle and in spinning a news report to arouse readers' emotions. Sensationalism was something these writers were familiar with and it was not too difficult for them to sensationalize the paper and to accentuate the emotional appeal of virtually all news stories.

In this context, modern sensationalism flourished in the news-papers launched in the late 1890s and 1900s, aiming at an upper-working-class, low-middle-class or middle-class readership. In addition to the *Evening News*, the *Star* and the *Sun*, the *Daily Graphic*, 1889, the *Morning Leader*, 1892, the *Daily Mail*, 1896, the *Daily Express*, 1900, the *Daily Dispatch*, 1900, the *Daily Illustrated Mirror*, 1904, and the *Daily Sketch*, 1909, were launched during these years. With the exception of the *Daily Graphic*, which special-ized in society news, and the *Daily Express*, which made a mod-erate use of sensationalism, the other popular newspapers made quite a widespread use of the discursive strategy.

The first indication that this was the case was given by the net increase in the amount of sensational news in these newspapers compared to previous ones. For example, page 2 of the 11 May 1896 issue of the *Daily Mail*, representative of the newspaper at this period, included the following headings: 'A Spanish Lady's Death in Pimlico'; 'Death From Excitement'; 'Murder near Matlock: An Unaccountable Crime'; 'Extraordinary Scare at Forest Hill'; 'Corpse in a Burning House'; 'Ghastly Scene in Camberwell'. If, as suggested in Chapter 4, a comprehensive definition of sensa-tional news is adopted which includes the coverage of any event with a particularly violent or bizarre character, it can be consid-ered that sensational material pervaded most sections of the paper, including the foreign news page. On 18 May 1896, page 5 of the *Daily Mail* read, *in extenso*: 'Texas Tornado: Two Hundred Lives Lost: Enormous Damage'; at Bida: 'Terrible Explosion: Two Hundred People Killed'; 'Fire in Glasgow: Exciting Scenes'; 'Rioting in Paris'; 'Zola on the Jews'; 'Brigandage in Italy'; 'Distress in Italy'; 'The Cholera in Egypt'; 'Tribal Fighting at Berbier'; 'Germans in Africa: Sensational Story'; 'The Transvaal: Suicide of a Prisoner'.

This extensive use of sensational material by the *Daily Mail* is quite revealing since Northcliffe's reputation is not tarnished by the charge of sensationalism. His biographers even insist that he was not a natural sensationalist and that he despised vulgarity and the use of sex-related news items in his newspapers (Fyfe, 1930, p. 64; Pound and Harmsworth, 1959, p. 416). Northcliffe, however, knew perfectly well that to increase circulations he had to have recourse to sensationalism in one form or another. This was a recurrent strategy of his which he employed with the *Evening News*, the *Daily Mail* and the *Daily Mirror*. Eventually, once the

Daily Mail had established its position in the market, the morning paper did become more respectable, although even at this stage Northcliffe underlined the danger of the *Daily Mail* becoming 'too respectable' (Pound and Harmsworth, 1959).

For those papers which were still struggling to get an audience, sensationalism remained the strategy of predilection to attract readers to the newspaper. During the 1900s the competition remained keen and thus popular newspapers kept on selecting sensational events. On 12 September 1905, page 5 of the *Daily Dispatch* read, among barely less sensational headlines: 'Plunged to Death: Passenger's Head Found Sixty Feet From Body'; from an earthquake: 'One Vast Cemetery: Weeping Women's Pathetic Appeal to Italian King'; 'Premature Burial'; 'Dragged to Death'; 'A Bridegroom's Suicide'; 'Attempted Suicide at 12'; 'Under a Traction Engine'. From the *Daily Mirror*: 'White Men and Women Slain in Savage Africa' (26 January 1904); 'A Bearded Lady Cyclist' (27 January 1904); 'East African Savages who Tattoo their Conquests on their Bodies' (28 January 1904); an Indiana physician aiming at making Blacks white: 'To Bleach the Negro' (29 January 1904); a woman certified dead was buried and then exhumed: 'Grave for the Living' (6 February 1904), and finally: 'Native Woman Burnt to Death by her Husband' (13 February 1904).

In addition to a news selection inclined to give much space to news of a sensational nature, many news stories were given a sensational spin. When a young woman was found mutilated on a railway line, the *Daily Mirror* ran a series of articles on the 'murder or suicide' theme (22 February 1904). The same journal entitled the police news section 'Law, Police, and Mystery'. Not only the angle but also the writing style of many stories testified to the intention of stirring readers' emotions. When 21 miners remained trapped down a mine for several days, their experience was 'terrible', their 'fight for life' 'desperate', their narrative 'thrilling', their meeting with the rescue team 'dramatic', their escape 'miraculous', their emotions 'indescribable', and the suspense 'dreadful' (*Daily Mail*, 31 March 1906).

The pathos that many news stories tried to convey was also blatant. Stories such as 'Heroic Mother's Futile Battle with the Flames' or 'Child's Pathetic Story of her Mother's Suicide' were balanced with happy-ending tales (*Daily Mail*, 1 September 1904, 1 October 1904). The *Daily Mirror* applauded the 'act of splendid heroism' of a boy who rescued a lifeboat crew and the 'heroic midshipman' who saved ten lives (4 October 1910, 15 October 1910).

The sensationalist policy of certain newspapers was also apparent in the prominence they gave to sensational events. In some newspapers the front page was progressively given over to dramatic happenings. The *Daily Mirror*, for example, reserved this space for full-page illustrations of murders, crimes, suicides and society scandals. The events selected for their dramatic qualities over more mundane news items were given much newspaper space and in the process were transformed into proper media events. Among the first media events manufactured by the British popular press, criminal trials figure prominently. During the hearing of Dr Crippen, condemned to death for the murder of his wife, the *Daily Mirror* published within three days some 12 pages of news and comments (18–20 October 1910). The trial was lavishly illustrated. During these three days, the *Daily Mirror* published 35 pictures, some of them two pages wide. The front pages and the central double pages were devoted to full-page photographs of the trial, representing the convict, the court room, or even the carriage of the judge. The whole three issues were suffused with the sombre atmosphere of the hearing.

Finally, as illustrated by this trial, editors made great use of the image to effect sensationalization. The use of appropriate images provided newspapers with the ability to stress the dramatic elements of a news story. Visuals gave to the audience a feeling of immediacy, of direct participation in an event. Most often popular newspapers skilfully combined the image with the printed word to maximize the emotional impact of news stories. This combination was employed to place the news story on an emotional plane and command reading at this level.

In sum, journalists have different ways of sensationalizing newspaper content. During the process of news selection, editors can take the decision to increase the quantity of sensational news or to raise the profile of events with good dramatic potential. At the news production stage, journalists can first select the story-angle and then pick up the words that have maximum emotional impact.

Sensationalism implies a relationship between readers and journalists which differs to a great extent from that between publicists and their public. Publicists had as their primary objective to maximize their readers' understanding of their social, economic and political environment. Some of the 19th-century working-class publicists hoped that this knowledge would compel some of their readers to express their discontent and thus bring forward social changes. As explained in Chapter 1, publicists wrote, maybe naively, to change the world. There is no clearer indication than sensationalism to illustrate that journalists do not write to transform the world but more simply and more modestly to brighten it up. Sensationalism is the surest sign that journalists have, as their sole ambition, to offer readers an escape from everyday life. Both publicists and journalists offer gratification to readers, but the journalist's promises are more immediate and more easily obtainable than those of the publicist. Even so, publicists aimed at empowering their readers through social and political knowledge, while journalists had no other goal than to amuse their audience. Whereas publicists gave their readers the world as it was, and sometimes as it could be, journalists presented them with a world of illusions and entertainment. Publicists tried to turn a dream into a reality, while journalists turned reality into a dream.

As a whole, sensationalism reflects the change of allegiance of the press in the course of the 19th century from the world of politics to commercial culture. Sensationalism suggests that this shift occurred well before the media entered the electronic age. Journalists strove to give 'wholesome and harmless entertainment to crowds of hard-working people craving for a little fun and amusement' (as Newnes told Stead in 1890) decades prior to the advent of television, a medium journalists often accuse of harbouring their own shortcomings by claiming it is better suited for entertainment than serious journalism. However, early-20th-century sensationalism shows that the rise of entertaining journalism has less to do with technology than the competitive pressure brought to the field of the press by the logic of the market.

7

The Polarization of the British Press

The usual implication in the discussions on the difference between the popular and quality press is that mass journalism exclusively would be market-oriented whereas quality journalism would be protected from the effects of market forces. John McManus developed this notion to the full, opposing 'market-driven' to 'normative' journalism (McManus, 1994, p. 183). According to the author, the 'market theory of news production', which sets as its aim the maximization of the audience, clashes with the 'journalistic theory of news production' for which the public understanding of events and issues is what matters most (ibid., pp. 86–90).

This chapter argues that the relationship between journalism and market forces is somewhat different and attempts to demonstrate that the division itself between quality newspapers and the popular press was originated and then perpetuated by market forces.

According to this perspective the logic of the market should not be opposed to that of journalism. Market forces have influenced many journalistic practices and, *inter alia*, have divided the discourse of journalism into two main genres. The division between popular and quality journalism is endogenous to journalism which, as a discourse, is characterized by the polarization of its texts towards the popular and quality formats. Popular and quality journalism obviously differ from each other, but it must be kept in mind that both journalistic genres have been created by the same market forces and belong to the same discursive entity. This chapter briefly traces the history of the polarization of the British press and then proceeds with the argument.

7.1   MARKET FORCES AND THE ORIGIN OF THE GAP BETWEEN POPULAR AND QUALITY JOURNALISM

In England, the division between entertaining and quality journalism became particularly apparent with the formation of the halfpenny press towards the closing years of the 19th century. Following the successful launch of a series of halfpenny morning papers from 1896 onwards, by the next decade two groups of newspapers could be distinguished amongst London dailies. In 1904, the halfpenny papers included the following titles: *Evening News, Star, Sun, Morning Leader, Daily Mail, Daily Express, Daily Dispatch, Daily Mirror, Daily News,* and *Daily Chronicle.* The second category of papers, sold for a penny or more, included the *Evening Standard,* the *Pall Mall Gazette,* the *St James's Gazette,* the *Westminster Gazette,* the *Echo,* and the *Globe; The Times,* the *Standard,* the *Morning Post,* the *Daily Telegraph* and the *Daily Graphic.*

The launch of the *Daily Mail* on 4 May 1896 was the turning-point in the creation of the halfpenny press, a fact highlighted by the mistake committed by Sir George Newnes. A month before the launch of the *Daily Mail,* Newnes had started the *Daily Courier.* Although Newnes' paper suffered from some notable editorial weaknesses, it would have undoubtedly survived longer than five months had its owner realized that the penny charge was too high for the lower-middle-class market the paper was aiming at. The point is that this mistake in the pricing strategy could only have occurred before the appearance of the *Daily Mail*; in the following years, it became evident for any press-owner that to reach a lower-middle-class audience, half-a-penny was the maximum that could be charged. The success of the *Daily Mail* crystallized that market by preventing other dailies aiming at a similar readership from selling them for more than half-a-penny. In 1889, there were 42 penny and 10 halfpenny morning newspapers in England, compared to only 10 penny and 19 halfpenny morning dailies in 1913 (Wadsworth, 1955, p. 26).

By 1904, the separation between the two groups of papers was marked.[1] Newspapers in the popular camp would include tit-bits of foreign news, a society column, gossip from the entertainment scene (theatres and opera houses), a good dose of human interest stories, a solid sports page with racing, cricket and football, numerous illustrations and a generous amount of sensational material. In most cases nothing too outrageous was printed but all halfpenny papers would offer their readers a good measure of crime news, bizarre events, natural disasters, accidents and melodramatic stories.

The book section, the serial and the magazine page were three of the regular features of the popular paper. Editors were eager to show advertisers that readers took home their copy and gave it to their wives, the holder of the household purse. Thus all popular papers had their magazine page with a typical layout including articles on fashion, sketches, portraits and a column of gossip and light comments entitled the 'Housewives column' in the *Sun* or 'Woman' in the *Star*.

Popular papers were depoliticized, but they still devoted some space to political news and political discussion. In their political commentaries, these papers showed a similar anxiety to abide by the common mind and express opinions that were as close as possible to the average reader's psyche. As a consequence, throughout the halfpenny press, political leaders were written from the same ostensibly commonsensical perspective, with the same matter-of-fact attitude and were suffused with the same populist overtones.

This was the common ground from which popular papers varied slightly. There were more illustrations in the *Daily Chronicle* than in the *Daily News*, more sensational material in the *Evening News* and the *Sun* than in the *Star*, more human interest stories in the *Daily Mail* than in the *Daily Express*, and more politics in the *Morning Leader* and *Daily Dispatch* than in the *Daily Mirror*. But the template was clearly established and popular papers did not vary much from this format. This process of standardization drifted the popular papers away from the penny papers, whose discourse was still centred on politics and public affairs.

Set upon their own logic, the two formats followed their own course during the interwar period and the two groups of newspapers moved further apart from each other. Concomitant with the process of polarization, homogenization within each group gathered pace also, with the result that within each group newspapers came to look increasingly similar to each other.

Both trends towards polarization and homogenization were detected by the 1947 Press Commission. The authors of the report first expressed concern with the fact that the 'gap between the best of the quality papers and the general run of the popular Press is too wide' and that there was a 'lack of newspapers more serious and better balanced than the popular papers but more varied and easier to read than the quality' (Royal Commission on the Press, 1949, p. 152). Second, the commissioners also noticed the 'considerable resemblance' between *The Times* and the *Daily Telegraph* on the one hand, and between the *Daily Express*, *Daily Herald*, *Daily Mail* and *News-Chronicle* on the other (ibid., p. 267).

Since the Second World War, the division between quality newspapers and the popular press has not receded. Observers of contemporary British media either argue that the difference between the two camps has been accentuated since 1945 (Sparks, 1992, pp. 37–40), or that it has remained unchanged (Seymour-Ure, 1996, pp. 142–8).

The question remains of exactly how market forces provoked the polarization of the British press. The division of the national press into two distinct types of newspapers was essentially triggered by journalists' constant effort to adapt their discursive production to the tastes and intellectual capabilities of their respective markets.

The polarization of the British press was the result of editors' and newspaper proprietors' unwearying endeavour to anticipate as much as possible the needs and desires of their readers. As the profitability of a newspaper partially depends upon the equation between market and product, journalists always search for the optimum formula to satisfy their audiences. Helen Hughes has noticed the 'experimental spirit' which 'dominates' the modern newspaper and this neatly describes this continuous research for the optimum match between product and consumers' tastes (Hughes, 1940, p. 26).

At the same time, the *rational calculation* that lay behind this adaptive effort also caused the trend towards standardization within each class of newspaper. Indeed, since it is likely that the marketing teams of rival newspapers competing for the same market reach similar conclusions, editors and journalists of these newspapers end up employing similar discursive strategies. In addition, with competing newspapers constantly watching and imitating each other, the competitive advantage gained by one is rapidly offset by emulators.

The whole process is best understood if compared to a model in which a mathematical function determines the value of a variable which tends towards the limit set by the function. The variable represents journalists' discursive production, the function the competition among newspapers, and the limit the market that journalists compete for. In other words, the limit represents the market to which the discursive production of the journalists who struggle for this market converge towards. By way of imitation and market research, journalists competing for a specific market come to use identical discursive strategies, and for this reason newspapers within this market converge towards the same limit and thus look increasingly similar. All news workers do not need to be aware of this process. News organizations hire editors, columnists and reporters whose skills and profile match the requirement of a specific commercial strategy and a specific audience. This is why journalists sometimes may hold the belief that they write for a public while they write for a market.

Other factors determine the use of discursive practices in the journalistic field so this model does not claim to be fully comprehensive. Determinants which need to be taken into account include the structure of the journalistic field at a given moment, the relative position of each newspaper within this structure and the state of the market journalists struggle for. Other factors which ensure that two newspapers within the same market will never be completely identical are the historical background of a newspaper and its ability, in terms of resources, to meet the demands of the market. Nonetheless this model is believed to be quite adequate in providing an account of the dynamic behind the processes of polarization and standardization in the British press.

The gap between the popular and quality press continued to increase throughout the first part of the 20th century and then never narrowed, notably because the split had created a series of inequities in the structure of revenues between the two types of newspapers. The first of these inequalities is related to the distribution of advertising revenue. When advertisers and their agents realized that the disposable income of readers differed from one class of newspaper to another, quality papers could command higher advertising rates per 1000 readers than popular dailies.

With the advent of the daily popular press, quality newspapers began to advertise the fact that some readerships were more equal than others. In the 1905 edition of the *Newspaper Press Directory*, the difference between papers advertising the quality of their readership and those which commended its size began to appear. Neither *The Times* nor the *Westminster Gazette* published their rates. The first, however, underlined that its readers were 'people of means', the second that its readership was composed of the 'wealthy and influential classes' and was not limited 'on mere party lines' (*Newspaper Press Directory*, 1905, pp. 3, 91). Newspapers with more ordinary readers, such as the *Daily Mail* and the *Daily Express*, placed the emphasis on the size of their readerships (*Newspaper Press Directory*, 1905, pp. 59, 61).

When newspapers began to publish their rates, it became evident that quality of readerships mattered as far as advertisers were concerned. In 1914, the *Daily Sketch*, claiming 663 000 readers, asked £70 for a page of advertising, while the *Daily Telegraph*, with an estimated circulation of 250 000 and a better-off readership, advertised the page at £200–250. A page in the *Daily Graphic*, a newspaper with a six-figure readership, cost £40, but the same page in the *Globe*, a London evening gazette with a confidential circulation, cost between £50 and £72 (*Newspaper Press Directory*, 1914, pp. 452, 455, 458).

In 1937, the advertising rate per 1000 readers was on average three times higher in the quality press than in the popular press. *The Times* could command a rate per 1000 readers of 3.75 pence, when the *Daily Express*, *Daily Mail* or *News Chronicle* could only get 0.67, 0.91 and 0.84 penny per 1000 readers. The column-inch for display advertisements cost £5 in the *Daily Telegraph*, with a circulation figure of 637 000, and only one pound more in the *Daily Herald*, whose circulation was over 2 million (Political and Economic Planning, 1938, pp. 84, 130).

Thus, as the purchasing power of the readership came to determine the advertising rate of a newspaper, the advertising income of the quality press came at a lesser cost than that of the popular press. A popular newspaper needed much larger circulation figures in order to attract an income from advertising that was equivalent to that of a quality paper, and thus it had to spend extra money on newsprint, ink, canvassing, promotion schemes and sophisticated production plants.

In addition to lower advertising rates, popular papers had to settle for cheaper cover prices. In the years preceding the First World War popular papers would usually sell for half-a-penny, half the amount charged by the cheapest upper-class papers.

During the interwar period, whereas some quality dailies hit the newspaper stands at two pence, the price of popular papers was fixed at a penny.

The combined effect of lower advertising rates and cheaper cover prices put the popular press in a different dynamic from that of the quality press. Popular papers became locked in a struggle for circulation because the only way for them to increase sales and advertising revenues was to expand paid readership. Popular papers could not raise cover prices unless competition followed suit, and could not substantiate claims for higher advertising rates unless their circulation increased. The consequences of this income inequality were first that the break-even point was set much higher for the popular papers than the quality press, and second that popular papers had to survive in a more competitive environment:

(1) For popular papers, the point in circulation where they would begin to get a return on investment was much higher than for the quality press. The Political and Economic Planning Group (PEP) optimistically estimated in 1938 that an established penny paper like the *Daily Express* with an advertising rate of 0.5 penny per column-inch per 1000 readers could break even at 400 000, while a twopenny paper with an advertising rate of two pence per 1000 readers could recover costs at 60 000 (Political and Economic Planning, 1938, pp. 82–3). In 1931 however, the *Daily News* and *Daily Chronicle* had to merge, with respective circulations of 765 000 and 828 000, while the *Morning Post*, a quality London newspaper, survived much of the 1930s with a circulation around 100 000 copies before being amalgamated with the *Daily Telegraph* in 1937 (ibid., p. 84; Koss, 1990, p. 932). Nonetheless, even an evaluation based on the figures provided above by the PEP indicates that during the interwar period a popular paper needed to sell approximately six to seven times more copies than a quality paper to break even.

In practice, the gap between the circulation figures of the popular and quality press was slightly bigger. According to the approximate figures given in Table 4.1, the average circulation of the 12 popular papers in 1922 was 9.2 times higher than that of the six quality papers (660 000 copies against 72 000). Eight years later the six popular papers sold on average 8.4 times more copies than the three quality dailies (1 350 000 compared to 160 000) (Royal Commission on the Press, 1949, p. 190).

(2) The second consequence of this inequality of income for popular papers was that they experienced a greater competitive pressure. Popular papers got caught in a vicious circle whereby more readers were needed to increase sales and advertising revenues which, in their turn, were needed to finance escalating running costs. Hence the ferocious circulation war which took place in the late 1920s to pass the two million circulation mark (see Chapter 2). Hence too the use of discursive strategies in the popular press that could only widen the gap between the popular and the quality press.

The Unintended Consequences of the Newsprint Shortage during the Second World War

As already noted by several scholars, the contrast between popular and quality papers was not as stark as usual during the Second World War. This particular feature of the British press during the conflict can be read as a confirmation of the influence of market mechanisms on the polarization of the press during peacetime (Curran and Seaton, 1991, pp. 80–3; see also Sparks, 1992, p. 38).

Following the German invasion of Norway in April 1940 the supplies of pulp and paper dropped to 25 per cent of pre-war levels in 1941 and 21 per cent in the following two years (Gerald, 1956, p. 227). This caused an acute shortage of newsprint and the government began to administer the distribution of paper. London dailies, which published up to 24 pages before the war, had to reduce their number of pages to eight in April 1940, six in July 1940, and four from April 1941 until the end of 1945 (ibid., p. 219). Advertising was limited to 40 per cent of available space in morning and Sunday papers and 45 per cent in evening papers (ibid., p. 225).

This had a series of impacts on the press that most newspapers' controllers found positive. In fact, 23 of them, out of 26, reported a healthier balance sheet in 1954 than in 1938 (ibid., pp. 82–3). Lord Beaverbrook even claimed that these restrictions 'had given the press a new set of four freedoms – freedom from competition, from advertising revenue, from newsprint, and from enterprise' (ibid., p. 34).

Beaverbrook was correct. Newsprint restrictions relieved the press of much of its pre-war competitive pressure. When advertisers were put on waiting lists for space, the size and purchasing power of readerships ceased to become determining criteria to set advertising rates (Curran and Seaton, 1991, pp. 80–3). Newsprint shortages counteracted the effects of market mechanisms on the press and it soon became apparent that the gap between the popular and quality press was waning. On this phenomenon the observations of George Orwell are particularly interesting. A year and a week after the entry of the Wehrmacht into Norway, he wrote the following:

> The tone of the popular press has improved out of recognition during the last year. This is especially notable in the *Daily Mirror* and *Sunday Pictorial* ('tabloid' papers of vast circulation, read largely by the army), and the Beaverbrook papers, the *Daily Express, Sunday Express* and *Evening Standard*. Except for the *Daily Mail* and certain Sunday papers these used to be the most lowbrow section of the press, but they have all grown politically serious, while preserving their 'stunt' make-up, with screaming headlines, etc. All of them print articles which would have been considered hopelessly above their readers' heads a couple of years ago, and the *Mirror* and the *Standard* are noticeably 'left'. [. . .] Nearly the whole of the press is now 'left' compared with what it was before Dunkirk – even *The Times* mumbles about the need for centralised ownership and greater social equality [. . .]. Ultimately this will bankrupt the newspapers and compel the State to take them over, but at the moment they are in an interim period when they are controlled by journalists rather than advertisers, which is all to the good for the short time it will last.
>
> As to the accuracy of news, I believe this is the most truthful war that has been fought in modern times. Of course one only sees enemy newspapers very rarely, but in our own papers there is certainly nothing to compare with the frightful lies that were told on both sides in 1914–18 or in the Spanish civil war (Orwell, 1968, pp. 112–13).

In light of what was said previously, the implications are that the newsprint shortage and the voluntary restrictions on advertising strongly modified the relations of production within the field by checking the economic competition among newspapers. This in turn had the effect of modifying the whole discourse of the press and notably to close the gap between the popular and quality press. What this episode shows is that if market forces recede then the division between popular and quality journalism disappears too, proving that the latter is the product of the former.

7.2 MANUFACTURING IGNORANCE

Communication experts are reluctant to commit themselves to value judgements on the popular press, but their comments and analyses generally imply that the quality press is on the whole more informative than popular dailies. First, quality papers devote more space to consequential news than popular dailies (see Royal Commission on the Press, 1949, pp. 247, 257–8; McQuail, 1977, pp. 15, 17–18). Differences in the news treatment between these two groups of newspapers is the second reason why quality newspapers are more informative than their popular counterparts. As seen in Chapter 6, the reporting style in popular newspapers is geared towards emotions rather than information. News stories focus on the dramatic elements of an event to the detriment of facts which may be more informative but less sensational. This strategy leads popular journalists to exclude contextual evidence in order to keep the story line simple, contrasting and emotional.

Although these considerations may seem judgemental, it remains a fact that journalists and editors working for the popular press have long ceased to pretend to be addressing the intellect of their readers and openly admit to pandering to what they think are the tastes of the masses for sensational material and trivialities. Among countless testimonies, Hamilton Fyfe, one-time editor of the *Daily Mirror*, confessed that 'nothing could be too silly, too vulgar or too sensational to print if it was reported to be what a particular public wanted' (Fyfe, 1949, p. 60).

Equally revealing was Hearst's fundamental distinction between the 'interesting' and the 'merely important' (in Breed, 1980, p. 253). Besides Hearst's confession that what is interesting is not necessarily important (and vice versa), there are two crucial points in this assertion. The first is Hearst's confession of his readiness to give readers what is of interest to them, regardless of whether it is important or not. The 'merely' further indicates Hearst's order of priority between the interesting and the important.

Secondly, what this reader-centred approach implies most fundamentally is that different readerships, as press-owners know, are not interested in the same news matter. This point was elegantly brought up by Northcliffe. In the following passage, the British newspaper proprietor contrasted the reading tastes of the 'highly educated class which ruled the British Empire' and the tastes of the new reader for whom Northcliffe designed the *Evening News*, *Daily Mail* and *Daily Mirror*: 'For this tiny class the big thing of one day would be a speech foreshadowing a change of Government or some new combination in politics; of another day a rise or fall in stocks and shares. The new sort of newspaper reader cares little about Governments: he has none' (in Fyfe, 1930, pp. 85–6).

In their efforts to please different types of readerships, these press barons were establishing the principle whereby each audience would get the paper best adapted to their immediate and commercially defined needs. Designing different newspapers for different classes of readers, the outcome of this marketing endeavour was that different readerships would not get the same type or the same amount of information. Those interested in politics would still get politically significant news, those known not to be interested by the 'merely important' would get a pre-digested diet of junk news.

Readership studies have confirmed the predictable, namely that the lower classes read the least serious newspapers while members of the upper middle class and upper class concentrate on the quality press. The first comprehensive readership survey conducted in Great Britain was commissioned by the Incorporated Society of British Advertisers and was published in 1937[2] (Coglan, 1937).

Table 7.1, relative to 1936, shows two interesting trends. The first is that newspaper consumption quadruples between the poor class and the upper class. While less than one poor person out of two bought a daily newspaper, readership patterns indicated an average of almost two papers per capita among the upper class. Second, the survey reveals reading preferences that are in sharp contrast between social classes (compare for example the readership patterns of the working classes and upper class or even upper middle class).

The patterns of consumption combined with the patterns of readership meant that while the upper middle class and the upper class read both quality and popular papers, the lower classes did

Table 7.1 Readership patterns and circulation profiles by social class in 1936

	Daily Herald	News-Chronicle	Daily Express	Daily Mail	Daily Sketch	Daily Mirror	Daily Telegraph	Morning Post	The Times	Total
% of poor class reading	20.66	7.55	7.83	4.46	2.14	2.01	.43	.01	.02	45.11
% of circulation in the poor class	27.24	16.18	10.53	7.57	11.06	7.78	2.67	.23	.30	n/a
% of working class reading	21.41	13.39	20.01	12.26	4.62	5.18	1.88	.16	.09	79
% of circulation in the working class	67.56	68.68	64.4	49.73	57.17	48.08	28.05	8.25	3.26	n/a
% of lower middle class reading	6.24	10.22	26.4	31.74	7.54	12.8	11.02	2.93	2.59	111.48[3]
% of circulation in the lower middle class reading	4.91	13.08	21.18	32.12	23.26	29.64	40.94	38.31	22.67	n/a
% of upper middle class reading	1.23	5.63	16.83	34.99	8.4	19.09	23.89	11.73	20.66	142.45
% of circulation in the upper middle class reading	.23	1.73	3.26	8.54	6.24	10.66	21.39	36.96	43.59	n/a
% of upper class reading	1.19	4.01	12.3	31.64	11.53	25.99	29.32	19.49	54.06	189.53
% of circulation in the upper class	.06	.33	.63	2.04	2.27	3.84	6.95	16.25	30.18	n/a

Source: Coglan, 1937, p. 1-A.

not buy quality newspapers. 0.5 per cent of the poor population, 2.1 per cent of the working class and 16.5 per cent of the lower middle class read either the *Morning Post*, *The Times* or the *Daily Telegraph*, while 56.3 per cent of the upper middle class and 102.9 of the upper class read one of these newspapers.

These diverging reading habits were reflected in the circulation profiles of the national newspapers. 10.5 per cent of the readership of the *Daily Express* was in the lowest income group, 64.4 was working-class, 21.2 was lower-middle-class, 3.3 was upper-middle-class and 0.6 was upper-class. By way of contrast, 0.3 per cent of the readership of *The Times* was given as poor, 3.3 working-class, 22.7 lower-middle-class, 43.6 upper-middle-class and 30.2 upper-class.

Subsequent readership surveys have confirmed strong differences between the readership patterns of the dominant and dominated classes. The first major readership survey of the postwar era, published in 1954, corroborated the contrasting newspaper circulation profiles and readership habits between social classes (see Gerald, 1956, p. 223). Data for the years 1966–94 show that very few among semi- or unskilled manual (D, E) and skilled manual (C2) workers read quality papers. One per cent only of these classes read either *The Times*, the *Independent* or the *Guardian*, and 2 per cent of the skilled manual class read the *Daily Telegraph* in 1994 (Seymour-Ure, 1996, pp. 146–7).

There is nothing new in the fact that the popular classes and the elites do not read the same papers. They never have. What has changed, however, is that the difference between high-class newspapers and the mass press came to be based on the quality of the discourse and the amount of information rather than on the ideological orientation of these newspapers. The masses have always been flooded with cheap and entertaining literature, as historians are never tired of recalling, but the unstampeds showed that before the advent of commercial newspapers the popular press was not entirely driven by emotions and not necessarily synonymous with the 'stunt press' or the 'gutter press'. During the 1820s and 1830s there was not much difference between the working-class press and the newspapers read by the middle classes such as the *Leeds Mercury*, the *Sheffield Independent* or the *Manchester Guardian*. Through the unstampeds the working classes had access to a rational and informative political discourse. This, together with the unstampeds' inflammatory character, was the main reason why middle-class political activists began to worry about unstampeds in the early 1830s. One of them, Charles Knight, published the *Penny Magazine* with the intention of diverting the masses from the publications of working-class publicists. The *Penny Magazine*, Charles Knight explained, 'enfeebles the intellect, but it does not taint it' (Knight, 1854, p. 299).

With the advent of the commercial press, this kind of protection against popular newspapers was to become superfluous. In the modern popular newspaper, there is much the elites can dislike, but not much they have to fear. The main differences between the press for the masses and the newspapers for the elite are no longer political or ideological but are related to the amount and quality of information on important and consequential events. The high proportion of working-class and lower-middle-class readers in the composition of the readership of popular papers, combined with the fact that very few members of these social classes read quality papers, are two of the factors which prompted the formation of a knowledge gap in the population.

The knowledge gap hypothesis postulates that the segments of the population with higher education and higher income learn more from the media than lower socio-economic groups. Since P.J. Tichenor and colleagues tried to measure knowledge gaps, numerous studies have confirmed their existence (Tichenor *et al.*, 1970). The author of an article reviewing 58 pieces of research on the topic concluded that '[a] great deal of empirical evidence for knowledge gaps exists' (Gaziano, 1983, p. 474).

Several factors have been identified as contributing to the formation of the knowledge gap. They include personal networks, a resource individuals can use to find information they may need, and information-processing skills such as the capacity to understand complex reading material (Kleinnijenhuis, 1991).

The determinant of the formation of the knowledge gap most relevant to our discussion is the phenomenon of *selective media exposure*. The information individuals get from the media depends upon the type of newspaper and television programme they are exposed to. As epitomized by the readership profiles of British newspapers, lower socio-economic groups tend to read newspapers whose information value is not as high as the newspapers read by the dominant social groups. Thus it comes as no surprise that communication scholars have consistently found that members of the upper classes are better informed on public affairs than members of the lower socio-economic groups. The authors of a recent research report write that the 'major demographic predictors of news information are education and income, which is consistent with almost 30 years' worth of other studies' (Robinson and Levy, 1996, p. 131).

What are the implications and consequences of the knowledge gap the media *contribute* to creating in the population? In light of this gap, it seems fair to question the taken-for-granted assumption that the media inform. In fact, it even appears possible to reverse the dominant paradigm and state that one of the main effects of the media is to manufacture ignorance.

The media inform but they do so unequally. They distribute knowledge along class lines and divide the population into information-rich and information-poor. It is this pattern of information inequity which makes the masses relatively more ignorant than if all socio-economic groups acquired the same information from the media. By allowing the higher socio-economic groups to get more from the media than the other segments of the population, the media manufacture the ignorance of the majority of the population. From a relational perspective, the knowledge of some creates the ignorance of many. Since the media participate in this pattern of information inequity, it is fair to say that the media increase rather than diminish the relative ignorance of the dominated classes and indeed of most segments of the population.

Another consequence and implication of the knowledge gap is that the media, in so far as they contribute to the formation of this gap, contribute therefore to the maintaining of the existing social order and to the reproduction of social hierarchies as they exist today. It is significant that in a class society such as Great Britain there exist two distinct schooling systems as two different presses. Distributing knowledge along class lines is presumably the best means of social control that can be invented. Those who lack the knowledge do not generally suspect that they may be missing something and thus do not feel any desire for more information, and then because their lack of knowledge limits their intellectual horizon, they cannot imagine other social conditions than those they presently experience. This greatly reduces the risks of discontent and goes a long way towards helping people to accept their fate.

The advantage of the present system is that it is regulated by market mechanisms, and thus the government does not need to artificially limit public access to information as was the case, for instance, with the taxes on knowledge. Although market mechanisms have the same long-term effects as any form of governmental control, they are not as detectable to the naked eye as obviously coercive measures. Under the present rules, the public can be led to believe that they get the press they deserve and read the newspaper they want.

In the final analysis, this means that the very same mechanisms under which the present economic system is based also ensure a favourable ideological and discursive environment for the reproduction of the system. The media provide information to those who need it and entertain those who may not find themselves particularly advantaged in the present social and economic order. The same mechanisms which dispossess the dominated classes deprive them of the means to comprehend the nature of their situation and to imagine ways to remedy it. Thus market mechanisms not only ensure that the distribution of information follows the distribution of wealth, but these mechanisms also contribute to the formation of the inequitable patterns of distribution of information which in themselves contribute to the maintenance of the economic inequities created by these same market mechanisms.

8

Journalists and Their Public

Once upon a time there was an old sow who sent her three little pigs out into the world to seek their fortune. The first little pig hastily built a house of straw. When the wolf came, he huffed and puffed and blew the house down and ate the little pig. The second built his house with sticks. When the wolf came, he again blew the house down and ate the little pig. The third little pig built his house with more care, and used bricks. When the wolf came, he could not blow that house down. After several unsuccessful attempts to attract the little pig out of his house, he threatened to get the little pig by coming down the chimney. As soon as the little pig heard this, he built a blazing fire to boil a large pot of water. The wolf, descending the chimney, fell into it and was boiled and eaten by the little pig who lived happily ever after.

This is the original version of an old English fairy tale. Today, however, most children know the version that Walt Disney transformed for commercial purposes. In the Disney version none of the little pigs is eaten. When the wolf blows down their houses, they escape to the last brother's house.

Disney expurgated from the fairy tale its most frightful passage probably because the American corporation estimated that the wolf's feasting on two little pigs would not be to parents' and children's tastes. In other words Disney anticipated consumers' tastes and adapted the tale in light of this calculation. This chapter argues that the difference between these two versions is symbolic of that between public and journalistic discourse. The following section tries to establish that the same discursive strategy employed by Disney informs certain journalistic practices. It examines, first, the nature of this strategy and the mechanisms which triggered its emergence in journalism and then it aims to understand the philological consequences for journalism of the use of this strategy. The second section concludes the book reflecting on the impact of market forces on the press and the ensuing changing nature of the role of the press in society.

8.1   POPULAR JOURNALISM AS A DISCOURSE OF SEDUCTION

Whether employed by Disney or journalists, this strategy emerges when the discursive producer is placed in a market environment. Within such an environment, discursive producers do not produce ordinary objects but commodities, and it is with this strategy that these producers commodify their discursive production. The following pages analyse the inside mechanisms of this operation and the way this transformation affects the mode of discursive production.

Commodities are ordinary objects with an added exchange value. Ordinary objects do not naturally possess an exchange value, and this value needs to be purposely created *during the process of production*: 'This division of the product of labour into a useful thing and a thing possessing value appears in practice only when exchange has already acquired a sufficient extension and importance to allow useful things to be produced for the purpose of being exchanged, so that their character as values has already to be taken into consideration during production' (Marx, 1976, p. 166).

In the realm of the press, the extension of exchange that Marx mentioned was induced by the opening of a market of readers for the penny press in the wake of the 1855 repeal of the Stamp Duty, followed by the development of a second market for the halfpenny press decades later. When press proprietors and editors started to sell newspapers on the market, they began to anticipate the consumption of their newspapers. From that time onwards consumer satisfaction became an influencing factor in journalists' mode of discursive production. Anticipating the moment of consumption, press proprietors and editors developed their understanding of readers' desires and then, overcoming journalists' eventual resistance, they progressively moulded journalists' discursive production according to the market's tastes. *The transition from a public of readers to a market of readers was the single most important historical event in the history of the British press in the last two hundred years.* The production for a market, instead of a public, was the most fundamental determinant in the transformation of publicists' discursive practices and the commodification of the public discourse. Competition for market shares added pressure to the process and resulted in added constraints for journalists to rationalize even more their pursuit of the reader.

From there developed a new breed of discursive producers whose only apparent reason to work in the press was 'to give the public what it wants'. Editors' and press proprietors' memoirs abound with useful tips on how best to seduce the public. Northcliffe's associate, Kennedy Jones, thought that 'what the public wanted [. . .] was the story of life as a whole, told in simple language and illustrated by intelligible pictures (Jones, 1919, p. 306). The successful editor of the *Daily Express* under Beaverbrook's ownership, R.D. Blumenfeld, had no doubt that 'modern newspapers give the public what it wants' and that was 'thrills, sensations, frivolities' (Blumenfeld, 1933, pp. 59, 209). There are many echoes in biographies on Northcliffe of his life-long quest to satisfy the public's tastes and preferences. Universally acclaimed as a master in crowd psychology, the press baron delivered lectures on many occasions to his fellow journalists on how to please the masses:

> The things [Northcliffe says] people talk about are news – and what do they mostly talk about? Other people, their failures and successes, their joys and sorrows, their money and their food and their peccadilloes. Get more names in the paper – the more aristocratic the better, if there is a news story round them. You know the public is more interested in duchesses than servant-girls. [. . .] Ask the Amalgamated Press [Northcliffe's periodicals concern] whether they do better in Lancashire with serial or periodicals stories of factory life, or stories of high life. Everyone likes reading about people in better circumstances than his or her own. Keep that in mind (in Clarke, 1931, pp. 200–1).

One of the many significant elements this abstract reveals is that it sounded natural for Northcliffe to design a newspaper around readers' tastes. The central place the reader occupied in Northcliffe's approach to journalism was also evident in his correspondence with his staff. Many of the press baron's communications with his managers dealt with the problem of identifying readers' tastes and ways to respond to this demand. Countless letters discussed the topic and related technicalities such as train schedules and printing problems.

J.H. Lingard was *Daily Mail* circulation manager from 1904 until 1919. In one of his frequent communications to Northcliffe, Lingard detailed the reasons why the *Weekly Dispatch* 'still does not satisfy the Sunday reader' and concluded his letter on two recommendations. Lingard called first for a better distribution of the paper, which was the task, he said, of the circulation department. The second recommendation concerned the editorial department, which Lingard asked '[t]o take care that the contents of the paper satisfy the requirements of the reader' (Lingard to Harmsworth, 16 November 1905, Northcliffe Papers, Add. MSS 62 211).

His successor in the position showed the same readiness to adapt the paper to fit market tastes. In a letter to Northcliffe, Valentine Smith explained:

> I know Leernock will also get up special stunts for me, but what I want to impress upon you is that it is no use our competing with the *Mirror* or *Sketch* with small pictures when they are given whole pages – we are wasting our money and doing ourselves no good by advertising. [...] I know the difficulties of space, but what I do not think the Editorial yet realize is the importance of these big local features, such as pageants, shows, regattas, etc.
>
> I am confident that our sole chance of getting more sale of the *Mail* is by producing several slip editions every night with good pictures and large ones, therefore certain news will have to be sacrificed. I know it is a sad thing when the general public want paltry pictures, but they do – evidenced by sale of the picture papers – and unless we give them what they want we shall not progress as we ought (Valentine Smith to Lord Northcliffe, 6 August 1913, Northcliffe Papers, Add. MSS 62 211).

During the interwar period, the most entrepreneurial newspaper proprietors yielded the rewards of their marketing effort, as the British press experienced an unprecedented commercial success. Between 1920 and 1930, while the total daily circulation of the provincial press remained almost unchanged to reach 9.3 million, the total circulation of the national press leaped from 5.4 million in 1920 to 10.6 million in 1939 (Wadsworth, 1955,

p. 28). This made the level of market penetration of the British press the highest in the world. The 19.9 million copies sold daily by the British press in 1939 represented approximately 424 copies per thousand inhabitants, against 320 in the United States and 261 in France[1] (Albert, 1983, p. 25; Mitchell, 1992, p. 8).

This hard-selling attitude was not to the taste of everyone and attracted strong criticism from the more traditional quarters of the press. Among the most virulent in their attacks were the editors of quality newspapers, who blamed the popular press for pandering to low instincts and debasing public taste. J.A. Spender, the long-time editor of the *Westminster Gazette*, pointed the finger at the 'new journalists' for making their opinion 'conform to the supposed prejudices of reader', and for seeing 'no objection to giving the public what the public is supposed to want', a diet of 'crime, sport, gambling, adultery and every sort of vulgarity' (Spender, 1925, pp. 103, 108–9). The editor of *The Times* between 1919 and 1922, H.W. Steed, was equally critical of the press which '"play down" to the public' (Steed, 1938, pp. 16–17). Finally, the editor of the *Spectator* raised the question of 'how far it is the function of the press to give the public what the public wants' (Harris, 1943, p. 11).

Ancillary to our central question of the attitude of journalists to the popular public, is the problem of what, exactly, the press gave to the public. This debate cannot be avoided as most media critics would refute the fact that the public got what it wanted. In fact, to answer this question a distinction needs to be made between what the popular classes need and what they want, and then establish that what they want is not necessarily what they themselves would consider as best for their own political interests.

Indubitably, journalists writing for a popular audience, and for any audience for that matter, are highly consumer-conscious and continually adjust their discourse to the demands of the market. This fact is certified by the gap between popular and quality journalism, which otherwise would be left unexplained. In addition, the mass circulation achieved by popular dailies during the interwar period showed that these newspapers were quite successful in designing a newspaper to the liking of the masses. On the basis of these observations, the problem can be reformulated the following way: why was this style of journalism popular with the masses, and why did the public seem to appreciate this diet of society news, sport, sensationalism and human interest stories?

A possible answer has been put succinctly by Theodor Adorno, whose comments on another form of mass entertainment, popular music, can be applied with profit to the present discussion:

> In our present society the masses themselves are kneaded by the same mode of production as the articraft material foisted upon them. The customers of musical entertainment are themselves the objects or, indeed, products of the same mechanisms which determine the production of popular music. Their spare time serves only to reproduce their working capacity. It is a means instead of an end. The power of the process of production extends over the time intervals which on the surface appear to be 'free'. They want standardized goods and pseudo-individualization, because their leisure is an escape from work and at the same time is molded after those psychological attitudes to which their workaday world exclusively habituates them. Popular music is for the masses a perpetual busman's holiday. Thus, there is justification for speaking of a pre-established harmony today between production and consumption of popular music. The people clamor for what they are going to get anyhow (Adorno, 1941, p. 38).

In spite of the strong deterministic overtones of this extract, Adorno has aptly put his finger on some of the reasons why the masses want what they get, and why what they get is not what they need. Our chief interest, however, rests with the nature of journalists' market-oriented discursive attitude. Although the empirical material presented in the previous pages helps us to understand the way journalists operate to commodify texts during the process of discursive production, we still have to name and qualify this operation. It may be called the *journalistic objectivation of readers' desires*. The mechanism of objectivation refers to a two-step process whereby journalists first identify readers' desires and then project these needs onto their discourse. This process is illustrated by Northcliffe's remark quoted above, which shows Northcliffe identifying a clear need for escapism among the popular audience and then his willingness to respond to this desire with more society and celebrity news.

Although intuition always plays an important role in identifying and responding to consumers' tastes, press proprietors' and editors' attempts to understand the reader's mind have increasingly become grounded on a rational basis. As shown by the correspondence between Northcliffe and his managers, media outlets began early in the century to collect data and information on readers. During the interwar period, media organizations started to commission these studies from polling and marketing experts.

The flow of information on readers' preferences has never run dry ever since, and many aspects of the evolution of the modern newspaper testify to the influence of this knowledge upon journalists' discursive production. Although Herbert Gans reported that the journalists he observed do not pay much attention to audience research (Gans, 1980, pp. 214–48), the long-term discursive trends in the press indicate just the contrary. The amount of space newspapers devote to sport, society news and human-interest stories denotes news selection considerations which strongly prioritize readers' interests. The division between a popular and quality press in Great Britain also demonstrates the editors' willingness to adapt their products to market tastes.

The process of objectivation of readers' preferences has important philological and sociological implications for the journalistic discourse. It means first that the ultimate referent of newspapers is not reality but readers' subjectivity. It is a twist that journalists operate when their discourse is not only the outcome of their personal beliefs and observations but is also the result of their conscious and subconscious interpretation of readers' preferences. In the popular press, for instance, where the process is made particularly visible due to the social difference between journalists and the readership, it is manifest that editors do not print what they believe is important, but what they feel their readers will find entertaining. Editors also engage journalists who they think reflect the readership's mindset and whose general opinions and predispositions naturally match those of the audience.

Secondly, while the journalistic objectivation of readers' desires has transformed the nature of the discourse of the press, it has also modified its function. On the basis of this discussion, the last section reflects on the nature of the role of the press in a modern and capitalist society.

8.2   THE MAGIC-MIRROR FUNCTION OF THE MEDIA

Part III of this book has mainly been devoted to the analysis of the influence of market mechanisms upon the discourse of the press. Ample evidence has been provided to show that economic competition and market-driven discursive practices had a significant impact on journalists' discourse. By way of consequence, it cannot be expected that the commercial press fulfils a role identical to that of public newspapers. The press, under the influence of market forces, has essentially become a magic mirror journalists hold to society.

The suggestion that the modern press has the function of a magic mirror was first put forward by Warren Breed, who conducted a study in America on the local press in the early 1950s. As it became increasingly clear to the sociologist that local newspapers rarely addressed communities' real problems, regularly dodged sensitive issues and abdicated their role of 'leadership and critical responsibility', Breed came to the following conclusion:

> the paper bestows upon the community a picture of how it would like to look, rather than how it would actually look from an impartial analysis. The 'nice' things are printed; other things are ignored or are exorcised, as with crime. Successes are applauded, failures are politely passed by; [. . .] The 'magic mirror' aspect of the paper seems not only that readers 'get what they want' as individuals, but that the community gets what it wants as a community (Breed, 1980, p. 396).

My own study of the British press has led me to similar conclusions. The following pages specify my understanding of the notion and spell out some of the consequences of the 'magic-mirror function' of the press for readers and society at large.

Newspapers only print a fraction of the daily information they receive. The difference between the input and the output is determined by the process of news selection, strongly influenced, as the gap between the popular and quality press certifies, by journalists' knowledge and intuition of their average reader's preferences, interests, reading skills and intellectual abilities. During this process the editorial staff define what may be called the *realm of the knowable* for their readers, that is, the fraction of information and the type of knowledge that they believe will be within their readers' reach. In other words journalists do not venture beyond what they think are the limits of their readers' cognitive abilities and seek to produce a newspaper without a cognitive gap with the average reader's mind. Newspapers, those reaching a popular audience in particular, may try to influence or even manipulate their readers, but they will never attempt to educate them. Unlike publicists, journalists never address the *possible consciousness* of their readers. Journalists safely remain within the boundaries of what they think their readers already know and already believe. As a result, journalists rarely challenge readers' preconceived ideas and prejudices or transcend readers' present state of consciousness. Journalists open no new levels of perception for their readers and do not expand their intellectual horizon.

This effect is reinforced by the fact that journalists addressing popular audiences may also deceive their readers about the amount of knowledge they really possess. The simplistic and emotional angle adopted for most news stories in the popular press and the oversimplified coverage given to many issues tend to give readers a false sense of understanding which in turn creates an illusion of knowledge. The way popular media select and then frame the news means not only that readers of the popular press do not learn much while reading their papers, but then, by giving readers the illusion of understanding, the popular press erases from readers' memory the infinity of the realm of knowledge. The realm of the knowable, or the fraction of information journalists decide to communicate to their audience, appears to readers as being the realm of knowledge itself. This reduction from knowledge to the knowable closes access to further learning because this tends to suppress the need and incentives for readers to seek further information. Thus the popular media not only put limits to their readers' intellectual horizon but, by making readers unaware of their lack of information, undermine the conditions for the appropriation of further knowledge. With such a relation to knowledge, the commercial popular press could only annihilate the promises of the project of enlightenment the public press contained.

The first facet of the magic-mirror function of the media is to provide the comfort of knowledge without the substance, thus misleading people about their knowledge of the world. The second facet of this function is that the popular media also deceive people about their position in the world.

Individuals who live in precarious conditions of life, as is often the case among the dominated classes, may either seek artificial means to escape from this reality, dream about the possibilities of miraculous transformation of their life conditions, or imagine that these life conditions differ from what they actually are. Henceforth, they either escape from reality, develop fantasies about unreal transformations of their life, or form illusions about what their life really is.

Historically, the first institution to respond to these needs was religion. Nowadays several institutions fulfil a similar task, notably the gambling industry (national lotteries, etc.) and more importantly the media. The reason why the media respond to these needs is entirely related to the market-oriented attitude of journalists and the process of objectivation of readers' desires. The existence of this mechanism is manifest in the increasingly escapist and entertaining nature of the media discourse, including its news section. This phenomenon is so pervasive that it affects journalists' discursive production at its deepest level.

What this phenomenon actually implies both for the press and the public may be illustrated with the two versions of the tale quoted in the opening section of the chapter. A likely symbolism of the tale is that the little pigs' houses represent one's self, while the wolf symbolizes the dangers and difficulties a human being is confronted with during his or her life course. The first version, in which the two pigs who built shabby houses are swallowed by the wolf, emphasized the necessity for children to build up strong characters in order to favourably overcome life's difficulties. In the Disney version, however, the fairy tale loses its original meaning. In the commercial interpretation, the two pigs find refuge in the brick house and thus the message seems to be that regardless of character, one will always be able to escape danger.

In other words the original version gave children an accurate image of their relation to the world. The tale warned children of life's difficulties first, their relative weakness as children second, and finally told them to carefully construct their selves if they want to survive in a world of adults. The tale symbolizes the process of growing up and presses on children the necessity to arm themselves properly for life.

By way of contrast, the Disney variant does not address the

problem of growing up and does not forewarn children of the difficulties ahead. Neither does this version give a realistic picture of children's position in life. By making children invulnerable and therefore unrealistically more powerful than they really are, the tale bypasses the reality of their conditions. Moreover, since danger can be easily overcome, children are not told of the necessity of making the effort to grow up.

The difference between the two versions illustrates the contrast between the working-class public press of the early 19th century and the popular commercial press that emerged in the 1890s. Publicists' objective was to change the working classes' conditions and thus gave them a true image of what these conditions were. Publicists never pretended to their readers that their life conditions were anything but what they really were, and thus never held a magic mirror in front of their eyes. Publicists stressed the fact that these conditions could be changed provided people made the necessary efforts to bring about these changes. On the other hand, journalists writing to a popular audience responded to the needs of the masses to artificially escape from their life conditions and thus incorporated within their discourse readers' demands for illusions. Journalism for the masses is a projection of readers' dreams of magically transforming their life conditions.

Thus, if the public discourse is essentially political, journalism for the masses is religious in character: in contrast to the political solution advanced by publicists, journalism offers a magic resolution to personal and social problems. In doing so, journalists bypass the social dimension of individuals, address their fantasies and reconstruct a world of illusions around their readers' dreams. Most differences between public discourse and journalism for the masses originate from the fact that publicists wrote to transform the world, journalists to brighten it.

A final, and crucial, aspect of the contrast between public and journalistic discourse is that publicists gave everyone the capability of becoming aware of political and social conflicts. Publicists built up this awareness by disseminating political information and analysis. With modern journalism the masses are only given the opportunity to escape from their own problems and those of the collectivity. This possibility of escape may have relieved the masses in their day-to-day life, but it has most certainly impaired their understanding of social reality and eroded their consciousness of social and political conflicts.

Notes

INTRODUCTION

1. Bakhtin's pseudonym in the late 1920s and early 1930s.

Part I   A Tale of Two Discourses

1   'KNOWLEDGE IS POWER': THE WORKING-CLASS 'UNSTAMPEDS' AS AN EXAMPLE OF PUBLIC DISCOURSE

1. The total of 44 713 is close to the 40 700 total circulation of the nine main dailies given by Howe for 1837 (Howe, 1943, p. 13).
2. A MORI survey in October 1995 revealed that of 726 journalists interviewed and working in a predominantly Tory press, 57 per cent would vote Labour 'at the next election and only 6 per cent Conservative' (*The Times*, 18 October 1995).
3. For the sake of conciseness, the following pages concentrate on the *Poor Man's Guardian*. This paper, one of the most prominent unstampeds of its time, is representative of confrontational unstampeds.
4. The Six Acts of 1819 (60 Geo. III cap. 1, 2, 4, 6, 8 and 9) were promulgated in the aftermath of the 'Peterloo massacre' on 16 August 1819 (named after St Peter's Fields where working-class demonstrators had died following cavalry action) and formed the legal basis for the repression of working-class agitation during this period. 60 Geo. III cap. 6, for example, forbade public meetings of more than 50 persons unless permission was granted by the Justice of the Peace. Two of these acts concerned public writings. 60 Geo. III cap. 8 aimed at the 'more effectual prevention and punishment of blasphemous [religious] and seditious [political] libels'. Sentences included banishment from the British Empire, or, if the banished was still within the dominions 40 days after the sentence, transportation. 60 Geo. III cap. 9 notably strengthened the security system imposed upon publishers. The deposits that publishers had to give to the Baron of the Exchequer to register their publications were increased by £100, to reach £200 out of London, and £300 within 20 miles of the capital. The preamble to the act, using terms similar to Chapter 8, made clear the intentions of the legislator; namely, to suppress pamphlets and papers 'containing observations upon public events and occurrences, tending to excite hatred and contempt of the government ... [which] have lately been published in great numbers, and at very small prices'.

5. One of the many campaigns these middle-class papers launched was a crusade against the ten-hour factory reform. The *Manchester Guardian*, for example, argued in 1832 that a reduction of children's work to ten hours in factories was an 'act of suicidal madness', considering that this bill would lower manufacturers' competitiveness, increase export prices and lead to a loss of foreign markets. In addition, the paper stated, this reform had the great fault of interfering with children's rights to labour (*Manchester Guardian*, 20 January 1832, in Read, 1961, p. 144).
6. At the theoretical level, this argument was first advanced by George Steinmetz and Margaret Somers, who both argued that the English working-class identity was constructed by social narratives (Steinmetz, 1992; Somers, 1992).

2   THE FORMATION OF THE JOURNALISTIC FIELD

1. These concerns were Northcliffe's, Pearson's and the Morning Leader group.
2. This section is based on the opening pages of an article published in *Media, Culture & Society* (see Chalaby, 1997).

3   BEYOND THE PRISON-HOUSE OF LANGUAGE: DISCOURSE AS A SOCIOLOGICAL CONCEPT

1. The first section of this chapter is an abbreviated version of an article published in the *British Journal of Sociology* (see Chalaby, 1996b).

Part III   Discursive Transformations in the British Press, 1850s–1930s

1. In America, in the absence of a duty on newspapers since 1766 and any noticeable governmental interference since the Independence of 1776, journalism, both as a field and discourse, has developed since the early decades of the 19th century, predominantly in urban centres (Mott, 1962; Schudson, 1978).

4   PRESS AND POLITICS: A NEW RELATIONSHIP

1. The *Star*, founded in January 1888 by the Irish MP T.P. O'Connor, is often labelled 'radical' and identified as a working-class paper. In fact, more than anything else, the *Star* illustrated the inability of the working classes to publicize their opinions. Although it earned the reputation as a champion of the poor and the labourer, this halfpenny

paper was more a milestone in the history of journalism than socialism. Backed by wealthy Gladstonians, O'Connor was at the forefront of the new journalism: he imitated most of the Steadian innovations, such as the use of interviews, feature articles, illustrations, headlines and crossheads. O'Connor introduced a gossip column, and, following the *Daily Telegraph*, he devoted several columns to sport. Ambitious and successful in terms of circulation, the *Star*'s ideology was closer to Pulitzer's populism than to the socialist creed. Far from being a working-class paper, the *Star* was among the first daily papers to set the pattern of the 20th-century popular press: popular readership, middle-class journalists, and bourgeois ownership (see also Schults, 1972, pp. 233–9).

2. See Marx's *Debates on Freedom of the Press and Publication of the Proceedings of the Assembly of the Estates* initially published in a May issue of the *Rheinische Zeitung*, in Marx and Engels, 1975, pp. 132–81.

3. Advertisers' preferences for light copy material emerged clearly in 1939, as it appeared that one of the reasons why some British newspapers denied the imminence of war was that advertisers thought the gloomy reports from Germany and consumer culture incompatible. Francis Williams, the editor of the *Daily Herald*, summarized the prewar advertisers' rationale: 'The optimistic paper, the paper that makes its readers feel gay and in a mood to spend and that assures them that there is no need for worry, is therefore likely to find more favour with advertisers' (in Royal Commission on the Press, 1949, p. 135). A former editor of *The Times* also claimed that advertising agents threatened editors to withdraw advertisements 'should they "play up" the international crisis and cause alarm which was "bad for trade"' (Steed, 1938, pp. 249–50). Although Steed's claim cannot be checked, advertisers' worries were echoed by many in the field of the press. Beaverbrook, the owner of the *Daily Express*, wrote to a friend that '[a] paper can't afford to prophesy disaster', and Elias, general manager of the *Daily Herald*, complained that 'the only idea our editorial people have is to depress and horrify our readers' (in Koss, 1990, pp. 983–4). The expert on the British press of the late 1930s confirmed that '[t]he business and advertising staff were opposed to anything controversial or depressing which might discourage advertisers' (Gannon 1971, pp. 39–40). He quoted the advertising manager of the *News-Chronicle*, who once asked his editor: 'Why all this foreign news?' (ibid.).

4. In 1947 and 1975 respectively, 13 and 12 per cent of the total news space of the *Daily Express* were devoted to this news category, 11 and 12 per cent in the *Daily Mail* and 23 and 11 per cent in the *Daily Mirror* (McQuail, 1977, p. 17).

5. As told by one of the paper's advertisements, Charles Dana was trying hard at this time to build up the circulation of his newly acquired daily: 'Its news is the freshest, most interesting and sprightliest current, and no expense is spared to make it just what the great mass of the people want' (in Mott, 1962, p. 374).

6. It is ironic that the *Daily Mirror* was published on Christmas Day, a

traditional day off for British press workers. To go to press on that day, Northcliffe had to breach the Unions' agreement and face the complaints of press workers' unions.

6 JOURNALISTIC DISCURSIVE STRATEGIES

1. On Pulitzer, see Juergens, 1966; on Hearst, see Swanberg, 1961.
2. Although at election times, Hearst's papers could become quite vocal in their support for the Democratic Party, the American press baron showed an awareness of the danger of partisan politics in journalism early in his career (see Chapter 2).
3. The *Daily Mail, Daily Express* and *Daily Mirror* took up a similar angle. The *Daily Mail*'s headline read 'White Boy, 15, Is Killed By Race Mob' and the story began as follows: 'A distraught mother wept last night for her son stabbed to death in a racial attack' (*Daily Mail*, 15 August 1994). The *Daily Express* story started the following way: 'Even his mother called him a big softie. Richard Everitt did not have an ounce of badness in him. But that did not stop a gang of thugs stabbing him to death allegedly for being white' (*Daily Express*, 15 August 1994). The *Daily Mirror*'s headline read 'This Gentle Teenager Was Killed Because He Was White' and the news story began with the following line: 'A heartbroken dad told last night how he found his teenaged son dying in a pool of blood – victim of a gang who knifed him because of the colour of his skin' (*Daily Mirror*, 15 August 1994).
4. In 1889, 'Jack-the-Ripper' had become a household name in the United States to the point that a club of reporters in Chicago opened its doors in 1889 under the name of the Whitechapel Club (Schudson, 1978, p. 69).

7 THE POLARIZATION OF THE BRITISH PRESS

1. With the exception of the *Daily Graphic*, a quality illustrated penny paper for the middle classes which had many common points, bar the price, with the halfpenny papers.
2. The results of this research must be taken cautiously since the author of the report did not specify the sampling method. It can be deduced however that the researchers did not use either representative or quota sampling methods, which may have had to be developed at that time, since the survey necessitated 82 613 interviews in 1232 places throughout the country (Coglan, 1937, p. xvii).
3. Readership totals for the lower middle class, upper middle class and upper class exceed 100 per cent because of multiple readership patterns among the members of these social classes.

8 JOURNALISTS AND THEIR PUBLIC

1. To calculate the sales per thousand inhabitant in the United Kingdom, and in the absence of a population census for this country in 1941, I arbitrarily opted for an intermediary value between the 1931 Census which set the population of England, Wales and Scotland at 44.8 million, and the 1951 Census which gave the figure of 48.85 million (Mitchell, 1992, p. 8).

References

Adorno, T.W. (1941) 'On Popular Music', *Studies in Philosophy & Social Science*, 9(1): 17–48.

Adorno, T.W. (1991) *The Culture Industry* (London: Routledge).

Adorno, T.W. and M. Horkheimer (1979) *Dialectic of Enlightenment* (London: Verso).

Albert, P. (1983) *La Presse française* (Paris: La Documentation française).

Althusser, L. (1965) *Pour Marx* (Paris: La Découverte).

Amaury, F. (1972) *Histoire du plus grand quotidien de la IIIe République* (Paris: PUF).

Anderson, B. (1991) *Imagined Communities* (London: Verso).

Andrews, A. (1859) *The History of British Journalism: From the Foundation of the Newspaper Press in England to the Repeal of the Stamp Act in 1855* (London: Richard Bentley).

Aspinall, A. (1949) *Politics and the Press: c. 1780–1850* (London: Home & Van Thal).

Bakhtin, M. (1981) *The Dialogic Imagination* (Austin: University of Texas Press).

Barthes, R. (1964) 'Eléments de Sémiologie', *Communications*, 4: 91–134.

Barthes, R. (1993) *Mythologies* (London: Vintage).

Baudrillard, J. (1977) *Oublier Foucault* (Paris: Galilée).

Baudrillard, J. (1981) *Simulacres et simulations* (Paris: Galilée).

Baudrillard, J. (1985) *Le Miroir de la production* (Paris: Galilée).

Baylen, J.O. (1988) 'Politics and the New Journalism: Lord Esher's Use of the *Pall Mall Gazette*' pp. 107–41 in J.H. Wiener (ed.) *Papers for the Millions: The New Journalism in Britain, 1850s to 1914* (New York: Greenwood Press).

Beaud, P. (1984) *La Société de connivence: media, médiations et classes sociales* (Paris: Aubier).

Bell, D. (1976) *The Cultural Contradictions of Capitalism* (London: Heinemann).

Bell, W.G. (1912) *Fleet Street in Seven Centuries* (London: Pitman).

Bellanger, C., J. Godechot, P. Guiral and F. Terrou (1969) *Histoire générale de la presse française*, vol. 2: *de 1815 à 1871* (Paris: PUF).

Bellanger, C., J. Godechot, P. Guiral and F. Terrou (1972) *Histoire générale de la presse française*, vol. 3: *de 1871 à 1940* (Paris: PUF).

Bérenger, L. (1897) 'Les Responsabilités de la presse contemporaine', *Revue Politique et Littéraire*, 8(25): 770–6.

Berridge, V. (1976) *Popular Journalism and Working Class Attitudes 1854–1886: A Study of Reynolds's Newspaper, Lloyd's Weekly Newspaper and the Weekly Times*, vol. 1 (University of London: PhD thesis).

Blondheim, M. (1994) *News over the Wires: the Telegraph and the Flow of Public Information in America, 1844–1897* (Cambridge, Mass.: Harvard University Press).

Blumenfeld, R.D. (1933) *The Press in My Time* (London: Rich & Cowan).

Bogue, D.J. (1985) *The Population of the United States* (New York: Free Press).

Bourdieu, P. (1992) *Les Règles de l'art: Genèse et structure du champ littéraire* (Paris: Seuil).

Bourdieu, P. (1993) *The Field of Cultural Production* (Cambridge: Polity Press).

Bourdieu, P. and J.C. Passeron (1990) *Reproduction in Education, Society and Culture* (London: Sage).

Bourdieu, P. and L.J.D. Wacquant (1992) *Invitation to Reflexive Sociology* (Cambridge: Polity Press).

Bourne, H.R.F. (1887) *English Newspapers*, vol. 2 (London: Chatto & Windus).

Boyd-Barrett, O. (1995) 'The Political Economy Approach' pp. 186–92 in O. Boyd-Barrett and C. Newbold (eds) *Approaches to Media: A Reader* (London: Arnold).

Breed, W. (1980) *The Newspaperman, News and Society* (New York: Arno Press).

Brendon, P. (1982) *The Life and Death of the Press Barons* (London: Secker & Warburg).

Brown, L. (1985) *Victorian News and Newspapers* (Oxford: Clarendon Press).

Butler, D. and G. Butler (1994) *British Political Facts, 1900–1994* (London: Macmillan).

Butler, and L.A. Sloman (1980) *British Political Facts, 1900–1979* (London: Macmillan).

Cadet, A. and B. Cathelat (1968) *La Publicité* (Paris: Payot).

Carey, J.W. (1986) 'The Dark Continent of American Journalism' pp. 146–96 in R.K. Manoff and M. Schudson (eds) *Reading the News* (New York: Pantheon).

Chalaby, J. (1996a) 'Journalism as an Anglo-American Invention', *European Journal of Communication*, 11(3): 303–26.

Chalaby, J. (1996b) 'Beyond the Prison-House of Language: Discourse as a Sociological Concept', *British Journal of Sociology*, 47(4): 684–98.

Chalaby, J. (1997) 'No Ordinary Press Owners: Press Barons as a Weberian Ideal Type', *Media, Culture & Society*, 19(4): 621–41.

Champagne, P. (1990) *Faire l'opinion* (Paris: Minuit).

Chisholm, A. and M. Davie (1992) *Beaverbrook: A Life* (London: Hutchinson).

Choisel, F. (1980) 'La Presse française face aux réformes de 1860', *Revue d'Histoire Moderne et Contemporaine*, 27: 374–90.

Clarke, T. (1931) *My Northcliffe Diary* (London: Victor Gollancz).

Clarke, T. (1950) *Northcliffe in History* (London: Hutchinson).

Coglan, W.N. (1937) *The Readership of Newspapers and Periodicals in Great Britain, 1936* (London: Incorporated Society of British Advertisers).

Cole, G.D.H. and R. Postgate (1946) *The Common People, 1746–1946* (London: Methuen).

Cole, M. (1953) *Robert Owen of New Lanark* (London: Batchworth Press).

Collet, C.D. (1933) *History of the Taxes on Knowledge* (London: Watts).

Cooke, G.W. (1859) *China, Being* The Times *Special Correspondence from China in the Years 1857–1858* (London: Routledge).

Compaine, B.M. (1980) *The Newspaper Industry in the 1980s* (New York: Knowledge Industry Publications).

A Conservative Journalist (1885) 'The Establishment of Newspapers', *National Review*, 5: 818–28.

Cox, G.W. and J.W. Ingram III (1992) 'Suffrage Expansion and Legislative Behavior in Nineteenth-Century Britain', *Social Science History*, 16(4): 539–60.

Crawfurd, J. (1836) *A Financial and Historical View of the Taxes which Impede the Education of the People* (London: Charles Ely).

Cummings, A.J. (1936) *The Press and a Changing Civilization* (London: Allen Lane/The Bodley Head).

Curran, J. (1977) 'Capitalism and Control of the Press, 1800–1975' pp. 195–230 in J. Curran, M. Gurevitch and J. Woollacott (eds) *Mass Communication and Society* (London: Edward Arnold).

Curran, J. and J. Seaton (1991) *Power Without Responsibility* (London: Routledge).

Dahlgren, P. (1991) 'Introduction', pp. 1–24 in P. Dahlgren and C. Sparks (eds) *Communication and Citizenship: Journalism and the Public Sphere* (London: Routledge).

Dauncey, H. (1996) 'French "Reality Television": More than a Matter of Taste?', *European Journal of Communication*, 11(1): 83–106.

Diamond, B.I. (1988) 'A Precursor of the New Journalism: Frederick Greenwood of the *Pall Mall Gazette*' pp. 25–45 in J.H. Wiener (ed.) *Papers for the Millions* (New York: Greenwood Press).

Ducrot, O. *et al.* (1980) *Les Mots du discours* (Paris: Minuit).

Dupuis, S. (1991) *Robert Owen, Socialiste utopique, 1771–1858* (Paris: Editions du Centre National de la Recherche Scientifique).

Durkheim, E. (1938) *The Rules of Sociological Method* (Glencoe: Free Press of Glencoe).

Fairclough, N. (1992) *Discourse and Social Change* (Cambridge: Polity Press).

Foucault, M. (1971) *L'Ordre du discours* (Paris: Gallimard).

Foucault, M. (1980) *Power/Knowledge, Selected Interviews* (New York: Harvester Wheatsheaf).

Foucault, M. (1989) *The Archaeology of Knowledge* (London: Routledge).

Fyfe, H. (1930) *Northcliffe: An Intimate Biography* (London: George Allen & Unwin).

Fyfe, H. (1949) *Sixty Years of Fleet Street* (London: W.H. Allen).

Gannon, F.R. (1971) *The British Press and Germany, 1936–1939* (Oxford: Clarendon Press).

Gans, H.J. (1980) *Deciding What's News* (New York: Vintage).

Gardiner, A.G. *Papers* (London: British Library of Political and Economic Science).

Garnham, N. (1986) 'The Media and the Public Sphere' pp. 37–53 in P. Golding, G. Murdock and P. Schlesinger (eds) *Communicating Politics: Mass Communications and the Political Process* (New York: Holmes & Meier).

Garnham, N. (1990) *Capitalism and Communication: Global Culture and the Economics of Information* (London: Sage).

Gaziano, C. (1983) 'The Knowledge Gap: An Analytical Review of Media Effects', *Communication Research*, 10: 447–86.

Gerald, E. (1956) *The British Press under Government Economic Controls* (Minneapolis: University of Minnesota Press).

Glasgow University Media Group (1976) *Bad News* (London: Routledge).

Glasgow University Media Group (1980) *More Bad News* (London: Routledge).

Golding, P. and P. Elliott (1979) *Making the News* (London: Longman).

Goldmann, L. (1971) *La Création culturelle dans la société moderne* (Paris: Denoël).

Goodbody, J. (1988) 'The *Star*: Its Role in the Rise of the New Journalism' pp. 143–63 in J.H. Wiener (ed.) *Papers for the Millions: The New Journalism in Britain, 1850s to 1914* (New York: Greenwood Press).

Graber, D.A. (1989) *Mass Media and American Politics* (Washington: Congressional Quarterly).

Grant, J. (1871) *The Newspaper Press*, vol. 2 (London: Tinsley Brothers).

Greimas, A.J. (1990) *The Social Sciences: A Semiotic View* (Minneapolis: University of Minnesota Press).

Gruder, V.R. (1992) 'Un Message politique adressé au public: les pamphlets "populaires" à la veille de la Révolution', *Revue d'histoire moderne et contemporaine*, 39(2): 161–97.

Habermas, J. (1991) *The Structural Transformation of the Public Sphere* (Cambridge, Mass.: MIT Press).

Hall, S. (1977) 'Culture, the Media and the "Ideological Effect"' pp. 315–48 in J. Curran, M. Gurevitch and J. Woollacott (eds) *Mass Communication and Society* (London: Edward Arnold).

Hall, S. (1980) 'Encoding/Decoding' pp. 128–38 in S. Hall, D. Hobson, H. Lowe, P. Willis (eds) *Culture, Media, Language* (London: Unwin Hyman).

Harris, M. and A. Lee (1986) 'Introduction' pp. 19–24 in M. Harris and A. Lee (eds) *The Press in English Society from the Seventeenth to Nineteenth Centuries* (London: Associated University Presses).

Harris, W. (1943) *The Daily Press* (London: Cambridge University Press).

Harrison, S. (1974) *Poor Men's Guardian: A Record of the Struggles for a Democratic Newspaper Press, 1763–1973* (London: Lawrence & Wishart).

Hart-Davis, D. (1990) *The House the Berrys Built: Inside* The Telegraph, *1928–1986* (London: Hodder and Stoughton).

Hobsbawm, E.J. (1975) *The Age of Capital, 1848–1875* (London: Weidenfeld and Nicolson).

Hollis, P. (1969) *The Poor Man's Guardian, 1831–1835: Introduction to the Reprint of the Original Journal*, vol. 1 (London: Merlin Press).

Hollis, P. (1970) *The Pauper Press: A Study in Working-Class Radicalism of the 1830s* (London: Oxford University Press).

Holsti, O.R. (1969) *Content Analysis for the Social Sciences and Humanities* (Reading: Addison-Wesley).

Holyoake, G.J. (1849) *The Life and Character of Henry Hetherington* (London: J. Watson).

Hopkin, D. (1988) 'The Left-Wing Press and the New Journalism' pp. 225–41 in J.H. Wiener (ed.) *Papers for the Millions: The New Journalism in Britain, 1850s to 1914* (New York: Greenwood Press).

Howe, E. (1943) *Newspaper Printing in the Nineteenth Century* (London).

Hughes, H.M. (1940) *News and the Human Interest Story* (New York: Greenwood Press).

Incorporated Society of British Advertisers (1924) *Truth About Circulation* (London).

Inglis, F. (1990) *Media Theory: An Introduction* (Oxford: Basil Blackwell).

Jameson, F. (1972) *The Prison-House of Language: A Critical Account of Structuralism and Russian Formalism* (Princeton: Princeton University Press).

Jamieson, K.H. (1992) *Dirty Politics: Deception, Distraction, and Democracy* (New York: Oxford University Press).

Jenkins, R. (1958) *Sir Charles Dilke: A Victorian Tragedy* (London: Collins).

Jones, K. (1919) *Fleet Street and Downing Street* (London: Hutchinson).

Juergens, G. (1966) *Joseph Pulitzer and the* New York World (Princeton: Princeton University Press).

Katznelson, I. (1986) 'Working-Class Formation: Constructing Cases and Comparisons' pp. 3–41 in I. Katznelson and A. R. Zolbert (eds) *Working-Class Formation: Nineteenth-Century Patterns in Western Europe and the United States* (Princeton: Princeton University Press).

Keane, J. (1991) *The Media and Democracy* (Cambridge: Polity Press).

Keeble, R. (1994) *The Newspapers Handbook* (London: Routledge).

Kennedy, P. (1980) *The Rise of the Anglo-German Antagonism* (London: Ashfield Press).

Kleinnijenhuis, J. (1991) 'Newspaper Complexity and the Knowledge Gap', *European Journal of Communication*, 6(4): 499–522.

Knight, C. (1854) *The Old Printer and the Modern Press* (London: John Murray).

Koss, S. (1990) *The Rise and Fall of the Political Press in Britain* (London: Fontana Press).

Kress, G.R. (1985) *Linguistic Processes in Sociocultural Practice* (Victoria: Deakin University Press).

Labour Research Department (1922) *The Press* (London: The Labour Publishing Company).

Laclau, E. and C. Mouffe (1985) *Hegemony and Socialist Strategy* (London: Verso).

Lansbury, G. (1925) *The Miracle of Fleet Street: The Story of the* Daily Herald (London: The Labour Publishing Company).

Lawrence, A. (1903) *Journalism as a Profession* (London: Hodder & Stoughton).

Lee, A.J. (1976) *The Origins of the Popular Press in England, 1855–1914* (London: Croom Helm).

Lippmann, W. (1920) *Liberty and the News* (New York: Harcourt, Brace, and Howe).

Maccoby, S. (1935) *English Radicalism, 1832–1852* (London: George Allen & Unwin).

MacDonagh, M. (1913) *The Reporters' Gallery* (London: Hodder & Stoughton).

Manévy, R. (1955) *La Presse de la IIIe République* (Paris: Foret).

Marx, K. (1976) *Capital*, vol. 1 (Harmondsworth: Penguin).

Marx, K. and F. Engels (1975) *Collected Works*, vol. 1: *1835–43* (London: Lawrence & Wishart).

Marx, K. and F. Engels (1980) *Collected Works*, vol. 14: *1855–56* (London: Lawrence & Wishart).

McCombs, M., E. Einsiedel and D. Weaver (1991) *Contemporary Public Opinion: Issues and the News* (Hillsdale: Erlbaum).

McCombs, M. and D.L. Shaw (1972) 'The Agenda-Setting Function of Mass Media', *Public Opinion Quarterly*, 36(2): 176–87.

McManus, J.H. (1994) *Market-Driven Journalism: Let the Citizen Beware?* (London: Sage).

McQuail, D. (1977) *Analysis of Newspaper Content* (London: HMSO, Cmnd. 6810–4).

Miller, W.L., H.D. Clarke, M. Harrop, L. Leduc and P.F. Whiteley (1990) *How Voters Change: The 1987 British Election Campaign in Perspective* (Oxford: Clarendon Press).

Mills, J.S. (1921) *Sir Edward Cook K.B.E.* (London: Constable).

Mitchell, B.R. (1992) *International Historical Statistics – Europe – 1750–1988*, Third edition (London: Macmillan).

Mott, F.L. (1962) *American Journalism* (New York: Macmillan).

Murdock, G. and P. Golding (1977) 'Capitalism, Communication and Class Relations' pp. 12–43 in J. Curran, M. Gurevitch and J. Woollacott (eds) *Mass Communication and Society* (London: Edward Arnold).

Nevett, T.R. (1982) *Advertising in Britain* (London: Heinemann).

Neveu, E. (1995) 'Les Emissions politiques à la télévision: Les années quatre-vingt ou les impasses du spectacle politique', *Hermès*, 17/18: 145–62.

Norris, J.D. (1990) *Advertising and the Transformation of American Society, 1865–1920* (New York: Greenwood Press).

Northcliffe (Alfred Harmsworth, Viscount Northcliffe) *Papers* (London: British Library).

Northcliffe (1922) *Newspapers and their Millionaires* (London: Associated Newspapers).

Nossiter, T.J., M. Scammell, and H.A. Semetko (1995) 'Old Values versus News Values: The British General Election Campaign on Television' pp. 85–103 in I. Crewe and B. Cosschalk (eds) *Political Communication: The General Election Campaign of 1992* (Cambridge: Cambridge University Press).

The Office of *The Times* (1939) *The History of* The Times, vol. 2: *The Tradition Established, 1841–1884* (London: *The Times*).

The Office of *The Times* (1952) *The History of* The Times, *The 150th Anniversary and Beyond, 1912–1948*, vol. 4, part I, *1912–1920* (London: *The Times*).

Orwell, G. (1968) *The Collected Essays, Journalism and Letters of George Orwell*, vol. 2: *My Country Right or Left, 1940–1943* (London: Secker & Warburg).

Owers, J., R. Carveth and A. Alexander (1993) 'An Introduction to Media Economic Theory and Practice' pp. 3–46 in A. Alexander, J. Owers and R. Carveth (eds) *Media Economics: Theory and Practice* (Hillsdale: Erlbaum).

Palmer, M. (1978) 'The British Press and International News, 1851–99: Of Agencies and Newspapers' pp. 205–19 in G. Boyce, J. Curran and P. Wingate (eds) *Newspaper History* (London: Constable).

Palmer, M. (1983) *Des petits journaux aux grandes agences. Naissance du journalisme moderne* (Paris: Aubier).

Patterson, T.E. (1980) *The Mass Media Election: How Americans Choose Their President* (New York: Praeger).

Pendleton, J. (1890) *Newspaper Reporting in Olden Time and To-day* (London: Elliot Stock).

Picard, R.G. (1993) 'Economics of the Daily Newspaper Industry' pp. 181–203 in A. Alexander, J. Owers and R. Carveth (eds) *Media Economics: Theory and Practice* (Hillsdale: Erlbaum).

Polanyi, K. (1957) *The Great Transformation* (Boston: Beacon Press).

Political and Economic Planning (1938) *Report on the British Press* (London: PEP).

Postman, N. (1986) *Amusing Ourselves to Death* (London: Heinemann).

Potter, J. and M. Wetherell (1987) *Discourse and Social Psychology* (London: Sage).

Pound, R. and G. Harmsworth (1959) *Northcliffe* (London: Cassell).

Pugh, M. (1993) *The Making of Modern British Politics, 1867–1939* (Oxford: Blackwell).

Purvis, T. and A. Hunt (1993) 'Discourse, ideology, discourse, ideology, discourse, ideology, . . .' *The British Journal of Sociology*, 44(3): 473–98.

Quéré, L. (1982) *Des Miroirs équivoques: Aux origines de la communication moderne* (Paris: Aubier).

Read, D. (1961) *Press and People: 1790–1850: Opinion in Three English Cities* (London: Edward Arnold).

Read, D. (1992) *The Power of News: the History of Reuters, 1849–1989* (Oxford: Oxford University Press).

Ricoeur, P. (1969) *Le Conflit des interprétations* (Paris: Seuil).

Riffaterre, M. (1984) *Semiotics of Poetry* (Bloomington: Indiana University Press).

Robinson, J.P. and M.R. Levy (1996) 'News Media Use and the Informed Public: a 1990s Update', *Journal of Communication*, 46(2): 129–35.

Romano, C. (1986) 'The Grisly Truth about Bare Facts' pp. 38–78 in R.K. Manoff and M. Schudson (eds) *Reading the News* (New York: Pantheon).

Royal Commission on the Press (1949) *Report* (London: HMSO, cmnd. 7700).

Saussure, F. de (1959) *Course in General Linguistics* (New York: McGraw-Hill).

Schalck, H. (1988) 'Fleet Street in the 1880s: the New Journalism' pp. 73–87 in J.H. Wiener (ed.) *Papers for the Millions: the New Journalism in Britain, 1850s to 1914* (New York: Greenwood Press).

Schlesinger, P., H. Tumber, and G. Murdock (1991) 'The Media Politics of Crime and Criminal Justice', *British Journal of Sociology*, 42(3): 397–420.

Schudson, M. (1978) *Discovering the News* (New York: Basic Books).

Schudson, M. (1986) 'Deadlines, Datelines, and History' pp. 79–108 in R.K. Manoff and M. Schudson (eds) *Reading the News* (New York: Pantheon).

Schudson, M. (1994) 'Question Authority: A History of the News Interview in American Journalism, 1860s–1930s', *Media, Culture & Society*, 16(4): 565–87.

Schults, R.L. (1972) *Crusader in Babylon: W.T. Stead and the* Pall Mall Gazette (Lincoln: University of Nebraska Press).

Seitz, D. C. (1928) *The James Gordon Bennetts* (Indianapolis: Bobbs-Merrill).

Semetko, H.A., J.G. Blumler, M. Gurevitch and D.H. Weaver (1991) *The Formation of Campaign Agendas: A Comparative Analysis of Party and Media Roles in Recent American and British Elections* (Hillsdale: Erlbaum).

Seymour-Ure, C. (1996) *The British Press and Broadcasting since 1945* (Oxford: Blackwell).

Siebert, F.S. (1965) *Freedom of the Press in England, 1476–1776: The Rise and Decline of Government Control* (Urbana: University of Illinois Press).

Sigal, L.V. (1986) 'Sources Make the News' pp. 9–37 in R.K. Manoff and M. Schudson (eds) *Reading the News* (New York: Pantheon).

Simonis, H. (1917) *The Street of Ink: An Intimate History of Journalism* (London: Cassell).

Somers, M.R. (1992) 'Narrativity, Narrative Identity, and Social Action: Rethinking English Working-Class Formation', *Social Science History*, 16(4): 591–630.

Somers, M.R. (1996) 'Class Formation and Capitalism. A Second Look at a Classic', *Archives Européennes de Sociologie*, 37(1): 180–202.

Soothill, K. and S. Walby (1991) *Sex Crime in the News* (London: Routledge).

Sparks, C. (1991) 'Goodbye, Hildy Johnson: the Vanishing "Serious Press"' pp. 58–74 in P. Dahlgreen and C. Sparks (eds) *Communication and Citizenship: Journalism and the Public Sphere* (Routledge: London).

Sparks, C. (1992) 'Popular Journalism: Theories and Practices' pp. 24–44 in P. Dahlgreen and C. Sparks (eds) *Journalism and Popular Culture* (London: Sage).

Sparks, C. (1995) 'Concentration and Market Entry in the UK National Daily Press', *European Journal of Communication*, 10(2): 179–206.

Spender, J.A. (1925) *The Public Life*, vol. 2 (London: Cassel).

Spender, J.A. (1927) *Life, Journalism and Politics*, vol. 2 (New York: Frederick A. Stores).

Splichal, S. (1994) *Media Beyond Socialism* (Boulder: Westview Press).

Statera, G. (1994) *Il volto seduttivo del potere* (Roma: Seam).

Stead, W.T. (1886a) 'Government by Journalism', *Contemporary Review*, 49: 653–74.

Stead, W.T. (1886b) 'The Future of Journalism', *Contemporary Review*, 50: 663–72.

Stead, W.T. (1902) 'Mr T.P. O'Connor, MP', *Review of Reviews*, 26: 473–9.

Steed, H.W. (1938) *The Press* (Harmondsworth: Penguin).

Steinmetz, G. (1992) 'Reflections on the Role of Social Narratives in Working-Class Formation: Narrative Theory in the Social Sciences', *Social Science History*, 16(3): 489–516.

Stephens, M. (1988) *A History of News* (New York: Viking).

Stevens, J.D. (1991) *Sensationalism and the New York Press* (New York: Columbia University Press).

Swanberg, W.A. (1962) *Citizen Hearst* (London: Longman).

Symon, J.D. (1914) *The Press and its Story* (London: Seeley).

Taylor, S.J. (1996) *The Great Outsiders: Northcliffe, Rothermere and the* Daily Mail (London: Weidenfeld & Nicolson).

Thompson, E.P. (1991) *The Making of the English Working Class* (London: Penguin).

Thompson, E.P. (1995) *The Poverty of Theory* (London: Merlin Press).

Thompson, J. B. (1995) *The Media and Modernity: A Social Theory of the Media* (Cambridge: Polity Press).

Tichenor, P.J., G.A. Donahue and C.N. Olien (1970) 'Mass Media Flow and Differential Growth in Knowledge', *Public Opinion Quarterly*, 34(2): 159–70.

Tocqueville, A. de (1990) *Democracy in America*, vol. 1 (New York: Vintage).

Todorov, T. (1978) *Les Genres du discours* (Paris: Seuil).

Twaites, P. (1996) 'News Photography in Britain: A Contested Site of Cultural Historicity', *A Century of the Popular Press Conference* (London: Institute of Contemporary British History).

van Dijk, T.A. (1988) *News as Discourse* (Hillsdale: Erlbaum).

van Dijk, T.A. (1991) *Racism and the Press* (London: Routledge).

Véron, E. (1995) 'Médiatisation du politique: Stratégies, acteurs et construction des collectifs', *Hermès*, 17/18: 201–14.

Verstraeten, H. (1996) 'The Media and the Transformation of the Public Sphere', *European Journal of Communication*, 11(3): 347–70.

Volosinov, V.N. (1986) *Marxism and the Philosophy of Language* (Cambridge, Mass.: Harvard University Press).

Wadsworth, A.P. (1955) *Newspaper Circulations, 1800–1954* (Manchester: Manchester Statistical Society).

Webb, R.K. (1955) *The British Working Class Reader* (London: George Allen & Unwin).

Weber, A. F. (1963) *The Growth of Cities in the Nineteenth Century* (Ithaca: Cornell University Press).

Weber, M. (1949) *The Methodology of the Social Sciences* (New York: Free Press).

Weber, M. (1968) *Economy and Society* (Berkeley: University of California Press).

Wickwar, W.H. (1928) *The Struggle for the Freedom of the Press, 1819–1832* (London: George Allen & Unwin).

Wiener, J.H. (1969) *The War of the Unstamped: The Movement to Repeal the British Newspaper Tax, 1830–1836* (Ithaca: Cornell University Press).

Williams, F. (1957) *Dangerous Estate: The Anatomy of Newspapers* (Cambridge: Patrick Stephens).

Williams, R. (1961) *The Long Revolution* (London: Chatto & Windus).

Wisan, J.E. (1934) *The Cuban Crisis as Reflected in the New York Press, 1895–1898* (New York: Columbia University Press).

Index